Fly-Fishing
Pioneers & Legends
of the Northwest

Fly-Fishing
Pioneers & Legends
of the Northwest

by

Jack W. Berryman

Northwest Fly Fishing, LLC
Seattle, Washington

NORTHWEST
Fly Fishing

Published by
NORTHWEST FLY FISHING, LLC
600 1st. Ave., Ste. 512
Seattle, WA 98104
www.matchthehatch.com

Distributed by
STACKPOLE BOOKS
5067 Ritter Road
Mechanicsburg, PA 17055
www.stackpolebooks.com

Printed in China

First edition

10 9 8 7 6 5 4 3 2 1

ISBN-10: 0-9779454-0-5
ISBN-13: 978-0-9779454-0-5

Library of Congress Control Number: 2006927976

"I still don't know why I fish or why other men fish, except that we like it and it makes us think and feel. But I do know that if it were not for the strong, quick life of rivers, for their sparkle in the sunshine, for the cold grayness of them under rain and the feel of them about my legs as I set my feet hard down on rocks or sand or gravel, I should fish less often. A river is never quite silent; it can never, of its very nature, be quite still; it is never quite the same from one day to the next. It has its own life and its own beauty, and the creatures it nourishes are alive and beautiful also. Perhaps fishing is, for me, only an excuse to be near rivers."

Roderick Haig-Brown,
A River Never Sleeps, 1946

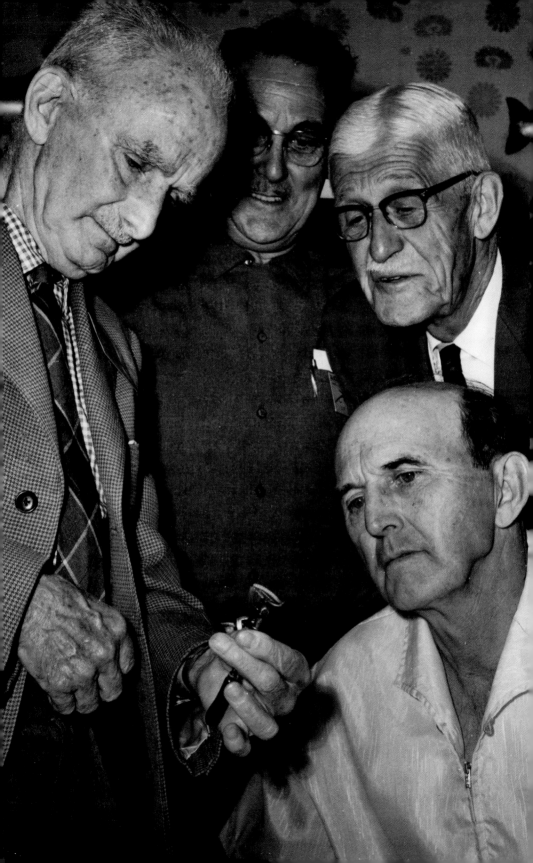

Contents

Foreword   Steve Raymond   **xi**

Acknowledgments   **xv**

Introduction   **1**

Part One: **British Columbia**
1. Arthur William "Bill" Nation (1881–1940):   **6**
   Kamloops Trout Guide and Innovative Fly Designer

2. Noel Money (1867–1941):   **12**
   Stamp River Steelheader and Fly Tier

3. Thomas "Tommy" Brayshaw (1886–1967):   **20**
   Angler, Artist, and Fly Tier

4. Roderick L. Haig-Brown (1908–1976):   **28**
   Writer, Conservationist, and Fly Fisher

Part Two: **California**
5. Peter J. Schwab (1887–1956):   **38**
   Klamath River Steelheader and Designer of Fly Rods, Lines, and Flies

6. C. James Pray (1885–1952):   **46**
   Eureka Fly Tier and Originator of the
   Popular "Optic" Series of Steelhead Flies

7. Harry M. Hornbrook (1915–1998):   **54**
   Legendary Steelheader on the Eel River

8. William E. "Bill" Schaadt (1922–1995):   **62**
   Pioneer Fly Fisher for Steelhead, Chinook Salmon, and Striped Bass

Part Three: **Idaho**
9. Cecil Whitaker "Ted" Trueblood (1913–1982):   **72**
   Outdoor Writer, Conservationist, and Legendary Fly Fisherman

Part Four: **Montana**
10. Franz B. "Frank" Pott (circa 1890–1955):   **82**
    Commercial Fly Tier and Designer of the Woven-Hair Series of Pott Flies

11. Norman Edward Lee Means (1899–circa 1984):   **88**
    aka Paul Bunyan, Inventor of the Bunyan Bug Series of Flies

12. Donald S. Martinez (circa 1900–1955):   **94**
    Popularizer of the Woolly Worm, Early West Yellowstone
    Fly-Shop Owner, and Pioneer in Western Dry Flies

13. Dan Bailey (1904–1982):   **100**
    Early Fly-Shop Owner, Innovative Fly Developer, and Staunch
    Western Conservationist

Part Five: Oregon
14. Maurice "Mooch" Abraham (1867–1936):   **110**
    Portland Fly Tier, Fly-Fishing Mentor, and
    Originator of the Double-Haul Technique

15. Jordan Lawrence Mott III (1881–1931):   **116**
    Novelist and Pioneer on the North Umpqua River

16. Zane Grey (1872–1939):   **124**
    Legendary Author, Angler, Northwest Fly Fisherman,
    and Devout Conservationist

17. Marvin K. Hedge (1896–1969):   **134**
    Champion Caster and Designer of Fly Lines and Rods

18. Ernest H. "Polly" Rosborough (1902–1997):   **142**
    Originator of Western Nymph Patterns and Nymphing,
    Techniques, Author, and Commercial Fly Tier

Part Six: Washington
19. Benjamin Letcher Lambuth (1890–1974):   **152**
    Innovator, Master Rod Builder, and Amateur Entomologist

20. Enos Bradner (1892–1984):   **160**
    Outdoor Writer, Fly-Fishing Advocate, and Conservationist

21. Ralph O. Olson (1902–1955):   **168**
    Judge and Pioneer Winter-Run Steelheader

22. Ken McLeod (1898–1987):   **176**
    Early Steelhead Fly Fisherman, Outdoor Writer, Innovator,
    and Environmentalist

23. Ralph E. Wahl (1906–1996):   **184**
    Photographer and Pioneer Winter-Run Steelheader

Selected Bibliography   **194**

Index   **200**

A GROUP OF THE NORTHWEST'S EARLY STEELHEAD FLY FISHERS GATHER AT A MONTHLY MEETING OF THE WASHINGTON FLY FISHING CLUB IN THE 1970S (FROM LEFT TO RIGHT): AL KNUDSON, HOWARD GRAY, KEN MCLEOD, SANDY BACON, AND RALPH WAHL (PHOTOGRAPH COURTESY OF ROBERT L. BETTZIG) (ABOVE)

TOMMY BRAYSHAW (FAR LEFT) SHOWS ONE OF HIS STEELHEAD FLIES TO ROY PATRICK, ENOS BRADNER, AND "POLLY" ROSBOROUGH (CLOCK-WISE) AT THE FIRST FLY FISHERS CONCLAVE (THE INAUGURAL MEETING OF WHAT WOULD BECOME THE FEDERATION OF FLY FISHERS) IN EU-GENE, OREGON, IN JUNE 1965 (PHOTOGRAPH COURTESY OF ROBERT WETHERN AND *THE CREEL*) (OPPOSITE CONTENTS).

PETE SCHWAB (LEFT) AND JIM PRAY (RIGHT), LOOK AT A CHOICE STRETCH OF STEELHEAD FLY WATER ON CALIFORNIA'S KLAMATH RIVER IN THE 1940S (PHOTOGRAPH COURTESY OF PAT AND GARY WALLER) (NEXT PAGE).

Foreword

Fly fishing, perhaps more than any other sport, depends on history and tradition. For hundreds of years it has progressed incrementally through the discoveries and innovations of countless anglers, each of whom has contributed at least one small thread to what has become a rich tapestry of tradition and lore.

From its European origins, fly fishing made its way to the New World and followed the trails of settlers to the western shore of the North American continent. Even as the western shore became the last frontier of settlement, it also became the continent's last frontier of fly fishing. Barely a century and a half has elapsed since the first anglers cast their flies over the virgin waters of the West, a period you would think scarcely long enough for any sort of historical tradition to become established. Yet not only has such a tradition bloomed, it has burst into full flower, with a great fund of literature and lore and a spectacular record of innovation and achievement. In fact, it would not be an exaggeration to say that, in its relatively brief period of development, western fly fishing has produced a richer, more colorful history than any other region of North America.

Considering the challenges that faced the first western fly fishers, it is perhaps not so surprising that this could have happened. To begin with, they were confronted with several species previously unknown to anglers: the explosive rainbow trout, the colorful cutthroat in all its permutations, the seagoing steelhead, and five North American species of Pacific salmon. Each required development of effective fly patterns and fishing methods.

But that wasn't all. Pioneer fly fishers also faced waters unlike any they had ever seen before: huge rivers, deeper and swifter than any previously encountered; estuaries that filled and emptied with tides more rapidly than any known before; and a multitude of other fishing environments, from brackish lagoons to high-elevation alpine tarns. Each required development of new fly-fishing techniques and tackle.

That our fly-fishing forebears were successful in meeting these challenges is evident from the fly patterns, tackle, and methods we have come to take for granted today. These have been handed down to us and we have accepted them as a matter of course, usually without even thinking about what it cost our ancestors to develop them, without realizing that we are the inheritors of a rich and well-established fly-fishing culture. But all these things—the flies, the lines, the leaders, the rods and reels and wading gear and accessories and all the sophisticated methods we now enjoy—are the result of painstaking effort and experiment, of lengthy trial and error, of some angler's toil, sweat, and maybe even tears. We owe them greatly for this, and the best way we can repay that debt is to remember them.

That's what Jack Berryman has done. In a remarkable series of columns titled "Pioneers & Legends" published in *Northwest Fly Fishing* magazine, he has chronicled the lives and contributions of 23 fly-fishing pioneers from British Columbia, California, Idaho, Oregon, Montana, and Washington. Now, for the first time, these columns have been gathered in a single volume where they can be enjoyed easily from beginning to end. Together they form an intricate mosaic of the fly-fishing history of the West, particularly the Pacific Northwest.

As Jack will tell you, space is the bane of every magazine writer's existence, and many of his columns had to be whittled down by editors to fit within the limited number of inches allotted in the magazine. Books, however, are free of such constraints, so portions deleted from the magazine columns have here been restored. What you have here, then, is the original, uncut version, so to speak, with more historical detail.

And there is plenty of historical detail, because Jack Berryman has impeccable credentials as a historian. He holds a doctorate in history and teaches the history of medicine at the University of Washington. He was also editor of the *Journal of Sport History*, formerly published on the U.W. campus, and he's a dedicated fly fisher. So in piecing together the personal histories of western fly fishers, he not only knows what to look for but where and how to look for it, and how to translate it into readable prose.

This was not an easy task. All the anglers profiled here have made their final river crossing, some long ago, so they were not available for Jack to interview; he had to learn about them from their own writings, if any, or from other anglers who knew them or wrote about them. This he did by digging relentlessly through libraries, collections of angling memorabilia, old diaries, and other sources. This is tough, tedious work, rewarded only by the occasional discovery of a long-sought nugget of information. Considering the success with which Jack was able to ferret out obscure facts from the lives of these pioneers, he could just as easily have become a private detective instead of a historian.

Even among modern fly fishers, some of Jack's subjects—men such as Roderick Haig-Brown, Dan Bailey, Polly Rosborough, and Zane Grey—remain household names. Others, such as Harry Hornbrook, Frank Pott, and "Mooch" Abraham, have mostly faded from collective memory, but the importance of their contributions is chronicled thoroughly in these pages, and perhaps now their names will be accorded the attention they rightfully deserve.

It was my good fortune to have been personally acquainted with no fewer than nine of the 23 anglers profiled in this book, and three of them—Enos Bradner, Letcher Lambuth, and Ralph Wahl—were among my closest friends. So I can testify that Jack has got everything right in what he says about them. In fact, I'm amazed he was able to find out some things I never knew about them even after years of friendship. Reading about them now, and viewing the photographs Jack has uncovered, triggers many nostalgic memories, especially the photos of

Letcher Lambuth's basement workshop, where I spent so many fascinating hours learning from that master bamboo-rod builder and craftsman.

But a personal acquaintance with the subjects isn't necessary to enjoy this book. Even if you never met any of them, you'll feel you know a lot about them when you finish reading this book, and you'll have a much greater understanding of the role each played in developing fly fishing as we know and practice it in the West today. And with understanding will surely come greater appreciation for the work these men did to improve the sport.

Yet there's more to come. Jack Berryman still has a long list of anglers who deserve profiles similar to those you will read here. He's still busy prowling around libraries, interviewing old-timers, digging through musty collections, and doing all the dogged legwork a determined historian must do to learn the truth.

That means you can look forward to more "Pioneers & Legends" columns in *Northwest Fly Fishing* magazine, and perhaps someday a second book like this one, maybe even a third. And even while Jack continues rummaging around to learn more about the anglers of the past, others are working hard in the present to make their own contributions to fly-fishing culture. They will become subjects for future historians.

Count Jack Berryman himself as one of those future subjects. In his columns, and especially in this book, he has made his own lasting contribution to the literature and lore of western fly fishing—just like the men he writes about.

—Steve Raymond

Acknowledgments

This book is the result of research I began in the spring of 2000 after editor in chief Steve Probasco invited me to write a regular feature in *Northwest Fly Fishing* magazine called "Pioneers & Legends." After writing 23 features over the next six years, I felt it was time to put all of that information in one location: a book. I am grateful to Steve for getting me involved with the magazine and giving me this opportunity to do the type of research and writing I love.

During the past six years of researching and writing about the "pioneers and legends" of Northwest fly fishing, I was faced with regular deadlines to meet a publication schedule of four magazine issues per year. It was during these times that I came to know and appreciate the other members of the *Northwest Fly Fishing* team. Publisher Steve Cole kept us all organized and on time, art and production director Jon Luke put it all together and made it look good, copy editor Miriam Bulmer corrected my mistakes and brought consistency to my writing, and, more recently, managing editor John Shewey has helped considerably with his vast knowledge of flies, fly fishing, and fly tying. This same team came together with a great combination of skill, excitement, and optimism to produce this book. I am particularly pleased to thank publisher Steve Cole for having faith in the content of this book and for moving the manuscript toward printing in a fairly short time.

In a work such as this where our debt to those who have gone before is patently clear, I still must mention several individuals whose appreciation for the history of fly fishing greatly aided my own research. Although I make every effort to acknowledge their contributions in the text and bibliography, I would like especially to thank Frank Amato, Bob Arnold, Trey Combs, George Grant, Art Lingren, Steve Raymond, Paul Schullery, Pat Trotter, Pete Van Gytenbeek, and Bob Wethern for their significant earlier research and writing. In addition, Steve Raymond read and commented on the entire manuscript and provided special assistance with editing. I would also like to thank him for his most gracious foreword to the book. Bob Wethern also read each of the chapters, provided many details that I had overlooked, and was especially helpful in securing photographs of many of the "pioneers and legends" whom he knew personally. The contributions of both of these men materially improved the final product, but I am responsible for any errors that remain.

The staffs at the following libraries and societies were very helpful during my research: American Museum of Fly Fishing (especially Gary Tanner, Sara Wilcox, and Yoshi Akiyama); Big Hole River Foundation; Center for Pacific Northwest Studies (especially Elizabeth Joffrion and Ruth Steele); Douglas County (Oregon) Museum of History and Natural History; Humboldt County

(California) Historical Society; Humboldt (California) Public Library; Multnomah County (Oregon) Library; North Umpqua Foundation; University of Washington Special Collections; and Washington Fly Fishing Club.

Others who provided me with assistance, information, documents, or photographs are Nick Amato; Richard Anderson; Ron Appel; John Bailey; Robert Bettzig; Dan Blanton; Karen Bratton; Todd Collins; Dale Dennis; Don Edge; Gary Estabrook; Dr. Loren Grey; Valerie Haig-Brown; Bob Hart; Dave Hornbrook; Sherri Hornbrook; Kim Koch; Deborah Lipman; Bob Nauheim; Mary Randlett; Stephen Rosenberg; Dee Snodgrass; Bill Sprague; Ward Tonsfeldt; Terrence Wahl; Tim Wahl; Pat and Gary Waller; Debbie Waterman; and Mike Wilkerson. The state and provincial maps preceding each part were prepared especially for this book by Peter Chadwell, and I thank him for his artistic talents. I would also like to thank Jon Luke for tying the beautiful flies featured as insets on the photographs that begin many of the chapters.

All of the typing of this book was done by others, and I am particularly thankful for the work of Amber Curtis, Jennifer Johnson, Jeff Curtis, and my wife, Elaine, who also helped with many other aspects of the book preparation.

Last, but certainly not least, I would like to thank the 23 "pioneers and legends" featured in this book for all of their many contributions to fly fishing. We certainly would not be experiencing the success and joy of the sport today in the same way without their prior accomplishments. Therefore, it is very rewarding for me to have this opportunity to pay tribute to these men and to honor the many things they have given us over the years.

Introduction

An exciting new fishing magazine made its debut in 1999, with my long-time friend and fishing partner Steve Probasco as its editor. The first issue of *Northwest Fly Fishing* appeared that summer, and the magazine quickly attracted a large readership. The following March, Steve called to ask if I would be interested in writing a regular feature in the magazine called "Pioneers & Legends." I accepted and, as the old saying goes, "the rest is history."

The purpose of "Pioneers & Legends" was to profile the anglers who helped make Western fly fishing what it is today. I began researching and writing about the lives of individuals who had developed innovative techniques, designed new fly patterns, invented new equipment, written classic books and articles, built special rods, taken beautiful photographs, opened-fly fishing shops, or contributed in other ways to the traditions and lore of Western fly fishing.

Since the first column appeared in the Winter 2000 issue of *Northwest Fly Fishing*, I have written 22 more. The 23 men who were the subjects of those columns are now the subjects of this book. But there is one big difference: due to space limitations in the magazine, some material was omitted from the published version of most columns. Now, thanks to the much greater space available, all of that material has been restored. In addition, a bibliography of references has been provided, along with a detailed index to help readers navigate the book.

Some of the individuals profiled here remain household names, such as Roderick Haig-Brown, Ted Trueblood, Dan Bailey, and Zane Grey. Others, such as Harry Hornbrook, Frank Pott, and "Mooch" Abraham, are not as well known. The exploits of some have been reported previously in such angling histories as Charles Waterman's *A History of Angling* (1981) and Paul Schullery's *American Fly Fishing: A History* (1987); others were subjects of profiles in regional publications such as *The Creel*, journal of the Flyfishers Club of Oregon, or many of the magazines and books published by Frank Amato Publications in Portland. Books and articles by Trey Combs, Art Lingren, Steve Raymond, Pat Trotter, Bob Wethern, and a few others, also were helpful. All of these individuals and their publications have helped to keep alive the memory of earlier generations of fly fishers.

The history of fly fishing in North America had its beginnings in the East, and for many years Eastern traditions of fly fishing were dominant in books and magazines. But as the 19th century neared its end, fly fishers were traveling west to sample new waters and different fish. Arnold Gingrich, publisher of *Esquire* magazine, noted this trend in his preface to Steve Raymond's classic book *The Year of the Angler* (1973). "The preponderance of American quality angling has been moving steadily westward for now very nearly half a century," he wrote. "The great days of the storied Eastern streams had peaked by 1925, and by midcentury mid-Pennsylvania had become the last Eastern redoubt of the kind of fishing from which Legend is engendered. . . . History, with its peculiar propensity for repeating itself, now appears to be restaging the same play of Legend for the West Coast." Indeed, it was!

Fly fishing in the West actually began much earlier than most suspect. Transplanted Bostonian James Swan was fly fishing for trout in a tributary of Washington's Shoalwater Bay (now Willapa Bay) as early as 1852. *Rod & Gun* magazine reported angling success for trout with a Gray Professor fly pattern on the Tongue River in Wyoming Territory in 1876; it also reported a Pacific salmon was caught on a fly in the mouth of the Columbia River that same year. Northern California's McCloud River was producing rainbows for fly fishermen in the mid-1870s as well, and in 1878 the McCloud Fishing Club was formed. A. S. Trude was fly fishing Idaho's Henrys Lake and the North Fork of the Snake by 1881, and *Forest & Stream* reported a salmon caught on a fly in Oregon's Clackamas River in 1886. The correspondent noted that his "favorite fly is of a reddish cast and is a hard one to describe. . . . The most killing fly is one with wine body and brown speckled wings."

As early as 1888, coastal cutthroat trout were being caught on flies in Washington's Chambers Creek, and the following year *Forest & Stream* claimed that "for the first time in tributaries of the Columbia River the steelhead salmon or Gairdner's trout have been taken in large numbers with artificial flies." The author concluded by happily reporting that "Gradually, but surely, the salmon and trout of the West are becoming fascinated by the attractive devices of the fly-fishermen, and new sources of enjoyment are continually being discovered, where at first the disciples of Walton met with many discouragements." By the early 1890s, the great Kamloops trout of British Columbia were being caught in lakes on a number of different fly patterns.

The pioneers and legends featured in this book, for the most part, were of the next generation, those who built on these early encounters between western fish and flies. Most were born in the 1880s and 1890s; the youngest of the 23 was born in 1922. They drew attention to fly fishing in the West through the pages of popular outdoor magazines, books, and newspapers, while simultaneously introducing fish such as steelhead, sea-run cutthroat trout, the five species of Pacific salmon, and Kamloops trout to a national audience.

The chapters that follow describe the contributions of these 23 pioneers and legends. I have attempted to document their lives in a manner that shows why and how they did what they did, what they thought, what they were passionate about, how important they were to their contemporaries, and, most of all, why they are still important to the current generation of fly fishers. This is history using a biographical approach, and I hope you will enjoy these "backcasts" into waters already downstream and around the bend, but not so far out of sight as to be forgotten.

Yet this roll call of great names in Western fly fishing is only the beginning. There are many more who deserve recognition, more still who are even now making innovative and lasting contributions to the sport. They will be the subjects of future columns in *Northwest Fly Fishing* magazine and, hopefully, another book.

Part One:

British Columbia

Bill Nation poses with a large trout caught by one of his clients. The handwritten note reads, "Rainbow trout on fly rod from a high altitude lake—Mr. H.G. Sheldon of Hong Kong with Wm. Nation, guide. June 10th, 1935." (photograph courtesy of Steve Raymond) Nation's Silver Tipped Sedge, tied by Jon Luke (inset)

"[T]here is no better Kamloops fisherman than Nation, and he may well claim credit for many of the traditions and methods that already belong to the sport of fly fishing for Kamloops trout."
—Roderick Haig-Brown, The Western Angler

Chapter 1

Arthur William "Bill" Nation, (1881–1940):

KAMLOOPS TROUT GUIDE AND INNOVATIVE FLY DESIGNER

Bill Nation was born in Bristol, England, on June 29, 1881, and immigrated to the Kamloops area of British Columbia, Canada, in the 1920s. While little is known about his early career, he apparently was a trained pharmacist. One fact that is known, however, is that when he arrived in British Columbia, Bill possessed well-developed skills in both fly tying and fly fishing and he soon put his talents to good use as a Kamloops trout fishing guide on the Little River. Soon thereafter, he relocated his guiding services to Echo Lodge on the west end of Paul Lake, a beautiful lake in a valley off the North Thompson River near Kamloops. Although he was headquartered there, he also guided on many of the other lakes in the Kamloops region.

Nation's reputation as an expert on Kamloops trout quickly spread. He was a pioneer guide and amateur scientist/biologist who spent most of his waking hours studying the Kamloops trout and experimenting with new ways to catch them. Bill was also a legendary fly tier who developed and popularized at least a dozen patterns. These flies remained favorites of Kamloops trout anglers for more than 40 years.

While Bill Nation and the Kamloops trout were known by serious regional anglers in the late 1920s and early '30s, the writings of Roderick Haig-Brown helped popularize both throughout the world. Haig-Brown's classic, *The Western Angler* (1939), featured four Nation-dressed nymphs in the frontispiece and included extensive information on Kamloops trout and Nation. Haig-Brown had befriended Nation, fished with him on several occasions, and corresponded with him regularly. In fact, Haig-Brown believed "there is no better Kamloops fisherman than Nation, and he may well claim credit for many of the traditions and methods that already belong to the sport of fly fishing for Kamloops trout." Later, in his revised edition of 1947, published seven years after Nation's death, Haig-Brown remembered that Bill Nation "brought to Kamloops trout fishing the most original mind it has yet known" and that "in a very real way he made the Kamloops trout his own special fish." Specifically in reference to the Kamloops trout, Haig-Brown suggested that "for me and for many another Bill will always be the true pioneer of the fishing, the man whose life was closer to those particular fish than any other man's had been or is likely to be."

During his years at Paul Lake, Nation also worked closely with Charles Mottley, a provincial fisheries biologist who conducted the first serious studies of the life cycle of the Kamloops trout. And, as Haig-Brown observed in *A River*

TWO BILL NATION FLIES, PHOTOGRAPHED ON NATION'S LETTERHEAD FROM ECHO LODGE, PAUL LAKE, KAMLOOPS, BRITISH COLUMBIA (PHOTOGRAPH COURTESY OF ARTHUR LINGREN)

Never Sleeps (1946), "Charlie learned a great deal from Bill . . . and Bill learned a great deal from Charlie; I was lucky enough to come between and learn from both of them." Bill also experimented with transplanting the famous "traveling sedge" to Paul Lake, persuaded fisheries managers to introduce crayfish to Paul Lake, helped run a small hatchery on the lake, and suggested the sterilization of Kamloops trout so their sexual maturity would not stunt their growth.

Two of fly fishing's keenest observers, Arthur Lingren and Steve Raymond, have both written convincingly of the importance and popularity of Bill Nation's flies. In Lingren's *Fly Patterns of British Columbia* (1996), he suggested that "British Columbia's fly development took a leap forward when Bill Nation produced his wet-fly patterns." Raymond, in his seminal book, *Kamloops: An Angler's Study of the Kamloops Trout* (1971), testified that "Bill Nation also was an innovative and prolific fly tier. Some of his patterns became standards for several decades." Raymond also noted that Nation flies were losing their popularity by 1970, but suggested that "if the future of Nation patterns is uncertain, their place in the past is assured." And, in a concluding statement, he argued for the overall significance of Nation and his flies: "Both the flies and the man who tied them occupy a place of honor in the history and traditions of Kamloops trout fly fishing that is unlikely ever to be eclipsed."

Nation produced at least a dozen patterns, including what Lingren believes were the first Chironomid pupa and dragonfly nymph imitations in British Columbia, if not the world. Nation's Black, one of his first flies, was a famous Chironomid imitation. Nation's Grey and Nation's Green were his small dragonfly nymph and mature dragonfly nymph imitations. His Nation's Red and Nation's Blue were made to replicate mating dragonflies and damselflies, respectively. Nation's Silver and Mallard was designed to look like a sockeye fingerling, and Nation's Green Sedge, Nation's Silver-Tipped Sedge, and Nation's Silver-Tip each represented various colors and sizes of sedges. Nation's Fancy and Nation's Special were two of his most popular flies. Both were excellent

attractor and exploratory patterns that sported a silver tinsel tag end as well as a silver tinsel rib. One of his least-known patterns was Nation's Grizzly King.

Haig-Brown's revised *Western Angler* included a list of Nation's flies, which Bill had sent him in 1938 (only the Grizzly King and the Silver and Mallard were absent). Enos Bradner's *Northwest Angling* (1969) featured Nation's Fancy and Nation's Silver-Tip. Raymond's Kamloops included a full-color plate of most of Nation's flies as well as descriptions and tying instructions for each. Lingren's *Fly Patterns of British Columbia* featured all 12 of Nation's flies. Regarding Nation's style and his tying trademarks, Raymond observed, "His flies are distinctive not only for the style of tying, but also for the materials used." Specifically, he divided "the bodies into radically different sections and ribbing, both with tinsel," frequently used "mallard breast and turkey for wing materials," and liked golden pheasant tippets for color and decoration. Later, in his *Rivers of the Heart: A Fly-Fishing Memoir* (1998), Raymond explained that Nation "was not a strict imitationist, apparently believing instead that a fly pattern should merely suggest the appearance of a natural insect, or create an impression of it." In Lingren's opinion, Nation "observed his natural world, formed beliefs and devised fly patterns to suit those beliefs, but most of all he presented the fly in such a way that brought reality to his hypotheses."

WILLIAM NATION

ANGLERS' GUIDE

Specializing in
Fly Fishing
for

KAMLOOPS RAINBOW TROUT

Headquarters
at
ECHO LODGE,
PAUL LAKE,
KAMLOOPS, B. C.

Wm. Nation, with day's catch of trout on flies tied by himself. Taken with a client from Hong Kong, August, 1934, in one of the number of high altitude lakes fished from Paul Lake in July and August only.

Fishing Paul Lake and day trips to Knouff, LeJeune, Pillar and Pinantan Lakes, and the Thompson, Adams and Little Rivers—all within easy distance on the car road.

Hyas Long, Pemberton, Devick and Beaver Lakes are reached by car and from four to six miles on horseback in day trips, or stay a few days in cabins.

Jewel, Winfield Beaver, Dee, Canim, and Big Bar Lakes can be reached by car, and are from four to six day trips.

Hi-Hiume Lake, especially good for fly fishing from mid-July to end of August, is a two hour run by car and a ten-mile pack, with comfortable cabins at the lake.

A guarantee of at least 100 trout a week. Each season I net for clients up to 70 trout a day in number, and of larger fish, up to 60 lbs. weight of trout a day, all on the fly.

Season April 16th to November 16th. Bookings, in advance, $35.00 a week.

Special flies tied for Kamloops Rainbow, guaranteed to kill, $2.50 a dozen.

Taupo and Rotorua Lakes in New Zealand in their season.

For further information or reservations, WRITE OR WIRE

WILLIAM NATION
Echo Lodge, Paul Lake, Kamloops, B. C.

AN ADVERTISEMENT FOR BILL NATION'S GUIDING SERVICES THAT WAS PUBLISHED IN A 1937 FISHING GUIDE (PHOTOGRAPH COURTESY OF STEVE RAYMOND)

Presentation was indeed crucial to Nation's success, and as an observant naturalist he was able to convert his knowledge of life in the lakes into applicable fishing techniques. Evidence of his biological abilities was made clear in a letter he wrote to Haig-Brown in the late 1930s, in which he suggested, "Underwater life movements might be classified into those that flick like a prawn, the large dragon nymphs; those that crawl like a snake on a boardwalk . . . , as the *Enallagma* nymphs; [and] those that walk like a sheep, as many of the sedge nymphs." He went on to emphasize that "the working of the fly that imitates these forms should also imitate the action of the particular nymph." Further testimony to Nation's ingenuity can be found in a statement he made to Haig-Brown: "For the Green Sedge it is advisable to carry peroxide of hydrogen to bleach the body to the desired shade of that of the sedge or nymph the fish are feeding on."

Bill Nation's unique and significant contributions to Northwest angling were beginning to fade by the 1990s. Then, in 1995, Bill Jollymore, who owned a fly-fishing shop in Kamloops during the 1960s and had as an employee and friend one of Nation's former assistant guides, Jack Morrill, was informed that Morrill had saved a trunk full of Nation artifacts and that Morrill's widow was giving the trunk and its contents to him. Jollymore contacted Steve Raymond, who assisted in Nation's "rediscovery" by writing an article for *Fly Fishing* magazine and devoting a chapter to Nation in his *Rivers of the Heart*.

Jollymore and Raymond learned that a monument honoring Nation had been erected in a Kamloops cemetery; it bears this inscription: "Erected in Memory of Bill Nation of Paul Lake, Kamloops, by His Many Fishermen Friends and Admirers. Died Nov. 27, 1940." Raymond used some of the Nation artifacts in an exhibit on the history of Northwest fly fishing displayed at the Whatcom Museum of History and Art in Bellingham, Washington. And, in the spring of 2000, a special event to honor Bill Nation on the 60th anniversary of his death was held in Kamloops, in conjunction with the annual meeting of the British Columbia Federation of Fly Fishers. Fittingly, Steve Raymond spoke on what it would have been like to fish with Bill Nation, while Arthur Lingren and Bill Jollymore discussed Nation's flies.

General Noel Money, circa 1930's (photograph courtesy of Robert Wethern and *The Creel*)

Chapter 2

Noel Money (1867–1941):

STAMP RIVER STEELHEADER AND FLY TIER

Noel Money was born in 1867 in Montreal, Canada, where his father, Captain Albert Money, was serving with the British Army. Soon thereafter, Captain Money returned with his family to his native England. There, young Noel grew up on the family estate in the west of England, doing what young male aristocrats did in the last quarter of the 19th century: attend private school and participate in a variety of field sports, most notably hunting and fishing. Noel, as part of the gentry, learned to shoot birds, ride to the hounds, and ride in point-to-point steeplechase races. And, as was expected of his class, Noel received an exceptional education, attending both Radley College in Abingdon, Oxfordshire, and Christ Church College of the University of Oxford.

It was during his collegiate days that Money began the first of what would eventually be eight hunting and fishing diaries, known in that era as "gamebooks." Spanning the period from the 1880s through 1940, these leather-bound volumes filled with the details of his hunting and angling exploits, along with photographs, provide some of the best information about this man and his passion for guns and fishing. Trey Combs examined the gamebooks in the early 1970s, thanks to Money's son, Gordon, who lived in Victoria, British Columbia. Combs then published a two-part article on Money in *Salmon Trout Steelheader* in 1972. The next year, for an article in *The Creel*, Fred Auger, retired publisher of Vancouver's *Province* newspaper, also looked at the diaries. And, more recently, British Columbia fly-fishing historian Arthur Lingren utilized the diaries in his book *Fly Patterns of British Columbia* (1996).

In 1885, at the age of 22, after college graduation, Money followed his father and joined the British Army. He became a commissioned officer and served in India, where he hunted wild boars and tigers. When the Boer War broke out in 1899, he served in South Africa. He commanded the First Squadron and, during this stint,

"In some of the big rivers on our West Coast we have a run of these big trout starting in May and going to October. This fly fishing I consider the best in Canada, except for Atlantic salmon in the East, but our steelhead are better fish than salmon—much more lively and jump more." —Noel Money

was injured. He returned to England in 1901 at the conclusion of the war, where he was awarded both the Queen's and King's Medals. Two years later, in 1903, Money married. He and his wife took ownership of the family estate, Culmington Manor, Shropshire, and began to raise their two children, Mary Evelyn and Gordon.

While serving in the British Army and living the life of an upper-class gentleman during the Edwardian era (1890–1914), Money hunted and fished with regularity. He hunted bear in Siberia, and elk, bear, and mountain sheep in Montana. His fishing included Scottish Atlantic salmon and English chalk-stream trout. Then, in 1913, at the age of 50, Money ventured to the Campbell River on British Columbia's Vancouver Island to fish for the famed tyee salmon. On this trip he became enamored with the little town of Qualicum Beach, south of Campbell River. The following year he sold the estate in England and moved his family to a large plot of land on Qualicum Bay, where the water sweeps in from the Strait of Georgia. Here, he began the construction of his Qualicum Inn and golf course, a landmark on Vancouver Island dedicated to angling, hunting, and military life through the early 1940s. It was also in 1914 that Money hooked his first steelhead, a late-March fish in the Little Qualicum River.

Just as he was getting settled and established on Vancouver Island, Great Britain entered World War I. Money reenlisted as a commissioned officer, took command of the 159th Brigade, and fought in Palestine and Egypt. By the end of the war, when he was 54, Money was promoted to the rank of brigadier general in the British Army. After the armistice was signed, General Money returned to his family and the Qualicum Inn to begin a life of dedicated attention to fly fishing for steelhead, salmon, and cutthroat trout in British Columbia, Washington, and Oregon. During the late teens and early 1920s, Money began to apply and institute in the Pacific Northwest the traditions, equipment, flies, and angling ethic that he had learned on the Atlantic salmon rivers and chalk streams in Scotland and England. Spey rods, Atlantic salmon flies, and highly machined reels became part of his Vancouver Island fishing experience.

During the 1920s, many times accompanied by his children, Money fished up and down the old Island Highway north of Nanaimo. He drove a large McLaughlin-Buick limousine bearing B.C. license number 1, testimony to the fact that British Columbians held him in high esteem. Photographs from this era show Money wearing a white collar, jacket, and necktie, standing about 6 feet tall and, as Auger described him, "straight as befits a soldier, lean, bronzed, grey-eyed, and serene." It was at this time that Money first fished the Stamp River near Port Alberni. He pioneered steelhead fly fishing on this river as well as its two major tributaries, the Sproat and the Ash. He also fished the lower Stamp or the Somass River before it entered Alberni Inlet and studied steelhead run size, timing, and specific angling techniques.

On the general's first trip to the Stamp, on September 15, 1920, he landed six "rainbows," the descriptor he used for steelhead. It was "love at first sight,"

MONEY'S POOL, OR "THE LONG RUN," ON THE STAMP RIVER (PHOTOGRAPH COURTESY OF VAN EGAN AND ARTHUR LINGREN)

and Money began to fish the upper Stamp and Ash rivers on a regular basis, with September being his favorite month. He landed 77 steelhead on the Stamp in 1922, and during that year he bought some property on a bluff overlooking the Stamp just below its junction with the Ash. It was here that Money built a cottage to serve as his base camp while fishing the Stamp. The beautiful pool at the base of the hill he named the House Pool, or Great Pool. He also referred to it as the Junction Pool because of its location. (As time went on, this great piece of Stamp holding water became known as Money's Pool, the Money Pool, or the General's Pool to the anglers who fished it since

GENERAL MONEY NO. 1, A SUMMER-RUN STEELHEAD FLY DEVELOPED BY GEN-
ERAL MONEY DURING THE 1920S FOR FISHING THE STAMP RIVER (PHOTOGRAPH
COURTESY OF ARTHUR LINGREN)

ANOTHER POPULAR GENERAL MONEY SUMMER-RUN STEELHEAD FLY, GOLDEN
RED, DEVELOPED IN THE 1920S FOR FISHING THE STAMP AND ASH RIVERS (PHO-
TOGRAPH COURTESY OF ARTHUR LINGREN)

the 1930s.) During the next season on the Stamp (1923), Money landed 109 steelhead. And, in one day in 1924, the general landed 10 steelhead.

Although General Money loved to fish the local Vancouver Island streams and rivers for steelhead and cutthroat, he did fish for other species in a variety of locales. For instance, he fished Oregon's famed Rogue River in 1928, cast for coho in Duncan Bay, just north of Campbell River, and hired Indian guides to float the Cowichan River. But summer-run steelhead were by far his favorite fish. For example, in a letter to Harold Smedley (author of *Fly Patterns & Their Origins*, 1943), in Michigan, Money noted, "In some of the big rivers on our West Coast we have a run of these big trout starting in May and going to October. This fly fishing I consider the best in Canada, except for Atlantic salmon in the East, but our steelhead are better fish than salmon—much more lively and jump more."

It was during the 1920s and '30s that Money experimented with a variety of steelhead flies and began to dress some of his favorites on a regular basis. In *Fly Patterns of British Columbia* (1996), Arthur Lingren attributes nine specific steelhead patterns to Money. However, Money did not always give names to his flies—just their color combinations, main ingredients, and unique characteristics. His flies were Black, Orange, and Jungle Cock; Black, Tippet, and Yellow (Lingren says this was the first British Columbia steelhead pattern to incorporate golden pheasant tippet in the wings); Dick's Fly (named after his regular fishing companion, Billy Dick from Alberta); General Money No. 1; General Money No. 2; Golden Red (which preceded Zane Grey's introduction of the Golden Demon to California summer-run steelhead by at least 10 years); Grey Fly; Prawn Fly (the main steelhead shrimp pattern up until the 1960s, when Colonel Esmond Drury's General Practitioner was popularized); and Rainbow (Lingren believes this fly was British Columbia's first locally designed steelhead pattern). For most of his patterns, Money used hook sizes ranging from 2/0 down to 4. For his Rainbow fly, Lingren says, he used blind-eyed salmon hooks. A testimony to the popularity and acceptance of the general's patterns is that Harkley & Haywood sporting goods store in Vancouver noted that Money's flies topped their steelhead-fly sales lists every year into the 1970s. Trey Combs included photographs of the General Money No. 1 and General Money No. 2 in his pioneering book, *The Steelhead Trout* (1971).

Money's angling exploits did not go unnoticed by another Vancouver Island resident and fellow traditional English sportsman—Roderick Haig-Brown. Haig-Brown and Money became friends during the 1930s, and Haig-Brown learned much about steelhead fly fishing from Money. In fact, Haig-Brown dedicated his classic book, *The Western Angler: An Account of Pacific Salmon & Western Trout in British Columbia* (1939), to Money with the following inscription: "To General Money of Qualicum Beach, finest of western anglers, and to his own Stamp River, loveliest and most generous of western streams." The color frontispiece of volume two shows three Money patterns—the General

A GROUP OF GENERAL MONEY STEELHEAD FLIES, PHOTOGRAPHED ON HIS PERSONAL INSCRIBED FLY BOX (PHOTOGRAPH COURTESY OF ARTHUR LINGREN)

Money (General Money No. 2), Dick's Fly, and the Prawn Fly. Later in the book, Haig-Brown refers to Money as "the finest and most experienced fly fisherman in British Columbia" and provides a list of dressings for the three flies pictured. Much later, long after Money's death, Haig-Brown remembered in an article on "The Evolution of a Steelhead Fly" (1976) that "[t]he first fly I ever saw that was specifically tied for steelhead was the General Money Special [No. 2]." He went on to say that "General Money also showed me his Prawn Fly which I found extremely good for winter fish."

General Money, and later Haig-Brown, must also be given much credit for popularizing fly fishing for winter-run steelhead. In fact, in an interview with Fred Auger for an article on Money for *The Creel* in 1973, Haig-Brown remembered, "It was General Money who first persuaded me that winter steelhead could be taken on a fly as a regular thing and not just a fluke." In addition, in his chapter "Winter Steelhead" in the 1947 edition of *The Western Angler*, written after he had fished with General Money, Haig-Brown said, "During the winter of 1938–1939 I began to use the fly at least as frequently as the minnow and found myself doing not too badly with it. Since then I have used the fly exclusively and, as nearly as I can judge, its effectiveness is at least seventy per cent that of the minnow." By 1951 and the publication of *Fisherman's Spring*, Haig-Brown admitted to being a total convert to fly fishing for winter steelhead. In fact, in the chapter "The Maculate Purist," he explains, "It is only within the last five years that I have rigidly abstained from fishing for steelhead with anything but the fly. . . . I am quite satisfied now that any good fisherman can get himself a fair share of winter steelhead on the fly, and have a much more interesting time doing it than he would have in catching more fish by some other means." So, it is clear that Money directly influenced Haig-Brown, who in turn had a major impact on anglers throughout the Northwest. Because of this, as well as his innovative fly patterns and pioneering work on the Stamp River system, Trey Combs refers to Money as the "dean emeritus of Canadian steelheading" and Lingren calls him the "father of British Columbia steelhead fly fishing."

In 1939, while fishing on the Stamp, Haig-Brown introduced General Money, then 76, to the famed "greased line technique" used and popularized by Atlantic salmon fishermen and passed along to other anglers in the popular book *Greased Line Fishing for Salmon/Compiled from the Fishing Papers of the late A.H.E. Wood, of Glassel, by "Jock Scott"* (circa 1930s). Haig-Brown wrote about the incident in his chapter "June" in *A River Never Sleeps* (1946) and recalled later in his interview with Auger the "day when the Stamp was extremely low, that I showed him [Money] Woods' greased line technique." Haig-Brown said Money caught a steelhead using the technique and was so enamored of it that he "promptly sent for suitable rods and low-water flies." Money called the experience "wonderful sport" and, after telling Haig-Brown "I'm getting old," exclaimed, "But we've found something new for the river after all these years."

Money continued to fish and be involved in fishing matters on Vancouver Island during the last few years of his life. He served as president of the Qualicum Fish and Game Association in 1939 and devoted considerable attention to raising and stocking brown trout in the area's streams. His last diary entry described a steelhead fishing experience on Whisky Creek in mid-December 1940. The general died at the Qualicum Inn, after a short illness, on May 26, 1941.

TOMMY BRAYSHAW WITH A STEELHEAD CAUGHT ON THE CAMPBELL RIVER IN 1943 (PHOTOGRAPH COURTESY OF THE LATE STANLEY READ AND ARTHUR LINGREN). WITH IT IS HIS COQUIHALLA ORANGE, TIED BY JON LUKE (INSET)

"Brayshaw was undoubtedly one of the more capable amateur fly dressers of his era."
—*Arthur Lingern,* Fly Patterns of British Columbia, *1996*

Chapter 3

Thomas "Tommy" Brayshaw (1886–1967):

ANGLER, ARTIST, AND FLY TIER

Thomas "Tommy" Brayshaw was born March 3, 1886, in Stackhouse in the parish of Giggleswick in Yorkshire, England. His father was in the legal profession; served as governor of the Giggleswick School, where Tommy was educated; and owned land and fishing rights on the nearby River Ribble. When Tommy was 8, he was presented with a small fly rod and began to fish the local waters with his father and uncle. He remembered, "I was only allowed to fish fly. I didn't catch anything that year, but when I was nine I caught about half a dozen."

At age 11 he began to tie all of his own flies and benefited greatly from the advice and encouragement of Sir Edward Grey, who was best known for his book *Fly Fishing* (1899). Tommy also fished the Aln and the Coquet, famous Northumbrian streams, and caught his first trout in Malham Tarn in 1900. It was at this time, when he was about 14, that the youthful fly tier established a correspondence with G. M. Kelson, the noted author of *The Salmon Fly* (1895).

By 1904 and his 18th birthday, Tommy left home to serve a six-year apprenticeship in drafting at Jarrow-on-Tyne, near Newcastle. Here he joined the Northumbrian Anglers' Federation and began to make drawings of fish. One of his first such sketches, *Brown Trout and Creel*, was published in his company's newsletter in 1909.

Brayshaw left England in 1910 and moved to Vancouver, British Columbia, where he was employed by the Yorkshire Trust. While in the region, he began to fish the Capilano, Seymour, and Coquihalla rivers and caught his first steelhead. He also discovered the large chinook salmon at Campbell River on Vancouver Island and caught two in the upper-40-pound range. Tommy returned to his native England during World War I, joined the Yorkshire Regiment, and was wounded in 1915. Thereafter, he became a revolver specialist in charge of the Tees Garrison revolver school and authored a training manual, *The Service Revolver as a Fighting Weapon*, which he illustrated with line drawings and photographs. He married Edith Rebecca "Becky" Sugden on July 5, 1916, and was discharged from the service as a captain in 1918.

Tommy and his wife returned to British Columbia in 1920, this time buying a small orchard and home in Vernon. Besides growing fruit, he taught mathematics at the Vernon Preparatory School, owned and operated by brothers Austin and Hugh Mackie, also from England. Both of the Mackies were avid fishermen, and throughout the next 10 or more years Brayshaw fished with them in the lakes and streams of the greater Kamloops region. Tommy's targets were the large rainbows, or Kamloops trout, and he became quite proficient at catching them. He fished most of the "Bill Nation Lakes," including Lac Le Jeune, Pinantan Lake, Knouff Lake, and Paul Lake, and always carried his "bible" with him—a compact fly-tying kit suitable for pocket or pouch. Because he never used a vise in his tying, the kit did not weigh much. He also regularly fished the Little River and the Adams River and was often accompanied by his wife and their son, Christopher, called Kit by his father.

Brayshaw was particularly fond of the large Knouff Lake trout and the thrill of catching them on the surface with Traveling Sedge patterns. However, by the early 1930s he noticed that the average weight per fish had been dropping rapidly every year. In a manner that would only get stronger as he witnessed the destruction of fishing opportunities in his home province, Brayshaw exclaimed that this was a perfect example of "a first-class lake ruined by overstocking."

In the early 1930s Brayshaw began making his own rods out of hickory or greenheart, started his fishing diary, and continued his annual trips to Campbell River seeking the large tyee salmon. It was on the Campbell River Spit in the fall of 1933 that Tommy first met Roderick Haig-Brown, who would become his lifelong friend. Haig-Brown remembered that Tommy "was bending over a massive tyee salmon, making little sketches and notes about its shape, color, condition." Little did he know that Brayshaw was preparing to carve his first wooden salmon model, which he completed the following year. When they met, Haig-Brown was only 25 and Brayshaw was 47.

From the start, Brayshaw and Haig-Brown became friends. Both were from England and enjoyed fly fishing, and they had a great influence on each other. They began to correspond and fish together quite frequently. Brayshaw started to fish for "cohoes" in Duncan Bay, just north of Campbell River, with his white and orange polar bear streamers (rather than the more common bucktail), and explored the Campbell for steelhead.

By 1936, Tommy had achieved an international reputation as a carver of life-size wood replicas of trophy trout and salmon, and he received further notoriety when an article about him, titled "Wooden Fish Trophies," was published in *Field & Stream* magazine. A 54-pound tyee carved by Brayshaw was sent on a Canadian tour on its way to a display at the New York Sportsman's Show, and a 52-pound tyee model he carved was hung on the wall of the Angler's Club of New York.

Haig-Brown learned much from Brayshaw about Kamloops trout. When Haig-Brown's book *The Western Angler: An Account of Pacific Salmon and Western Trout in British Columbia* was published in 1939, the color plate labeled "Interior Flies" featured not only "Nation's flies," but "Mr. Brayshaw's sedges for interior lakes" and "Mr. Brayshaw's large wet flies for Little River fishing." The sedge pattern was probably his Olive Sedge, which Art Lingren believes he developed around 1932. The wet flies were Tommy's Little River No. 1

J. J. Weston (left) and Tommy Brayshaw (right), weigh a 14-pound hen steelhead caught in the Coquihalla River in 1951 (photograph courtesy of the late Stanley Read and Arthur Lingren)

and Little River No. 2, which Lingren says he started making around 1934. Haig-Brown said they were "attractive to look at, ingeniously worked out and thoroughly practical." Another of Brayshaw's flies from this period started out in 1935 as the Queen Mary, which Haig-Brown called Brayshaw's Nameless and later named Brayshaw's Fancy. Brayshaw's two other most popular trout flies were his Yolk Sac, later named Alevin, and the Maggot. Lingren's *Fly Patterns of British Columbia* (1996) offers much more detail on all of these.

As World War II began, Brayshaw became an army recruiting officer and later a counselor, eventually retiring with the rank of major. While serving his country and residing in Vernon, Tommy still had time to fish, carve, and tie flies. He was angling friends with some of British Columbia's most notable fishermen and writers, including A. Bryan Williams, author of *Rod and Creel in British Columbia* (1919), *Game Trails in British Columbia* (1925), and *Fish & Game in British Columbia* (1935), and Francis C. Whitehouse, who wrote *Sport Fishes of Western Canada, and Some Others* (1946).

Nearing retirement from the army, Brayshaw and his wife bought land and built a home on the bank of the Fraser River, just across from the mouth of the Coquihalla River, in the town of Hope. They moved into their new home, which they named "Stackhouse" after his native home, in 1946, and established a spacious workshop and garden. Here, Tommy and Becky regularly entertained fishing friends since they were geographically at a crossroads for those heading to the interior lakes or local rivers.

The move to Hope and his retirement form the army marked a dividing point in Tommy's life. Haig-Brown had introduced him to Letcher Lambuth, the noted Seattle rod maker, in 1944, and Letcher taught Tommy to make split-cane fly rods. He used 13- and 14-foot rods on the Thompson, and for his home stream, the Coquihalla, he built 10.5-, 11-, and 11.5-foot rods weighing from 8.5 to 12.5 ounces. He noted that "all were double-handed . . . and of an easy action for Spey or roll casting."

It was in 1946 that Brayshaw began to regularly fly fish the Coquihalla for summer-run steelhead, and he landed his first one in early August. Later that month he caught his first Coquihalla steelhead on his own pattern, the Coquihalla Orange. He carved a wooden model of one of his first steelhead and presented it to Ralph Wahl, another pioneer steelheader and friend from Bellingham, Washington.

Brayshaw's career as an artist and illustrator began the following year, when he was invited to supply the artwork for a revised edition of Haig-Brown's *The Western Angler*, his first professional assignment. He did several line drawings, two color paintings of cutthroat and rainbow trout and "cohoe" and steelhead, and the cover. By the late 1940s, as his reputation as an artist was spreading, Tommy became primarily a steelhead fly fisher. He made infrequent trips for

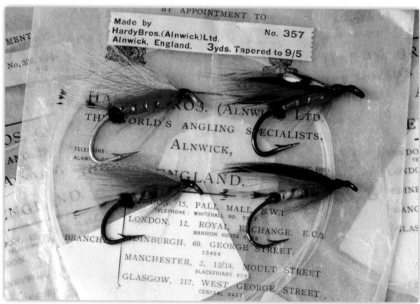

A GROUP OF STEELHEAD FLIES DEVELOPED BY TOMMY BRAYSHAW IN THE 1940S AND '50S FOR FISHING THE COQUIHALLA RIVER (PHOTOGRAPH COURTESY OF ARTHUR LINGREN)

A Tommy Brayshaw drawing, in colored pencil on paper, titled Cutthroat (above) and Rainbow Trout, used on the cover of Roderick L. Haig-Brown's *The Western Angler*, 1947 (courtesy of the Washington Fly Fishing Club)

trout and finally stopped fishing for Pacific salmon, disgusted with too many boats, derbies, and the long and boring days of trolling. He was content fishing near home and served as the founding president of the Hope Rod and Gun Club from 1948 until 1961.

Brayshaw was probably known best in steelhead fly-fishing circles for his Coquihalla series of four flies. He developed the first, his Coquihalla Orange (Light), in 1946 and the Dark variation in 1949. The Silver came in 1947, and his Latest, which became his Red, appeared first in 1950 and changed its name sometime in the early 1950s. Art Lingren, in his *Fly Patterns of British Columbia* (1996), also identified his Black and Silver, sometimes called Brayshaw's Black and White, and Brayshaw's Dusk, the first developed in 1946 and the other in 1947. In Lingren's opinion, "Brayshaw was undoubtedly one of the

A Tommy Brayshaw drawing, in colored pencil on paper, titled Cohoe (above) and Steelhead, used to illustrate Roderick L. Haig-Brown's The Western Angler, 1947 (courtesy of the Washington Fly Fishing Club)

more capable amateur fly dressers of his era." Tommy primarily fished the Coquihalla, where he took his largest steelhead, a 13.5-pounder, in 1952, and the Thompson, where he took the first fly-caught steelhead from the famous Y Run the following year on a trip with Haig-Brown.

During the 1950s and early 1960s, Brayshaw's reputation as a steelhead fly fisherman, painter, carver, rod builder, fly tier, and devout conservationist spread throughout Canada and the Pacific Northwest. He provided fish art for several of Haig-Brown's publications, the Canadian Department of Fisheries, the provincial government of British Columbia, and the Vancouver Public Aquarium, among others, and had his work shown in galleries in Victoria and Vancouver. Other paintings and drawings were done as gifts or by special order for a nominal fee. Haig-Brown referred to Tommy's fish as "those sleek, water-surrounded creatures he created with such affection and exactitude on river-blue paper."

As for his unique style, Brayshaw said, "I specialize in pictures of fish and work particularly in crayon, though switching to water-colour or pastel to get any particular effect I may wish, some pictures may be a combination of two, or even all these." His fish were always on the move, chasing a fly or another fish, or were being chased by predators. Today, Brayshaw's art is cherished by its owners, and some is housed in museums.

He also continued to make his wood models of steelhead, salmon, and cutthroat trout, and gave them to his fishing friends and to officers of fly-fishing clubs he had become associated with into the early 1960s. His primary connections were with the Washington Fly Fishing Club (Seattle), the Fly Fisher's Club of Oregon (Portland), and the McKenzie Flyfishers (Eugene). Brayshaw's last carving, a 17-inch sea-run cutthroat, which he referred to as "the last of the run," was done for Bob Wethern, former president of the Fly Fisher's Club of Oregon and early editor of their newsmagazine, *The Creel*. This model, like each of his earlier ones, was very lifelike, with exact color, texture, and proportion. In fact, as was the case with his earlier carvings, they rivaled that which could be accomplished by taxidermy.

In late 1963, Brayshaw and his wife sold their home in Hope and moved into an apartment in Vancouver. At age 77, Tommy was having health problems and could not keep up with his rural property. This was sadly clear in his only fishing diary entry for that year: "Took out my license and never went fishing either for trout or steelhead—the first year I've completely missed since I started fishing in 1894."

While ill, Brayshaw still kept active with some painting, carving, and regular correspondence with fishermen in the Pacific Northwest. On one of his last trips, he was a member of a panel on "Reflections and Philosophies of Fly Fishing" at the first national conclave of the Federation of Fly Fishers (FFF), held in Eugene, Oregon, and hosted by the McKenzie Flyfishers. Tommy's angling ethic was well known and he was a perfect panelist, bringing to the table the long tradition of British fly fishing fostered in the United States and Canada by anglers like himself and Haig-Brown. It was a memorable occasion for Tommy, and in a letter to one of his hosts he remarked that "that meeting was one of the highlights of my long angling life, never have I run into such a big group of congenial people." The following year, the FFF honored Brayshaw with their President's Award "for outstanding contributions to the Federation."

Even after suffering what he described as "a nasty heart attack" in 1967, Tommy tried to keep active. He authored a short article, "Hints on Making Wooden Fish Models," for *The Creel* and continued to paint. In early October 1967 he mailed "4 little pics of fish" to the Washington Fly Fishing Club. A few days later, on October 10, Tommy Brayshaw died.

Brayshaw's contributions to fly fishing have continued long after his death. He donated his entire collection of angling literature to the University of British Columbia's (UBC) Harry Hawthorn Foundation, including his diaries and letters. In 1968, the Washington Fly Fishing Club began the Tommy Award, which bears a wooden fish-shaped "priest" carved by Brayshaw. The Tommy goes to a member "who displays the traits held in highest regard by fellow anglers: enthusiasm, wisdom, humility, honor." His gift to the UBC Libraries stimulated the publishing of *The Contemplative Man's Recreation: A Bibliography of Books on Angling and Game Fish in the Library of the University of British Columbia*, compiled by Susan Starkman and Stanley Read in 1970; it included a short essay titled "Tom Brayshaw—Artist, Craftsman, Flyfisher" by Haig-Brown. The following year, Steve Raymond chose one of Brayshaw's pastel paintings of a brace of Kamloops trout as the cover of *Kamloops: An Angler's Study of the Kamloops Trout*. In 1977, Stanley Read, a professor at UBC and former friend of Brayshaw, published his extensive book on Brayshaw's life, *Tommy Brayshaw: The Ardent Angler-Artist*. J. David "Skip" Hosfield of Eugene, Oregon, the high bidder for several Brayshaw originals and a member of the McKenzie Flyfishers, began offering the first high-quality limited-edition prints of some of Brayshaw's art in 1982, and Tommy's fish carvings were recognized in 1992 in an article on fish models published in *The American Fly Fisher*.

Well-known British Columbia fly-fishing historian Art Lingren has published much about Brayshaw, his art, his flies, and his pioneering days on the Coquihalla in *Fly Patterns of British Columbia* (1996) and *Famous British Columbia Fly Fishing Waters* (2002). It was also Lingren who tied Brayshaw's Coquihalla Orange when in 1998 Canada Post honored the fly as one of six in a commemorative fishing-flies stamp set. Of the six, three were from British Columbia—Brayshaw's and two by Roderick Haig-Brown. One of Brayshaw's rods is on display at the Royal BC Museum in Victoria.

RODERICK HAIG-BROWN TRIMS THE TIPPET OFF HIS FLY ON HIS BELOVED
CAMPBELL RIVER IN 1965 (PHOTOGRAPH © MARY RANDLETT/MSCUA).
RODERICK HAIG-BROWN'S COHO BLUE, TIED BY JON LUKE (INSET)

"I am [an] author, pure and simple and anything else I do in this life is merely done in pursuit of that profession."
—*Roderick Haig-Brown*

Chapter 4

Roderick L. Haig-Brown (1908-1976):

WRITER, CONSERVATIONIST, AND FLY FISHER

Roderick Haig-Brown, known affectionately throughout his life as Roddy, was born February 21, 1908, in Lancing, Sussex, England, and had two sisters. His father, Alan Roderick Haig-Brown, taught at Lancing School and wrote poems and articles about hunting and fishing. Roddy's mother, Violet Pope, was the daughter of Alfred Pope, head of a prominent family that ran a Dorset brewing company. Roddy's grandfather, William Haig-Brown, was headmaster of Charterhouse School and was a well-known Victorian educator. His godfather, Sir Robert Baden-Powell, was founder of the Boy Scout movement. It was from this group of men that Roddy learned, at a very young age, the British amateur traditions of duty, fair play, honor, decency, and civility.

In 1918, when Haig-Brown was 10, his father was killed during World War I while fighting in France. After this tragedy, Roddy's uncle Decimus Pope and family friend Major H. M. Greenhill taught him the essence of the gentleman's sporting ethic and took him hunting and fishing whenever possible. Roddy remembered that his uncle taught him to fish on the Frome and became a member of the Fly Fishers' Club of London. From Greenhill, he said, "I learned most of the things about fishing and wing shooting that a boy generally learns from his father."

Haig-Brown entered Charterhouse School in 1921, at the age of 13, and studied there for three years until he was expelled for not following the rules. After attending a few other private schools and working with tutors, young Roddy, at 18, was stunned when Major Greenhill shot himself. Later that year, in 1926, Roddy sailed to New York and took a train to Seattle, where he was promised a job in a logging camp near Mount Vernon, Washington. He was hired by Alex McEwan, father of his Uncle Decimus's wife, and began to explore the fishing opportunities in the vicinity. He fished the Pilchuck and Stillaguamish rivers and caught his first steelhead in Deer Creek. The following year he continued his logging work at another of the company's camps near the Nimpkish River on Vancouver Island in British Columbia. Here, in late 1927 through most of 1929, he worked as a logging surveyor, guide, and trapper, and began to write adventure stories for the *Fishing Gazette*. He also bought a book, *Narrative Technique*, and developed plans to be a writer of fiction.

In late 1929, Haig-Brown sailed back home to England, where he did some journalism work and began to write his first book. In 1931, *Silver: The Life Story of an Atlantic Salmon* was published, and one reviewer reported that the author "knows [his] subject . . . from [the] standpoint of a naturalist and from that of an angler." He returned to British Columbia in late 1931 and revised his second book, *Pool and Rapid: The Story of a River* (1932), on the ship. Both novels dealt with what would become his two favorite writing topics: fish and rivers. Roddy was receiving money from his mother to support his writing, and in a 1932 letter he stated, "I am [an] author, pure and simple and anything else I do in this life is merely done in pursuit of that profession."

In 1933 Haig-Brown spent more and more time in Seattle visiting Ann Elmore, a bookstore clerk whom he first met in 1929, and he also established a lifelong relationship with Harold Ober, a New York City literary agent. He rented a house along the Campbell River on Vancouver Island and, while still a bachelor, continued his writing and worked as a guide on his beloved Nimpkish River. He and Ann were married on January 20, 1934, and in that same year *Panther*, another novel, was published. He and Ann lived in the rented house until 1936, when they purchased a home on 20 acres just up the river, with Kingfisher Creek running through their land. On this property, which they called Above Tide, the Haig-Browns resided for the next 40 years and raised four children.

It was also during the early 1930s that Haig-Brown met and became great friends and fishing companions with fellow Englishmen and British Columbians General Noel Money, Bill Nation, and Tommy Brayshaw. Together, these four gentlemen helped transfer the British sportfishing ethic to North America and began to experiment with flies and methods to catch rainbow trout, sea-run cutthroat, salmon, and steelhead. All the while, Haig-Brown was actively researching and writing his first book of nonfiction, *The Western Angler: An Account of Pacific Salmon and Western Trout in British Columbia* (1939). This fact-filled book included much information from his friends, but Roddy himself introduced at least a dozen of his own fly patterns to the eager readers of this two-volume Derrydale Press book. According to Arthur Lingren, in *Fly Patterns of Roderick Haig-Brown* (1993) and *Fly Patterns of British Columbia* (1996), the Silver Lady, Silver Brown, and Bullhead (fry patterns); Dark Caddis, Gammarus, Cedar Borer, and Brown, Black, Fiery Brown, and Orange Caterpillar (insect and crustacean patterns); and Coho Golden and Coho Blue all made their public debut in this book. *The Western Angler* established Haig-Brown as a serious and astute fish and fly-fishing authority and one who was seriously concerned about the conservation of British Columbia's fish stocks and their habitat. A revised edition of the book was published in 1947 with the addition of Tommy Brayshaw's artwork and new material.

Haig-Brown published the third of his three "animal biographies," *Return to the River: A Story of the Chinook Run*, in 1941, and that same year, without any legal training or college education, he was appointed a "lay magistrate" in his hometown of Campbell River. He held court on Saturday and Monday mornings and served in this role until 1975. In 1942 he published *Timber:*

RODERICK HAIG-BROWN WALKING THE TRAIL FROM HIS HOME TO THE CAMPBELL RIVER IN 1965. (PHOTOGRAPH © MARY RANDLETT/MSCUA)

A Novel of Pacific Coast Loggers and began his service in the Canadian Army during World War II. *Starbuck Valley Winter*, another novel, but more for the young reader, came out in 1943.

After the war, and much thought about writing and fly fishing, Haig-Brown returned to his home, family, and home river, ready to accomplish new things. Paramount was the writing of his soon-to-be-published book *A River Never Sleeps* (1946), thought to be his most eloquent publication by literary scholars. It was also at this time that he developed his three popular steelhead-fly patterns—Golden Girl, Steelhead Bee, and Quinsam Hackle. The Steelhead Bee, his only dry-fly pattern, evolved from a series of experiments during the late 1940s when he "began to notice that floating flies commonly produced more action from summer steelhead than wet flies." He published *Saltwater Summer*, a novel for youngsters, in 1948, and his final work of fiction, *On the Highest Hill*, in 1949.

STEELHEAD BEE (TIED BY JON LUKE)

Between 1950 and 1964, Haig-Brown published 12 more books and established himself as a literary giant in North America. *Measure of the Year* (1950), about his own life, nature, life in the country, and conservationism, was followed by the first of his famous four-volume tetralogy, *Fisherman's Spring* (1951). In this book he introduced more of this own fly patterns—Humpback Fry, General Fry, Stickleback, Perla, and Golden Girl—and, in the chapter "The Maculate Purist," made a powerful case for catching winter steelhead on a fly. It was also in *Fisherman's Spring* that he made it clear that he was first and foremost a writer, admitting that "I am a writer first and a fisherman second. I go fishing quite a lot and I think about fishing a lot, but I write all the time." He published an account of his two-month fishing trip to Chile and Argentina in early 1952 as *Fisherman's Winter* (1954) and also published the first of his children's history books, *Mounted Police Patrol* (1954). After this came *Captain of Discovery: The Story of Captain George Vancouver* (1956), *Fisherman's Summer* (1959), and another juvenile history, *The Farthest Shores* (1960). He published two more history books for children in 1962, *Fur and Gold* and *The Whale People*, just after authoring a large volume called *The Living Land: An Account of the Natural Resources of British Columbia* (1961), in which he discussed the public ownership of natural resources and how to best mange them. His final two books before a 10-year hiatus were *A Primer on Fly Fishing* and *Fisherman's Fall*, both appearing in 1964.

RODERICK HAIG-BROWN AND RALPH WAHL LISTEN INTENTLY TO A PRESENTATION AT THE NORTHWEST CONCLAVE OF THE FEDERATION OF FLY FISHERS IN OCEAN SHORES, WASHINGTON, IN MARCH 1969 (RALPH E. WAHL PHOTOGRAPHIC COLLECTION, CENTER FOR PACIFIC NORTHWEST STUDIES, WESTERN WASHINGTON UNIVERSITY).

During this period of extensive book writing, Haig-Brown also developed an elaborate freelance writing career. He published numerous articles in popular magazines such as *Field & Stream, Outdoor Life, The New Yorker, Maclean's, Argosy, Life, and Sports Illustrated*; authored movie and radio scripts; and penned essays, government bulletins, and encyclopedia entries. He was also a popular speaker at fish and wildlife functions, book fairs, and fly-fishing clubs. In order to be closer to the rivers and fish he loved so dearly, he took up skin diving at the age of 54 and explored the Campbell on a regular basis. In an essay for *Trout* in 1964, he remarked, "Watching the various salmon runs come home last fall was one of the supreme satisfactions of my life." He also helped popularize dry-fly fishing for steelhead at this time, first in *Fisherman's Summer* (1959) and later in *Fisherman's Fall* (1964).

Haig-Brown and his writing had profound influences on many leading personalities in Northwest fly fishing, including his neighbor on the Campbell since 1955, Van Gorman Egan, Letcher Lambuth, Enos Bradner, Ralph Wahl, Frank Amato, and Bill McMillan, among numerous others. Amato started the magazine *Salmon Trout Steelheader* in 1967 because of Haig-Brown's encouragement, and Haig-Brown wrote "Will the Chinook Take a Fly?" for the inaugural issue. For McMillan, *Fisherman's Summer* (1959) changed his life at the age of 14 as he came to "realize I wanted to see and feel as Haig-Brown did" and "I found a mentor with whom I did not feel alone through the otherwise lonely turmoil of adolescence."

During the late 1960s, Haig-Brown turned more of his attention to public service and conservation work than writing. While he had the occasional article published in *The Flyfisher* and *Fly Fisherman*, he spent large amounts of his time as the chancellor of the University of Victoria and as one of six commissioners on the International Pacific Salmon Fisheries Commission. He continued his involvement with a number of fly-fishing clubs and accepted leadership and advisory positions with associations that he believed were doing valuable work. For example, he was director of the National Second Century Fund, trustee of the Nature Conservancy of Canada, adviser to B.C. Wildlife, adviser to Trout Unlimited, adviser to the Federation of Fly Fishers, member of the Federal Saltwater Sport Fishing Advisory Commission, and member of the Federal Fisheries Development Council.

Haig-Brown published some extraordinary fly-fishing essays in the early 1970s in the *Financial Post* ("The World of the Fly Fisherman"), *True* ("Winter's Toughest Fishing Challenge: The Steelhead Trout of the Pacific Slope"), and *The Flyfisher* ("Steelhead Angling Comes of Age"), and he was interviewed by other notable writers such as Thomas McGuane and Ernest Schwiebert. His next-to-last book, *The Salmon* (1974), was commissioned by Environment Canada, and his final book, *Bright Waters, Bright Fish: An Examination of Angling in Canada* (1980), was completed in manuscript form in October 1976, the month he died from a heart attack at the age of 68 after mowing his lawn at Above Tide. This last book was a commissioned work, sponsored by the Department of Fisheries and Oceans Canada. In all, 11 of Haig-Brown's 24 books dealt with fish or fly fishing.

Haig-Brown's funeral was held October 13, 1976, at St. Patrick's Church across the field from his home, just a few weeks earlier than he would have preferred. In *A River Never Sleeps*, in the chapter "November," he wrote in the section "Before I Die" that "If one has to die, I should think November would be the best month for it. It is a gray, stormy month; the salmon are dying, and the year is done." His son Alan and eldest daughter Valerie agreed that they wanted the first part of "The Death of the Salmon" from *Fisherman's Fall* (1964) read at their father's funeral, so Valerie read aloud to the audience, "Do they all die after spawning? Yes. . . . Yes, they all die. . . . It is natural for a man to resent this, I suppose, to feel it is wasteful and shocking, in some way unnatural. . . . Now I have lived so long with this fact of collective, simultaneous death that I no longer resent or question it. Instead I find it fitting and beautiful. . . . I am still curious about the manner and meaning of it, but I do not question that it has manner and meaning." Roddy's wife, Ann, spread his ashes on the garden at Above Tide, and she continued to reside there until her own death on June 2, 1990, when her ashes were joined with her husband's.

Some individuals of great stature and importance, like Haig-Brown, continue to "live" long after their death. Probably more has been written about Roddy than about any other writer who ever wrote about fly fishing, and he has been honored repeatedly over the years. Certainly, his thoughts and ideas continue to exist in all of his many books and publications still in print, and it seems that every new generation eventually "discovers" this man's writing.

In the years following his death, the Haig-Brown Fly Fishing Association (Victoria) was formed, Roderick Haig-Brown Provincial Park was established on the banks of the Adams River in British Columbia, Mount Haig-Brown was named in Strathcona Park in the center of Vancouver Island, Above Tide was designated a B.C. Provincial Heritage Site, the Haig-Brown Kingfisher Creek Society was formed, the B.C. Book Award Society and the Federation of Fly Fishers named awards after him, and Valerie Haig-Brown has edited at least five books of his writings and diaries. More recently, in 1998, two of the six flies chosen to be part of Canada Post's commemorative "Fishing Flies" series of stamps were Haig-Brown patterns—Coho Blue and Steelhead Bee. And there is much, much more. Most of Haig-Brown's manuscripts, letters, and diaries are housed in the University of British Columbia Library, and a small collection of his flies and equipment is on display at the Haig-Brown house, a popular bed-and-breakfast and travel destination in Campbell River.

Part Two:

California

PETER J. SCHWAB WITH A KLAMATH RIVER STEELHEAD IN 1945.
NOTICE THAT HE IS STILL WEARING HIS FAMOUS WORDEN'S
"BELLY REEL" (PHOTOGRAPH COURTESY OF PAT AND GARY
WALLER). ORIGINAL SCHWAB PAINT BRUSH (INSET)

"Pete Schwab was one of the greatest artists with the fly rod who ever lived, comparable only to such modern experts as Joe Brooks and Lefty Kreh. As a steelheader, Pete was the supreme regional oracle, and his ability in dressing super steelhead flies was unsurpassed." —Joseph D. Bates, Jr., Streamers and Bucktails: The Big Fish Flies, *1979*

Chapter 5

Peter J. Schwab (1887–1956):

KLAMATH RIVER STEELHEADER AND DESIGNER OF
FLY RODS, LINES, AND FLIES

Although Peter J. Schwab was born in Conshohocken, Pennsylvania, in 1887, it did not take him long to begin traveling to the Midwest and West in search of better fly-fishing opportunities. He began fly fishing when he was 8 years old and loved to fish for trout and bass in his home state. By the early 1900s, Schwab had learned the craft of tanning hides, and he earned a living at the trade through the 1940s. While this line of work put bread on the table for him, his wife, Bess, and their daughter, Schwab's real passions were traveling and fly fishing.

By the early years of the 20th century, Schwab had become more involved in fly casting and fly-rod construction, and he spent considerable time in the Chicago area with champion casters Fred Peet and Call McCarthy. It was also in Chicago, in 1922, that Schwab was invited to join other conscientious and concerned fishermen as a director of the newly formed Izaak Walton League of America. Schwab and Peet, who was also an initial director, were members of the Izaak Walton Club of Chicago, which was formed that same year with 54 members. Shortly thereafter, Schwab began an illustrious outdoor writing career when he was named the motor-camping editor for Chicago-based *Outdoor Recreation* magazine. He and his wife pulled a large "motor coach" around behind their car and spent months at a time visiting fishing destinations that were considered exotic in the 1920s—Montana, Wyoming, Idaho, Northern California, Oregon, Washington, and British Columbia. His articles about these trips appeared regularly.

It was on one of these "forays" in 1926–1927 that Schwab discovered the steelhead of the Pacific Northwest. He searched up and down the coast from Eureka, California, to Vancouver, British Columbia, looking for steelhead fly fishermen, but found only a few. Notably, however, he did meet Harry Van Luven of Portland, Oregon, whom Schwab referred to as "my old friend and mentor." Van Luven's famous Red Fly, which evolved from the great Royal Coachman—he omitted the peacock herl, added a red tail, and replaced the white goose wings with white bucktail—stimulated Schwab to move into a steelhead fly design mode that would continue until his death in the 1950s. In 1927–1928, Schwab first dressed his well-known Wood Pussy Bucktail and Paint Brush Bucktail flies, both of which used deer hair to replace the previously used feathers in most steelhead flies. In 1928–1929, enamored with steelhead and the rivers of Northern California and Oregon, Schwab put together his small but innovative "Steelheadin Directory." It was also about this time that he began collecting information for a book on fly fishing that he worked on for the remainder of his life.

Over the next two decades, from the early 1930s through the early 1950s, Schwab and his wife spent as much time as they could living in their travel trailer in Montana, Idaho, and Northern California. But Schwab's favorite spot was on Northern California's Klamath River near the town of Yreka. Here, Schwab became part of the early evolution of steelhead fly fishing and the design of steelhead flies, and developed close friendships with Eel River anglers Lloyd Silvius (who designed the Nite Owl pattern) and C. Jim Pray (who developed the Optic series of flies). He also befriended Lew Stoner, cofounder and chief rod maker for the R. L. Winston Company in San Francisco; helped Stoner design rods; and fished with him on a regular basis. Although Schwab did fish elsewhere, especially the Shasta, Rogue, Trinity, Eel, and Umpqua rivers, for all intents and purposes the Klamath was his home river. And it was on the banks of the Klamath, near the town of Hornbrook, California, that he made the majority of his most significant and pioneering contributions to Northwest fly fishing.

Beginning in 1935, when Schwab started an almost 20-year writing relationship with *Sports Afield*, his national reputation as a respected fly fisherman began to take off. Joseph D. Bates, Jr., the author of *Streamers and Bucktails: The Big Fish Flies* (1979), and a well-known historian of fly patterns, noted that "Pete Schwab was one of the greatest artists with the fly rod who ever lived, comparable only to such modern experts as Joe Brooks and Lefty Kreh. As a steelheader, Pete was the supreme regional oracle, and his ability in dressing superb steelhead flies was unsurpassed." Similarly, Donald Zahner, the editor and publisher of *Fly Fisherman* in the early 1970s, referred to Schwab as "the legendary, even if in his lifetime, angler and caster . . . [who] was very influential in the development of several lines of West Coast fly rods."

Schwab's second article for *Sports Afield*, which appeared in 1936, was on the "Challenge of the Steelhead" and featured the Klamath, Umpqua, and Rogue rivers. Zane Grey's pioneering article on North Umpqua steelhead had appeared in the same magazine just a year before, and Ray Bergman, fishing editor for *Outdoor Life*, included a chapter on "Steelhead of the Umpqua" in his book *Trout* (1938). These were the early days of the popularization of Northwest steelheading, and Schwab was one of the prime proponents of the wonderful "sea-going rainbow trout." Trey Combs, in his historical book *The Steelhead Trout* (1971, 1988), referred to this area divided between California and Oregon as "a kind of steelheading breadbasket." In this region "were rivers where the fly reigned supreme," Combs wrote, and he noted that the connecting highways helped give birth to "the steelheading circuit rider, a fisherman here for all seasons." Steelhead, steelhead flies, steelhead rods, steelhead lines,

PETER J. SCHWAB TESTING
ONE OF HIS PERSONALLY DE-
SIGNED "LETTLE FELLER"
FLY RODS AT THE WINSTON
ROD COMPANY IN SAN
FRANCISCO IN 1938 (PHO-
TOGRAPH COURTESY OF PAT
AND GARY WALLER).

and steelhead rivers gained a national reputation, and anglers throughout the world began to take notice. At the center of much of this newfound attention was Pete Schwab, who generally stayed on the Klamath until the bitter cold and snow drove him out in December.

During the late 1930s, Schwab began to write about fly lines, fly rods, and fly casting in *Sports Afield* on a regular basis. He discussed new fly lines in 1937 and cited several specifications for his silk line tapers. Later that year he authored two articles on "The Fly Rod Balance Controversy," and he wrote another for the 1938 *Sports Afield Fishing Annual* on "Fitting the Fly Line to the Rod Action and Fishing." It was also in 1937 that Lew Stoner built Schwab a 7-foot, 2.25-ounce fly rod that became the prototype for R. L. Winston's "Leetle Feller" series. The following year Winston produced a 6-foot, 1.5-ounce rod for Schwab. Both were featured in Schwab's 1939 *Sports Afield* article "Short Rods and Long Casts." He became a spokesman for Winston rods and used their San Francisco headquarters as his "official West Coast post office" when he was traveling. Schwab argued that Lew Stoner was "the greatest rod builder of all time" and that Winston rods were superior because they used better cane, had finer precision tools, and had the patented "fluted hollow construction of the butts."

The challenge of steelheading—wide and fast rivers that demand long casts and, in general, a deeply sunken fly—led Schwab to design his own fly lines.

He painstakingly cut and spliced as many as seven sections of different-size silk lines to provide the type of performance he expected. Specific diameters and lengths were spliced together, varnished, and left to dry in his trailer. While he did write about lines—for example, his "Torpedo Head Distance Fishing Lines and How to Use Them" appeared in the 1941 *Sports Afield Fishing Annual*—he was generally quite secretive about his line designs. He shared his materials, techniques, and specifications with a few friends, but was waiting until he was "satisfied with them and can give them to the cockeyed steelhead world."

From years of experimentation, Schwab ascertained that the lightest fly rod was the most efficient. After seeing a newly invented "belly winder reel" or "belt reel" produced by the Worden Company in Yakima, Washington, Schwab put the two ideas together and began steelheading without a reel on his rod. Rod builder Dan Brenan built him a rod with no reel seat to use with his "belt reel," and Schwab wrote about it in an article in the 1942 *Sports Afield Fishing Annual* titled "A Better Fly Rod Grasp." Schwab used this setup regularly and drew crowds to watch him fish with it. His article "Carry Your Fly Reel on Your Belt" appeared in a 1941 issue of *Sports Afield*, and toward the end of the 1940s he authored an article on the advantages of the "belly reel" for *Field & Stream*.

More national notoriety for Schwab and for steelheading came in 1946, when he wrote a two-part "Steelhead Diary" followed by another two-part article on "Bucktails for Steelheads" for *Sports Afield*. In "Diary" he noted that his trailer was "parked under the locusts, within 20 feet of the swirling Klamath," and he wrote of his regular fishing partners, George Bellamy and Bobbie Dunn, who fished with him most of September, October, and November. He

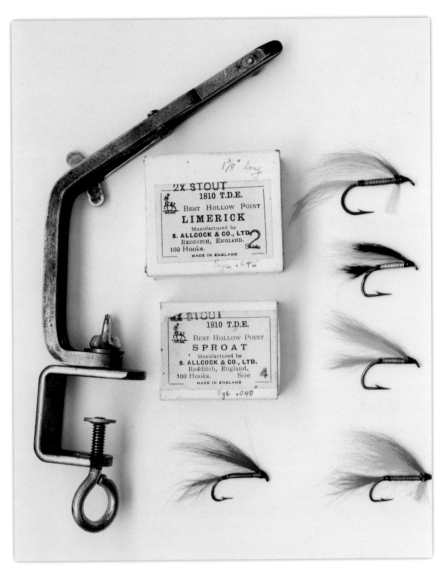

SCHWAB'S PERSONAL VISE AND TWO BOXES OF HIS FAVORITE S. ALLCOCK LIMERICK (SIZE 2) AND SPROAT (SIZE 4) STEELHEAD FLY HOOKS. THEY ARE OUTLINED BY SEVERAL OF HIS ORIGINAL PATTERNS IN DIFFERENT SIZES AND VARIATIONS (COUNTERCLOCKWISE FROM TOP RIGHT): QUEEN BESS, QUEEN BESS, PAINT BRUSH, PAINT BRUSH, AND BOBBIE DUNN (PHOTOGRAPH COURTESY OF PAT AND GARY WALLER).

fished with Lew Stoner for almost two weeks in September. In October, after an early snowfall, Schwab admitted, "Still I can't keep off the river. Neither can anyone else. It's that way with steelheading. It does things to you. Gets under your skin. Spoils you for any other kind of fishing." Still later in 1946, also in *Sports Afield*, he wrote "Torpedo Head Lines" and "Fly Rods for Steelheads."

Schwab is probably best remembered for the group of wire-bodied bucktails

"All I did was discover that hard wire, polished, was better under many conditions than covered wire. It was a mental accident that worked. . . . I thought I was achieving results from added weight, only to discover slowly . . . that the success of the flies lay in their slender streamlining, action and flash." —*Peter J. Schwab*

he developed and showed the world in his "Bucktails for Steelheads" series in *Sports Afield.* Schwab, along with others, realized the need to present flies deeper for winter steelhead, and he experimented with weighted flies by wrapping wire under the fly body. In the course of working on what became his Bellamy fly, he discovered that the steelhead's "sharp teeth soon tore the red wool covering from the body, but they hit the bare copper wire just as eagerly." From then on, he began to tie several of his patterns with bodies visibly made from wrapped copper, brass, silver, or gold wire. He would shine the body, wipe it clean, and then cover it with a thin lacquer to prevent tarnish with age. All of his flies were identified as bucktails, since he believed "a hair fly becomes a bucktail when the wings are roughly twice the length of a standard-length hook and thus give pronounced swimming action to the lure." In all, Schwab introduced the Wood Pussy, Bellamy, Bobbie Dunn, Brass Hat, Paint Brush, and Queen Bess. Other flies dressed in his style and ones directly related to his influence were the Princess, Orange Steelheader, Van Luven, and Copper Colonel. Besides the uniquely exposed wire wraps, his flies also had from one to three bucktail wings held up at a 45-degree angle by several wraps of thread. For the three-winged models, the first two wings were tied tandem in the usual position and the third was tied midshank.

In a letter to Ralph Wahl of Bellingham, Washington, in 1952, Schwab elaborated upon his unique wire-bodied flies and told Wahl that "all I did was discover that hard wire, polished, was better under many conditions than covered wire. It was a mental accident that worked. . . . I thought I was achieving results from added weight, only to discover slowly . . . that the success of the flies lay in their slender streamlining, action and flash." Schwab was convinced that his flies worked because of "the combination of wire body, tail and hair wings, plus the *flash and action*." He also used fairly stout hooks, and his favorite colors were yellow, red, white, and black. His favorite fly was the Queen Bess, which he named after his wife, followed closely by the Bobbie Dunn and Brass Hat.

When one considers that the two classic books on steelhead fly fishing, Claude Krieder's *Steelhead* and Clark Van Fleet's *Steelhead to a Fly*, were not published until 1948 and 1951 respectively, it is apparent why Pete Schwab is recognized as a true pioneer in Northwest fly fishing. Although he never did finish his own book, his contributions to the sport were truly astonishing. After finishing the 1950 season on the Klamath, Schwab's health began to falter. He had heart problems, frostbitten toes, and constantly burning eyes, all of which interfered with fishing, writing, and transporting his large trailer. Consequently, after visiting friends and relatives in Arizona, New Jersey, and Pennsylvania, Pete and Bess settled on a small farm in Florida in 1954. He died there two years later.

Thanks to vintage-fishing-tackle collectors Pat and Gary Waller of Grants Pass, Oregon, the memory of Peter J. Schwab lives on. They have many of his personal fly-fishing items, including rods, reels, hooks, and flies, as well as a collection of correspondence between Schwab and pioneering Washington steelheader Ralph Wahl, written during the early 1950s. In 1998, the Wallers made much of this fine collection available for display at the International Fly Fishing Center in Livingston, Montana.

C. James Pray in his Eureka, California shop in 1951. Note the fly he is tying using his thumb and forefinger as a vise. Black Optic, tied by Jon Luke (inset)

Pray was "one of the outstanding professional fly-tyers on the west coast and noted as an expert steelhead fisherman." —William Bayard Sturgis, Fly-Tying, 1940

Chapter 6

C. James Pray, 1885–1952:

EUREKA FLY TIER AND ORIGINATOR OF THE POPULAR "OPTIC" SERIES OF STEELHEAD FLIES

Claire James Pray was born February 2, 1885, in Ann Arbor, Michigan, where he was raised by his mother and older sister after his father died when Jim was 1. He also had two brothers. Even at a young age he never used his first name—all of his friends throughout his life just called him Jim. Young Pray began tying flies when he was 8 years old and fished regularly for smallmouth bass in the Huron River on the outskirts of his hometown. He perfected his tying by disassembling flies that were given to him and by reading Mary Orvis Marbury's classic, *Favorite Flies and Their Origins* (1892). His fly fishing was further enhanced by a new rod, reel, and line presented to him by his mother and sister. Interestingly, even as a youngster, Pray learned to tie his flies without a vise and never used one throughout his illustrious career as a commercial tier in Eureka, California. For Pray, it was always quality over quantity, and he noted that he "never made flies to see how many I could tie. My aim always was to see how well I could put each one together."

Pray attended the University of Michigan for a year before dropping out to work and support his mother. After her death in 1908, when he was 23, Jim left Michigan for the West. He stopped briefly in Denver and in Ogden, Utah, but settled and stayed in Northern California. He lived in Scotia in 1910, working as a timekeeper for a lumber mill, and it was here, on the banks of the Eel River, that Pray caught his first steelhead and shot his first valley quail. His passions were hunting and fishing, and he could not have found a better geographic locale for these pursuits. Pray later worked in real estate and owned a car dealership in Oroville until the mid-1930s, when the Depression hit him hard financially. He lost his business, property, and money, and, in 1934, moved back to the Eel River area and settled in Eureka. Here, near the famous "River of the Giants," Pray began a career of innovative steelhead fly tying that was highlighted by the invention and popularization of his famous Optic flies.

When Pray first arrived in Eureka, homeless and out of money, he camped near the edge of town and traded his flies for groceries. At 50 cents a fly, he eventually earned enough money to rent a room and moved his fly tying to the mezzanine of a local bakery. During these early years, in 1934 and '35, Pray first tied his Carter's Dixie Bucktail, named after Harley Carter, a famous Stanford football player during the 1920s, who used the fly with great success on both the Klamath and the Rogue rivers. Also in 1934, Pray developed the Orleans

Barber for his barber friend John Berisa of that town on the Klamath.

In 1935, because of the popularity of New Zealand's Golden Demon, introduced to the United States the previous year by Fred Burnham and Zane Grey, Pray followed with his Silver Demon, tied Cains River style. The Silver Demon was tied with a silver rope tinsel body, barred wood duck tail, orange throat, and a wing of barred gadwall feathers. No jungle cock cheeks were used. Pray's records for 1935, the fly's first year, showed that his Silver Demon outsold the Gold Demon 1,300 to 300. Pray's Black Demon made its debut in 1937. The Black Demon was originally tied with a silver body, no tail, orange throat, and a black bucktail wing. The Silver Demon was most popular on the Eel River, the Black Demon on the Klamath. It was about this time that Pray also originated his Cains River Steelhead Streamer for Klamath River steelheaders.

One of Pray's most successful flies, and one of the most famous western steelhead patterns, was invented on Christmas Day, 1936. Pray was about to throw away some materials at the end of a day of tying, but instead created a new fly. He combined a piece of red chenille, an orange hackle, some white buck hair, and a Rhode Island Red saddle hackle, and put the result on a size-6 hook. He gave the fly to his friend Walter J. Thoresen of Eureka, and on the following day, using his new fly in the Eel, Thoresen hooked and landed five steelhead averaging 12 pounds each. The largest weighed 18 pounds and won first place in that year's *Field & Stream* "Western Division Rainbow-Steelhead Class." Pray used the first four letters of his friend's last name to give his new invention the name Thor in honor of Thoresen's achievements. Two years later on Christmas Day, 1938, Gene Sapp of Ferndale landed a 17.75-pound steelhead on a Thor in the Eel to also capture first place in the *Field & Stream* competition. Pray's original recipe for the Thor called for a black head, a small bunch of stiff orange hackle fibers for a tail, a medium-thick body of dark

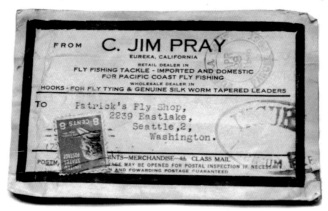

An original C. Jim Pray mailing label (photograph courtesy of Pat and Gary Waller)

red chenille, several turns of a mahogany saddle hackle applied as a collar and tied back but not gathered downward for a throat, and a wing composed of a medium-size bunch of white bucktail extending to the end of the tail.

As a result of the success and notoriety of his flies, Pray and his small Eureka fly shop began to be sought out by steelheaders from far and near. His earliest more permanent shop, called The Stump House, was located on the corner of Broadway and Clark streets in Eureka. Here, Pray specialized in steelhead flies and a few pieces of basic steelhead equipment: three types of rods, one brand of fly reel, one brand of fly line, the finest gut leaders he imported from Spain, one brand of waders, and his own signature hooks made especially for him by Mustad of Norway. He was friends with Lew Stoner, the famous rod maker for the R. L. Winston Company, outdoor writers Fred Burnham and Ted Trueblood, and former President Herbert Hoover. Pray and Peter Schwab, an avid steelhead fly fisherman and columnist for *Sports Afield*, were also close friends and often fished together on the Eel and Klamath and compared tying notes. It is interesting to note that Schwab's Queen Bess was the twin of Pray's Silver Demon.

During the late 1930s, Pray began to tie several of his own versions of older flies, especially for his friend Fred Bair of Klamath Lodge. He produced Bair's Black Joe and Bair's Demon for the Klamath fishery, and Bair's Railbird and Black Gnat Bucktail for the Eel as well as the Klamath. In 1938, Pray's friend Harley Carter asked for a black hair fly to be used on the Klamath and the Rogue. Accordingly, Pray invented the Carter, which sported a glossy black bear-hair wing. At about this same time, Pray originated his Improved Governor Bucktail for steelhead on the Eel and Klamath rivers. All of these flies, as well as a few of Pray's earlier flies, were featured in William Bayard Sturgis's book *Fly-Tying*, published in 1940. The steelhead flies on the colored frontispiece plate were all tied by Pray, and Sturgis referred to Pray as "one of the outstanding professional fly-tyers on the west coast and noted as an expert steelhead fisherman" in the chapter "Steelhead Flies." Here, Pray selected 26 of his favorite flies, at least 11 of which were his own creations or his variations on earlier patterns. Readers were encouraged to contact Pray for specific information on steelhead flies and fly fishing.

Just as Pete Schwab and a few other steelheaders were experimenting with a new fly variety that would sink quickly, be tough enough for big fish and rocky rivers, and have some glitter and flash in the water, Pray developed the first of his famous Optic Bucktails. It was early in 1940 that he first clamped a large split brass bead just behind the eye of a short, stout hook. He put it on top of a body of gold rope tinsel, tied on a wing of black buck hair immediately in back of the eye, and used tying thread to taper the head down to the body. Finally, he lacquered the brass head black to create large eyes, added a white iris, and upon that painted a black pupil. The new fly was christened the Black Optic. Pray made several more of the same fly that day, using two different-size brass eyes (three-sixteenth inch and 0.25 inch) and gave them a try the next morning in the Eel. By noon he had landed four steelhead and two silver salmon on the heavier of the two flies. He gave the remainder of his first Black Optics to friends who proceeded to take several limits of steelhead and salmon from the Eel's tidewater pools over the next few days. By then, Pray knew he was on to something special.

Optic eyes were not new to fly construction in general, but their use by Pray was the first instance specifically for steelhead. Knowing that red flies did well farther upstream in the Eel, Pray followed the Black Optic with his Red Optic. It had a silver rope tinsel body, a blood red buck-hair wing with a touch of yellow polar bear hair on top, and a black head with the same white-and-black "optic" eyes. The Red Optic was an instant success, and its fame spread rapidly. Even Preston Jennings, author of *A Book of Trout Flies* (1935), wrote and requested a sample in 1940. Pray replied that a great run of steelhead and salmon was in the Eel and "they are taking almost exclusively my Red Optic." He also told Jennings that his stock was low and "I have been working until 2 and 4 o'clock in the morning to get them out." The fly was the top producer of steelhead on the Eel, Mad, Smith, and Garcia rivers, among others, throughout the 1940s. By Pray's own records, his Red Optic caught more than 500 steelhead between 11 and 18 pounds from 1940 to 1947. The fly also accounted for at least four of the largest steelhead listed in the *Field & Stream* annual contest. This fly has also been known as Owl-Eyed Optic No. 1 and Pray's Red Optic.

AN ORIGINAL BOX OF C. JIM PRAY STEELHEAD HOOKS AND FOUR OF HIS FAMOUS OPTIC PATTERNS TIED BY PETE SCHWAB IN HIS FAVORITE COLORS (PHOTOGRAPH COURTESY OF PAT AND GARY WALLER)

Pray continued his Optic series in 1940 with the Cock Robin Optic, also known as the Owl-Eyed Optic No. 2 and named after Cock Robin Island near the Eel's tidewater. This was followed by the Red and Yellow Optic, sometimes called the Eel River Optic, and the Orange Optic. The Cock Robin had the same head and body as the Black Optic and Red Optic but had an orange hackle throat and a wing of ground squirrel or badger hair. The Red and Yellow Optic was characterized by a red bucktail wing topped with yellow polar bear and a white eye with a black pupil and a red iris. The Orange Optic was similar to the other Optics in head and body, but had a red hackle throat and a wing composed of orange bucktail or polar bear. Pray's Optic flies have frequently been referred to as Eel River Optics, Owl-Eyed Optics, and Pray's Optics.

Pray was very particular about the hooks he used for his flies and used only two styles of Mustad hooks. They were made to his specifications and packaged in boxes bearing his name and shop address. Both styles had a Limerick bend, were constructed from 5X heavy wire, and were bronze. One was a size-4 length with a size-1/0 bend, which he used for size-2 or -4 flies. The other was a size-6 length with a size-2 bend, which he used for size-6 flies. Pray specifically promoted the wide-gap, short-shanked, heavier hooks for steelheading. His belief was that they would help develop a compact fly that would sink quickly, cast with ease, and provide a wide enough gap to hook the hard-nosed steelhead. Additionally, Pray noted that short-shanked hooks kept the fly riding with the wing uppermost in the water, with the barb and bend acting effectively as a keel to prevent the fly from turning over.

Pray was a master tier without a vise. He held the hook between the thumb and forefinger of his left hand and dragged the tying thread across the top of a bottle of sticky shellac with his right. Then, instead of attaching the thread to the hook and leaving it there, he completed each step and tied off the thread before starting the next step. Accordingly, he was not fast. His record was 100 Optics in one day, but that consisted of working straight through from early morning until late at night. He also taught many of his customers to tie flies, even though he knew it could hurt his business. For Pray, however, quality always took precedent over quantity, and friends were always more important than profit.

By 1946, Pray moved into his last and most popular shop, located at 323 G St. in Eureka. It was across the street from the city hall and post office, and attracted a daily assemblage of fly fishermen. His shop, not much to look at, was a one-story frame building composed of three fairly small rooms. The front room housed his fly displays, pictures, books, a desk, and some tackle. The middle room was his tying area and his supply room. He lived in the back room, which he accessed by going up a few steps from his shop. Here, he read, listened to music, and entertained friends.

It was also during the 1940s that two other noted steelhead fly fishermen experimented with new fly designs and weighting techniques similar to Pray's. Pete Schwab, a regular Klamath River angler, developed his wire-bodied flies and wrote about them in two articles, "Steelhead Diary" and "Bucktails for Steelheads," in *Sports Afield* (both in 1946). Earlier, Ralph Wahl of Bellingham, Washington, who was a regular on the Skagit River, where several large steelhead were recorded, invented two bright heavy-bodied bucktails he named Lord Hamilton and Lady Hamilton. He followed with the Painted Lady in 1952. All three flies had Pray-like "optic" heads with white eyes and black pupils. And, like several of Pray's flies, they accounted for several large steelhead listed in the annual *Field & Stream* contest.

Pray and his flies were at the peak of their popularity in 1950 when Joseph D. Bates, Jr., published his very well researched book *Streamer Fly Fishing in Fresh and Salt Water*. Pray had established a viable mail-order business in addition to his regular shop customers and was receiving regular recognition in national magazines. His flies were all featured in Bates's book, and several of the other patterns shown were actually dressed by him. Because of additional exposure, he received even more accolades. Unfortunately, later that year Pray discovered he had cancer, which led to a very serious disease called uremia—a toxic condition produced by urine in the blood. He went through a number of operations at the University of California Clinic in Eureka, where he was under the care of his physician and friend, Dr. Stanwood Schmidt, formerly head of the clinic's Department of Urology. Although Pray amassed substantial medical costs, he never had to spend a dime because Schmidt and many of his other friends rallied to his support.

Pray was fitted with a rubber tube for urination and spent all of 1951 being cared for in his shop living quarters by his friends. Although very sick, he was still his congenial self, continued to tie flies, and waded the local rivers. In fact, he admitted to one writer that "Doc told me not to wade, but I've already been in way over this tube. Thank God, my heart and arms and shoulders still are good. I can cast." Pray finally succumbed to cancer on March 13, 1952, at the age of 67. Unfortunately, he never got to see the feature article about him titled "Wizard of West Coast Flies," written by Ted Trueblood under the pseudonym Thomas Hardin, published the following month in True. His pallbearers included Schmidt, Bair, and four of his other closest fishing friends. After the funeral a small group met one last time at his shop to drink a toast to his memory. They left a wreath on the door with a card that read: "gone fishing—c. jim pray, 1885–1952."

HARRY HORNBROOK AT FERNBRIDGE ON THE EEL RIVER CIRCA 1975
(PHOTOGRAPH BY STEVE ROSENBERG)

Chapter 7

Harry M. Hornbrook (1915–1998):

LEGENDARY STEELHEADER ON THE EEL RIVER

Harry M. Hornbrook was born on May 10, 1915, in the small town of Ukiah, California, south of Eureka. His parents, Nobel and Inez Hornbrook, resided in Ukiah all of their lives, and it was here that Harry graduated from high school in 1934. Like many other young men in Depression-era America, Harry joined the California Conservation Corps, a state branch of the nation-wide Civilian Conservation Corps, and began driving a supply truck in the Willits, California, area. About two years later, in 1936, Hornbrook accepted a temporary two-week painting job at the Pacific Gas and Electric power plant in Eureka. His "temporary" job as a painter evolved into the position of "watch engineer," and at the age of 21, Harry began a job that he held until he retired in 1978. By the time he retired, Hornbrook was plant operator of what had become the PG&E Humboldt Bay Nuclear Power Plant.

As fate would have it, the year Hornbrook moved to Eureka for his new job, the nearby Eel River was having one of the most profound steelhead years on record. With little or no fishing experience before 1936, Harry met and befriended a local fly fisherman, Ben Anderson, who had moved to nearby Ferndale from Denmark in 1909. Ben happened to be close friends with Art Dedini, who owned Art's Tackle Shop in Ferndale on the Eel River Delta. Together, Anderson and Dedini transformed fishing neophyte Hornbrook into one of the Eel River's legendary fly fishermen. In 10 years, Hornbrook was setting records for fly-caught steelhead on the Eel and was known locally as the "king" of the river.

> *"[T]he Eel became the first of our western waters to gain a national reputation specifically as a steelheading river" and was the "fountainhead of our modern steelhead heritage."* —*Trey Combs,* The Steelhead Trout, *1971*

California's Eel River watershed, with its flow running south to north, is the state's third largest, covering 3,684 square miles. The main-stem Eel, which is more than 30 miles long, is fed by rain, springs, and the snowpack from three mountains, each nearly 7,000 feet tall. The Middle Fork is the Eel's largest tributary, beginning in Trinity County and flowing on into Mendocino County, where it joins the main stem at Dos Rios. The North Fork tributary is about 35 miles long and flows only in Trinity County. The Van Duzen River, another major tributary, enters the main-stem Eel just south of Fortuna in Humboldt County, about 14 miles upstream from the Eel's mouth. The Eel's fourth tributary, the South Fork, originates in Mendocino County south of Laytonville, and travels about 105 miles before joining the main stem just north of Pepperwood. The Eel's mouth, where it enters the Pacific Ocean, is about 15 miles south of Eureka. The Eel flows through some of the most beautiful redwood groves in the state, including Humboldt Redwood State Park, and when it is running at its best, the Eel's emerald green color is majestic.

Historically, the Eel River was the mainstay of the California commercial salmon industry. Trolling, gillnetting, and seining, both in Humboldt Bay and in the river itself, accounted for millions of pounds of chinook and coho salmon annually. But, by the 1910s, the Eel River commercial salmon fishery was dying because of the depleted resource and damaged environment. After years of pressure from sport fishers and conservationists alike, gillnetting on the Eel was finally made illegal in 1922. By 1926, when commercial fishing was limited to trolling offshore, sportfishing for salmon began to dominate the lower river tidewater area. Commercial fish buyers' docks were quickly converted to rowboat rental facilities, and sports anglers started to troll spinners and spoons for salmon every fall. Here, some pioneer fly anglers also began to cast flies to the salmon, and as the steelhead began to move upstream to spawn, the anglers also tested their flies on the Eel's large run of winter steelhead, which began nosing into tidewater in November and ran through March. Not only were there plenty of fish, they were big too! In fact, outdoor writer H. L. Betten began to refer to the Eel as the "River of the Giants."

It was this early group of Eel River fly fishermen near Eureka that Trey Combs argues "gave us our steelheading birthplace." Combs, in *The Steelhead Trout* (1971), says "they were the first to set their calendars according to the steelhead's ascending habits, and the first to intercept them with flies of their own design that were of lasting importance." Accordingly, Combs concluded that "the Eel became the first of our western waters to gain a national reputation specifically as a steelheading river" and was the "fountainhead of our modern steelhead heritage." The Eel was fished by pioneers such as John Benn, Sumner Carson, Jim Hutchens, Josh Van Zandt, and Walter Thoresen, among numerous others in the early years. They were joined later by Clark Van Fleet, Lloyd Silvius, and Jim Pray, as well as others too numerous to recount. This group of innovative fly anglers became, as Paul Schullery suggests in *American Fly Fishing: A History* (1987), "national leaders in developing big-river fishing techniques." They invented shooting-heads, perfected distance casting, put the "double-haul" into daily use, experimented with rod design, and tied flies with bulk and weight unlike any previously used for trout or salmon.

In 1936, as a beginner, Harry Hornbrook stepped into this tradition-bound fly-fishing paradise and began to develop his own skills and talents.

HARRY M. HORNBROOK WITH A 17-
POUND, 5-OUNCE STEELHEAD CAUGHT
IN THE EEL RIVER ON JANUARY 9, 1947.
(PHOTOGRAPH COURTESY OF SHERRI HORNBROOK) RIGHT: HARRY M. HORN-
BROOK'S *FIELD & STREAM* CERTIFICATE FOR THE FOURTH LARGEST "WESTERN RAIN-
BOW TROUT, FLY-CASTING DIVISION," CAUGHT IN 1947 (CERTIFICATE COURTESY OF
SHERRI HORNBROOK)

That same year, as Harry was learning how to cast, assemble shooting-heads, and tie flies from Art Dedini and Ben Anderson, Walter Thoresen landed an 18-pound steelhead the day after Christmas on one of Jim Pray's flies, soon to be named the Thor after Thoresen. The large steelhead from the Eel placed first in the *Field & Stream* Western Rainbow Trout Fly-Casting Division that year. Two years later, on Christmas Day, Ferndale angler Gene Sapp landed a 17.75-pound steelhead on a Thor in the Eel to place first in the 1938 *Field & Stream* contest. Word of these large fish spread rapidly, and Hornbrook became a regular on the Eel. He had succumbed to steelhead fever. Because he worked different shifts, he could fish either before or after work on a regular basis. He

HARRY M. HORNBROOK ON THE EEL RIVER SHORE WITH A LARGE SALMON, CIRCA 1947 (PHOTOGRAPH COURTESY OF SHERRI HORNBROOK)

and his wife also had their first child at this time, a son named Dave.

By the early 1940s, Hornbrook was catching his share of Eel River "half-pounders," salmon, steelhead, and shad, which he called "poor man's steelhead." Besides tying flies, Harry began to make his own fishing rods and developed a love of photography. He also became good friends with Jim Pray. Harry's son Dave remembers sitting with his father at the potbellied stove in Pray's Fly Shop and said that Pray "was like a father to my dad." Hornbrook began using Pray's new Optic flies for salmon and steelhead, but also experimented with weighting flies on his own. In fact, Dave remembers his father's Telephone Wire Fly, which consisted of orange or red telephone wire wrapped around the hook shank. Hornbrook also became one of the best distance fly casters on the Eel. Eureka attorney Stephen Rosenberg recalls a story that his father told him about the day Harry hooked 22 steelhead at Miller Pool. "On this particular day," Rosenberg's father said, "the steelhead were lying by a sunken log and no one else could cast far enough to reach the fish."

To successfully fish the Eel, anglers had to combine exact timing with very specialized equipment and techniques, and Hornbrook was superb at all of the above. Much of the lower river was influenced by tides, water-color changes, and winds. Because of Hornbrook's work schedule and proximity to the river, he had the unique opportunity to "be at the right place at the right time doing the right thing." The prime steelhead pools, beginning just above the Van Duzen's entrance and going downstream to Fernbridge, could be reached fairly easily by driving right to the rocky shoreline. The pools below Fernbridge, namely Singley, Snag, Dungan's, and Fulmore, were influenced by the tides, had little or no current, and oftentimes required fishing from a pram. These slower and deeper estuary pools required a cast-and-strip technique that allowed a weighted fly to sink and then be retrieved to give the fly an up-and-down nodding or swimming action.

This water also required major distance-casting ability. In fact, as Russell Chatham noted in *Dark Waters* (1988), "Years ago, there was a saying in the West to the effect that if you fancied yourself a distance fly caster you had better be able to hold your own among the boys at Singley Pool." Dave Hornbrook said his father preferred to wade and cast for steelhead, but they each had an 8-foot plywood pram to fish the wider tidewater pools. Hornbrook was also an "absolute perfectionist," his son said, which pushed Harry to be the best at anything he took up. This trait kept him busy perfecting his gear and technique to become the best fly angler on the Eel.

> *"[I]n accordance with Harry's usual custom, he let everyone else go first." After four anglers had fished through the run without anything, "Harry hooked and landed a beautiful steelhead." —Stephen Rosenberg*

Hornbrook continued to master the Eel and its fish into the mid-1940s, when he had his most noteworthy success. From the 1946 winter steelhead season to the early 1948 season, Harry recorded the following steelhead catches: "1 @ 11 lbs., 2 @ 12 lbs., 2 @ 14 lbs., 2 @ 15 lbs., 2 @ 16 lbs., 1 @ 17 lbs., and 1 @ 17.5 lbs." He made no attempt to record the dozens of smaller steelhead, silvers, and chinook he also caught. His 17.5-pound steelhead caught on January 9, 1947, and his 17-pound steelhead caught on January 1, 1948, placed fourth in the *Field & Stream* Western Rainbow Trout Fly-Casting Division in their respective years. And, on the day in 1947 that he landed the 17.5-pound steelhead, he also landed four others, all over 15 pounds, for his five-fish daily limit. All were caught on Pray's Red Optic; not surprisingly, Stephen Rosenberg notes that "Harry caught more fish on Pray's Eel River Optic than any other person."

By the early 1950s, Hornbrook's reputation was moving beyond that of a local celebrity. Clark Van Fleet's pioneering book, *Steelhead to a Fly* (1950), had two chapters devoted to the Eel River in which he discussed the size of the steelhead there and the unique techniques used by the fly fishers. At one point, he proclaimed that "Eureka developed some of the best rod-wielders to be found on the West Coast" and went on to suggest that "the Eel was famous, not only for its monster fish, but for the expert fly-fishermen as well." He referred to Hornbrook specifically when he wrote, "Harry hooked a monster at Singley Pool early this morning, but it broke away." That same year, in The *American Angler* (1951), written by *Field & Stream* editor A. J. McClane, Hornbrook was identified as ranking 15th and 20th in the top 50 fly-caught "western rainbow trout" during the 1940s. Finally, in an article on Pray titled "The Wizard of West Coast Flies," written by Ted Trueblood for *True* magazine in 1952, Hornbrook's skills with the Red Optic were recorded for a national audience to read. Besides listing all of the large steelhead Harry landed in the mid- to late 1940s, Trueblood told his readers that on "one unforgettable afternoon on the Singley Pool he [Harry] hooked eighteen steelhead on the Red Optic." Trueblood, from Nampa, Idaho, was a well-known outdoor writer and regular columnist for *Field & Stream*, and wrote this piece under the pseudonym Thomas Hardin. He spent time with Pray in Eureka and learned quickly of Hornbrook's exploits.

Hornbrook continued to fish the Eel in the 1960s and '70s, but the lower river changed considerably after the flood of 1964. He also got involved in bowling, hot-rodding, and drag racing, and applied his perfectionist personality to these three activities. When Stephen Rosenberg began to fish the Eel in the 1970s, he finally got to know the "king" as his father had known him and was similarly impressed with Harry's skill, generosity, and gentlemanly behavior. On one cold morning on the Speedy Run, just below the mouth of the Van Duzen, Rosenberg remembers that "in accordance with Harry's usual custom, he let everyone else go first." After four anglers had fished through the run without anything, "Harry hooked and landed a beautiful steelhead."

After Hornbrook retired, he moved to a retirement home in Winston, Oregon, where he bowled on a team known as the Old Kids. At 71, Harry had a 170 average; in keeping with his personality, he told a reporter that "anytime I bowl, I'm trying to do the best I can at the time. I compete more with myself than any other bowler." Around this same time Stephen Rosenberg traveled to Roseburg, Oregon, to fish the North Umpqua and to visit his old friend Hornbrook. They fished together at the Elevation Pool, and Rosenberg was not surprised when "Harry promptly extracted two summer steelhead from it on this, his first ever visit to the North Umpqua."

Hornbrook later moved to Roseburg and died there on November 14, 1998, at the age of 83.

BILL SCHAADT IN 1989 WITH A 40-POUND CHINOOK SALMON CAUGHT
USING 8-POUND TIPPET ON CALIFORNIA'S SMITH RIVER. (PHOTOGRAPH
COURTESY OF DAN BLANTON) BILL SCHAADT'S GOLDEN GOOSE, TIED
BY JON LUKE (INSET)

Chapter 8

William E. "Bill" Schaadt (1922–1995):

PIONEER FLY FISHER FOR STEELHEAD,
CHINOOK SALMON, AND STRIPED BASS

*W*illiam E. "Bill" Schaadt was born in San Francisco in 1922 to a German father and Portuguese mother. There he attended Catholic school. His name, Schaadt, was pronounced "Shad," just like the fish. During his high school years he became an accomplished high diver; after graduation he attended San Francisco Junior College. He was described as "a tall, swarthy, athletic man with large, powerful hands, a large nose, piercing black eyes, and tight curly hair." Besides diving, Schaadt was also a talented artist, excelling at pen-and-ink drawing, painting, and wood carving.

After his father's death in the early 1940s, Schaadt was drawn from the city to the "Redwood Empire" near the Russian River to the north and bought a small lot in Monte Rio. While working at a garage in nearby Guerneville, he built a house for himself and his mother. Bill also began pursuing an art-related career and started painting signs for a living. Before long, his unique flowing style and signature, Shad Signs, appeared on storefronts and businesses in many small towns north and west of Santa Rosa. At this time, too, in 1944 and 1945, Schaadt began to fish for summer steelhead on the Klamath and purchased his flies at Jim Pray's shop in Eureka.

> *Bill "was using a line that I had never seen before. . . . . . He had taken lead-core trolling line and cut it into 27-foot lengths, each weighing 300 grains. A small loop, to which the monofilament running line could be attached, was tied into one end. The result was a lead-core shooting head that cast like a bullet and got down to the fish."*
> *Bob Nauheim, "The Line on the Big Fish,"*
> Outdoor Life, *1972*

With seasonal work and an immense interest in steelhead fly fishing, Schaadt had the right combination for success. He never married or had children, and once his mother passed away he worked when he had to and fished the remainder of the time. Influenced by Pray and the river's national reputation for big fish, Schaadt fished the Eel River in the mid-1940s. However, he soon realized that closer rivers, such as the Gualala and Garcia—and, more important, his local Russian River—were also top winter steelhead rivers. This was also the time that several members of the Golden Gate Angling and Casting Club (GGACC), who were some of the finest fly casters and fishermen in the world, began driving up the coast to fish the rivers practically in Bill's backyard. He befriended Jim Green, Myron Gregory, and Jon Tarantino, among numerous others, and learned much from them over the years.

In 1946, a pivotal year for both steelhead fly fishing and Bill Schaadt, he began a nearly uninterrupted 50-year streak of fishing Northern California's coastal rivers on an almost daily basis. If there were fish to cast to, Schaadt would be there. It was also in 1946 that Jim Green used shooting-heads and monofilament shooting line at the National Casting Tournament in Indianapolis, Myron Gregory used lead-core line for saltwater fly fishing, and Jon Tarantino was coming on the scene as a champion distance caster. In addition, Pete Schwab was experimenting with weighted steelhead flies and torpedo heads for distance casting and writing about it in *Sports Afield*; Harry Hornbrook was having his best years on the Eel; and Lloyd Silvius, a friend of Pray and Schwab, developed his Fall Favorite Optic fly pattern, modeling it after Pray's highly effective Black Optic and Red Optic. It was in this unique environment that Schaadt grew as a fly fisherman and a steelheader.

By the early 1950s, Schaadt had adapted many of these previous developments to his own fishing. He became such an accomplished caster that he could compete with Tarantino, and the two fished regularly with lead-core lines and shooting-heads for saltwater bottom fish as well as steelhead. Schaadt focused most of his fishing attention on steelhead in the Russian and the Gualala, where his two favorite patterns were the Red and Orange Fall Favorites. On the Gualala, he fished with Joe Paul and Alan Curtis, both associated with the GGACC, and they began to outfish him in the Snag Hole and Donkey Hole using a new pattern, soon to be called a Comet. It was an orange fly with a bucktail tail twice the length of the hook, a lead-wire body, and bead-chain eyes. Others started using Comets on the Russian River, and soon thereafter both Guerneville fly-shop owners, John Ferenz and Grant King, began tying and marketing the fly commercially. As a takeoff on the Comet-style fly, Forestville resident Virgil Sullivan created his Boss pattern, which Grant King named after his wife, Betty, "The Boss." King began marketing this fly as well. Both flies became Schaadt favorites.

Schaadt's fame and celebrity status, like his cohorts', began to develop in the early 1950s. On a day when Claude Krieder, the well-known author of *Steelhead* (1948), proclaimed the Gualala too muddy for fly fishing, Bill landed 33 steelhead, including one weighing almost 20 pounds. He also discovered that the shad in the Russian River would take a small, sparsely dressed, silver-bodied fly with a red head, and he was so successful that Idahoan Ted Trueblood came and fished with Schaadt and featured him in a *Field & Stream* article. On

Christmas Eve 1953, Bill caught a 17-pound steelhead in the Gualala, and the fish placed third in the *Field & Stream* Western Rainbow Trout Fly-Casting Division and tied for 20th place (with a fish caught by Harry Hornbrook) for large steelhead entered in the contest during the 1940s and early 1950s. During the 1955–1956 winter steelhead season, Schaadt fished either the Gualala or Russian almost every day from November through April and caught and released nearly 900 steelhead, including a 19-pound, 10-ounce fish from the Gualala on his Shad Roe fly, which placed fourth in the *Field & Stream* contest that season. For 1956, he placed fourth again in the *Field & Stream* contest with a 16-pound, 8-ounce steelhead from the Russian.

He used his Fall Favorite Optic and Comet patterns when river flows were strong, but pioneered with his Feeler Flies during clear and low water conditions during the mid-1950s. By cutting off the hackle on the bottom of the fly so as not to interfere with the hook, Bill could actually feel the fish and determine at what depth they were holding. He developed the Brown Nymph, Gold Nymph, Gray Nymph, Nasty Nymph, and Schaadt's Nymph for this style of fishing, generally tying them as small as size 14s and fishing them on 3-pound tippet.

Chinook salmon fishing with heavy traditional gear, mostly in salt water, was well developed and advertised by the 1940s. In fact, A. J. McClane's *The American Angler* (1954) included chinook records from the annual *Field & Stream* contests. McClane described the "King" as "a plug-chewing, spoon-slamming behemoth," and the prize-winning fish ranged from 61 to 82 pounds. Only 11 of the top 110 salmon were caught in California. Forty-eight were caught on spoons, 41 on plugs, and 21 on bait. Schaadt had heard about the big kings of Northern California's Smith River, but the fishery there was composed entirely of trollers and bait anglers who anchored in Suicide Row, Death Row, and You're Gone Row, at the river's mouth. Schaadt decided he could catch these salmon on flies and became a pioneer in that fishery in the late 1950s, fishing upriver in his 8-foot pram and using lead-core lines. He would tow his small travel trailer to the Smith River in early October and stay there until high water sent him back home in November.

During the late 1950s and early 1960s, the Russian River was at its steelhead peak and Schaadt was its recognized guru. He was seen on a daily basis fishing Watson's Log, Duncan's, and Freezeout from shore or in his old green pram, and he caught hundreds of winter steelhead every year. After the river was dammed and in places increasingly used as a gravel quarry, the steelhead fishing in Schaadt's beloved Russian went into serious decline. Later, in a late-1980s interview with Trey Combs, Schaadt admitted that the chain of events that destroyed the Russian "really hurt my soul!"

In the late 1950s Schaadt met two fellow anglers who became his close friends and who were instrumental in spreading his status as a legend throughout North America. Bob Nauheim, a Santa Rosa fireman and freelance writer, was in awe of the man he finally got to meet at the old Gualala Hotel after a day of steelheading. And Russell Chatham, as a young local teenager, watched for Schaadt's old, black 1937 Dodge along the Russian in hopes of seeing his hero. When Chatham finally was introduced several years later, he remembered that Schaadt's "manner was guarded," but when "he offered his immense hand . . . the legend had come to life." Nauheim and Chatham became Schaadt's regular fishing companions, joining a select contingent of local anglers who fished year-round from the Russian north to the Smith and Chetco rivers.

By the early 1960s, thanks largely to Chatham, Schaadt began to actively pursue striped bass with a fly in San Francisco Bay and the local rivers, including the Russian. Chatham caught stripers in the bay as early as 1962 and buoyed interest in the fishery even more with his 36-pound, 6-ounce record fly-caught striped bass, caught beside the Richmond–San Rafael Bridge in 1966. Schaadt began to pursue these fish in earnest during the summer and was so enamored of them that he regularly patrolled the lower Russian by bicycle, motorbike, or car looking for their very visible feeding activity. On one such occasion, after spotting a school of stripers, he fished for them all night, long past legal hours, only to lose his California fishing license for a year and pay a fine. Because he could not imagine having to stop fishing, he discovered that the king salmon in Oregon's Chetco River would also take a fly and once again he was in "on the ground floor," as he liked to say, of a magnificently popular fishery.

Schaadt perfected his chinook salmon fly fishing in the Smith and the Chetco during the 1960s and early 1970s, and Nauheim and Chatham were directly involved. In 1963, in the Smith's Early Hole, Schaadt caught four fish of more than 35 pounds, including a 47-pounder. On other occasions, in the Smith's Bayley Pool, Cable Hole, Lower Park, and Woodruff Pool, Schaadt landed many kings in the 40- and 50-pound range, including a 52-pounder and the fly-caught record fish of 56 pounds, 8 ounces. His 11-hour, 33-minute fight with a 49-pound fish received national notoriety in Chatham's article "Night of the Salmon," published in *True* in 1973. However, it was Nauheim's article "The Kings Come to the Smith," published in the October 1970 issue of *Outdoor Life*, that brought the Smith and Schaadt instant national acclaim. Bill was pictured with his record fly-caught king, and Nauheim referred to him as "one of the pioneers of the sport on the Smith." The article also highlighted his popular salmon fly, Schaadt's Golden Goose, along with Grant King's Explorer and local fly tier Jack Geib's Special.

Nauheim further popularized Schaadt and his extraordinary talents in other *Outdoor Life* articles, including "Gift of the Gualala" (December 1970), "A Season of Giants" (September 1972), and "The Line on the Big Fish" (October 1972). In the latter article, Nauheim noted that Schaadt was "not only an expert fly fisherman but also an innovator." He said Bill "was using a line that I had never seen before. . . . He had taken lead-core trolling line and cut it into 27-foot lengths, each weighing 300 grains. A small loop, to which the monofilament

BILL SCHAADT IN HIS 8-FOOT PRAM, PUTTING A LOT OF PRESSURE ON A LARGE SMITH RIVER CHINOOK SALMON IN THE 1970S (PHOTO-GRAPH COURTESY OF DAN BLANTON)

running line could be attached, was tied into one end. The result was a lead-core shooting head that cast like a bullet and got down to the fish."

Schaadt also applied his successful techniques to Babine River steelhead, Alaskan salmon, tarpon in Florida and Costa Rica, and trout in Montana and Oregon. Schaadt's fishing companions included some of the sport's other notables: Joe Brooks, Ted Trueblood, Bob Wickwire, Ed Rice, Jim Teeny, Tom McGuane, and Polly Rosborough, among others. Nauheim again featured Schaadt and his contributions in "Chinook Fly-Fishing in Theory and Practice," published in *Fishing World* in 1973. Chatham, who had moved to Montana and was embarking on a highly successful painting career, discussed Schaadt and striper fishing in a 1973 article in *Sports Illustrated* titled "By the Cellblock and the Bay." The following year, the same magazine published Chatham's "The World's Best," the most important article ever written about Schaadt. Therein Chatham told the world that "Bill Schaadt has more physical ability and coordination than any fisherman I have ever known," and that even though Jon Tarantino was considered "the greatest distance fly caster who ever lived, he was the only man clearly the equal of Schaadt." Chatham continued his praise, noting that Schaadt "has caught more big steelhead and salmon than any man who ever lived" and that his "overall sense of understanding, deep love of the natural world, energetic effort and his style are the qualities that set him apart from his contemporaries."

> *"Bill Schaadt has more physical ability and coordination than any fisherman I have ever known," and his "overall sense of understanding, deep love of the natural world, energetic effort and his style are the qualities that set him apart from his contemporaries."*
>
> Russell Chatham, *"By the Cellblock and the Bay,"*
> Sports Illustrated, *1973*

Schaadt exploits and stories also played significant roles in Chatham's *The Angler's Coast* (1976) and *Silent Seasons* (1978); Rosborough had a chapter on him in *Reminiscences from 50 Years of Flyrodding* (1982); Trey Combs devoted a chapter to him in *Steelhead Fly Fishing* (1991). California fly fisher and guide Dan Blanton, who first met Schaadt on the Smith in 1968, referred to his pioneering efforts and included photographs of Schaadt and several of his large salmon in articles titled "King Salmon: California & Oregon Style" and "Shooting Heads" in *American Angler* (1992) and *Saltwater Fly Fishing* magazine (1993), respectively.

By 1994, Schaadt realized he had lung cancer and found out the medical community could do nothing for him. He took a salmon fishing trip to British Columbia's Sustut River with Chatham and Mel Krieger that August and went to the Smith and the Chetco in October. By early November, Bill was back home, sick, exhausted, and too weak to live alone. He went to live with Bob and Helena Nauheim in Santa Rosa and told Bob, "I can't believe it's all over. I'm having so much fun!"

Chatham came from Montana to be with him at the Nauheims' home and at the nearby Kaiser Hospital, where, Chatham remembered, "we held his hand, all of us who were there, and in turn cried and prayed for him." Bill Schaadt passed away on January 17, 1995, at the age of 73.

More than 240 friends, mostly fly anglers, memorialized Bill on January 29 at the Calvary Chapel in Santa Rosa. The church overflowed, with loudspeakers broadcasting the service and testimonials to mourners on the lawn. It was here, amid the pain and sorrow, that many of the unique Schaadt stories were told once again: the time he stood on a stepladder in the river so he could cast even farther; the morning his car rolled over an embankment, only to have Bill emerge with his fishing equipment, fish all day, and have the car towed out after dark; how, after watching a boatload of gear fishermen fishing on one of his favorite Russian River holes, marked by a rag in a tree, Bill moved the rag in the middle of the night; Bill hiding his car and riding a bicycle to his favorite holes so he would not be followed; Bill tying on a "razor-blade fly" and pulling it through a hole if other anglers would not break off a foul-hooked fish; Bill laying naked in his pram in the Florida Keys to get a suntan when the tarpon were off the bite.

Schaadt was buried beside his mother and father in Holy Cross Cemetery in Colma, California, and Nauheim, who was the executor of Bill's estate, gave his home to the Kaiser Cancer Center. Also as Bill wished, Nauheim divided $70,000 in $5,000 bequests given to Bill's fishing friends. Both Nauheim and Chatham wrote touching obituaries for *California Fly Fisher*, and John Randolph published one in *Fly Fisherman*. Randolph astutely declared that "if Bill Schaadt lived for anything it was to have his fly in the bucket when the bite was on."

Nauheim, who passed away in 2005, remembered that "Bill's energy was limitless. That energy was directed primarily toward finding fish and staying on them. You always joined Bill already on the river. . . . And when you joined him, it was pretty certain he was over fish."

Chatham called Schaadt "the finest fly caster who ever lived" and remembered that Bill's "goal was clear and singular: to be there for the bite." For Chatham, Schaadt was "the hero I valued and worshipped . . . a rare and fragile genius," who saw fishing and life as "one inseparable entity." His attitude, too, said Chatham, "could always be counted on to be one of hope. He expected nothing, yet anticipated everything."

"No lost motion!"—Schaadt's favorite admonition—was also indicative of his life in fly fishing, and, as Chatham testified, "Bill Schaadt's life was an arrow straight to the bull's-eye."

Part Three:

Idaho

Ted Trueblood changing flies in the early 1950s as he appeared
in his book *How to Catch More Fish*, 1955. Trueblood's Otter
Shrimp, tied by Jon Luke (inset)

Chapter 9

Cecil Whitaker "Ted" Trueblood (1913–1982):

OUTDOOR WRITER, CONSERVATIONIST, AND
LEGENDARY FLY FISHERMAN

Ted Trueblood was born June 26, 1913, on a farm near Homedale, Idaho, in the southwestern corner of the state just west of Boise near the Snake River. His parents, Cecil and Elsie, had moved from Indiana to Idaho the year before to homestead on a 300-acre parcel of land. Farming with horses, the family raised corn, wheat, barley, potatoes, and alfalfa, and young Ted began to hunt in the surrounding woods and fields. He and his younger brother, Burtt, accompanied by their dog Barney, also fished regularly in the local streams, rivers, and lakes. Ted remembered that he began reading about hunting and fishing when he was 10 and bought his first shotgun when he was 13. His first fishing license was purchased the following year, and by the time he turned 17, Ted recalled, he "had become fairly proficient at tying flies." He received a 9-foot Horrocks-Ibbotson fly rod from his grandfather upon his graduation from nearby Wilder High School in 1931 and sold his first article, "A Certain Idaho Trout," to *National Sportsman* magazine under the pseudonym J. W. Wintring.

Ted loved to write and gained an appreciation for it from his mother, who was a prolific writer and diarist. He attended the College of Idaho (now Albertson College) in nearby Caldwell for about two years and continued to write. He published another article in 1932 under the name of Wintring and penned several short stories while still fishing and hunting locally with his brother. They regularly fly fished the Boise River for bass using Ted's Lord Jim pattern. In 1935 Ted enrolled in the University of Idaho in Moscow. That same year, he published an article in *Fur, Fish, and Game* using his own name. Soon thereafter, in 1936, he accepted a position as a reporter for the *Boise Capital News*, started a regular column called "Angles on Angling," and played a major role in organizing the Idaho Wildlife Federation. He moved to Salt Lake City to be a reporter for the *Desert News* the next year and in 1938 began a regular newspaper column, "Campfire Talks." Ted also continued his magazine writing, selling several articles to *Outdoor Life*.

Trueblood moved back to Nampa, Idaho, in 1939 and married Ellen Hinkson Michaelson, a reporter for the *Capital News*, then set out on a four-month honeymoon of camping, hunting, and fishing. Shortly thereafter, he was hired by the Idaho Fish and Game Department as a field researcher, public relations officer, and photographer. During this time he worked to save the lower Hells Canyon from dam building; explained to his readers how to catch chinook salmon on rod and reel, thus eliminating the need for the traditional spearing of salmon in Idaho; and published articles in *Natural History* and *Nature*. His wife, an expert on mushrooms and an avid outdoorswoman herself, accompanied Ted regularly on his many outdoor adventures.

In 1941 Ted was offered the position of fishing editor for *Field & Stream* magazine in New York, and he accepted. He and his wife moved to Pleasantville, New York, but due to internal changes at the magazine he soon lost his job. He then worked briefly as outdoor editor for the *Raleigh News-Observer* in North Carolina. After moving back to Nampa in 1942, he once more accepted the position of fishing editor at *Field & Stream* in 1944 and moved back to New York. By 1947, at the age of 34, Ted had had enough of East Coast city life and moved back to Nampa "determined to hunt, fish, and write about it." After seeing his recently retired New York neighbor suddenly die of a heart attack, Ted reassessed his own life and asked himself, "Why work hard and save money and then die before I had a chance to enjoy the things for which I had been saving it?" He continued to write for *Field & Stream*, as well as several other magazines, as a freelancer, but also started a column called "Outdoors by Ted Trueblood," in Boise's weekly newspaper, the *Statewide*.

By the late 1940s and early '50s, Trueblood had established a national reputation as a hunter and fisherman, which resulted in several book contracts. He coauthored *Fishing in America* with Lynn Hunt and S. Kip Farrington, Jr., in 1946 and combined with illustrator Walter Dower to publish *Trout Trouble and Other Trouble* in 1948. The following year, he published his largest and most comprehensive book, *The Angler's Handbook*. An abridged version appeared in 1951 as *Ted Trueblood's Fishing Handbook*. Ted and several other notable anglers coauthored The *Finest Split Bamboo Fishing Rods* for the E.F. Payne Rod Company in 1952, and his final fishing book, *How to Catch More Fish*, appeared in 1955. Trueblood also authored at least three other books on hunting, his most recent in 1978, titled *Ted Trueblood's Hunting Treasury*. While some of his books were compilations and anthologies of his previous writings in magazines, most notably *Field & Stream*, others contained completely original work.

It was also during the early 1950s that Ted began to write regularly for *True Magazine, Elks Magazine, True Hunting and Fishing Yearbooks*, and *Rod and Gun*, among others. In 1954 he started his regular column in *Field & Stream* as an associate editor. Covering subjects such as hunting, camping, fishing, dogs, outdoor cooking, and conservation, Ted's column spanned 28 years. In all, he published more than 500 articles in *Field & Stream*, 72 in *True*, 121 in *Elks*, and 74 in *True Hunting and Fishing Yearbooks*. He wrote every one of them on his trusty Underwood typewriter and referred to those articles never published as "misfires." He was read by millions, many on a monthly basis, and was a star writer in the eyes of most American outdoorsmen. Particularly appreciated was Trueblood's friendly, straightforward, and down-to-earth style, which readers could understand and identify with. Many of his own photo-

TED TRUEBLOOD PLAYING A TROUT, CIRCA 1949 (PHOTO). COVERS OF TED TRUEBLOOD'S BOOKS *HOW TO CATCH MORE FISH* (FAWCETT, 1955) AND TED TRUEBLOOD'S *FISHING HANDBOOK* (FAWCETT, 1951).

graphs accompanied his articles and books and were chosen from his personal collection of 4,000 slides, 28,000 negatives, and 2,500 prints.

Trueblood was a fly-fishing legend and, to a certain extent, a pioneer too, in the history of American fly fishing. One of his earliest and most lasting contributions came in the late 1940s, when he started to experiment with nymphs and nymph fishing. He soon discovered, much to his surprise, that exact imitation was not important. Instead, he realized, "the purpose of flies of this type was merely to suggest food so that trout would take them to investigate."

Making flies that were "suggestive" rather than "imitative" led Trueblood to use a variety of hairs and furs for dubbing. This, he argued, provided "insect-ness." As a result, he developed his most famous fly, the Otter Shrimp, also referred to as the Trueblood Otter or the Trueblood Shrimp, in 1950. He used a Mustad 7948A hook in sizes 6, 8, 10, and 12 and dubbed the body with pale otter belly fur with a little white seal hair mixed in. The dubbing was spun on Nymo, color 2042, and the throat hackle and tail were partridge. Trueblood developed other flies as well, but never gave them names that would last. All were "impressionistic" and were referred to simply as "My Tan Nymph" or "My Green Nymph." In fact, in an article in *Field & Stream* on "The Trout Flies of Ted Trueblood" in 1986, one of his closest fishing companions over the years, Peter Barrett, confirmed that "Ted Trueblood was modest about his flies and rarely dignified any with a name." Yet, Barrett did attribute the Integration, Pine Squirrel, Otter Shrimp, and Trueblood Fledermaus to him.

Fly-line development also received a major boost from Trueblood. He became aware of shooting-heads and monofilament running line through his association with the tournament casters at the Golden Gate Angling and Casting Club in San Francisco, and regularly used these unique lines, combined with the double haul, in his steelhead fly fishing.

"[Ninety] percent of the time I think fishing your fly where the fish are is more important then the kind of fly you use."
—*Ted Trueblood*

In 1960 Ted began a long association with Scientific Anglers (founded in 1945) and worked directly with owner Leon P. Martuch and his son, Leon L., or "Chum." He wrote several pamphlets and guidebooks and did considerable field research for them on lines, rods, and reels. Accordingly, he was instrumental in developing their first Sink-Tip lines and used some of the first graphite rods. He was one of the first to advocate a complete "fly-fishing system" where he carried a variety of different shooting-heads to match any water conditions he might encounter. Indeed, this method fit nicely into his basic belief that "90 percent of the time I think fishing your fly where the fish are is more important than the kind of fly you use." He also used a line with a floating tip and a sinking belly and experimented with leader color. He began dyeing his tippets a mossy brown-green color about 1950. This proved to be a wonderful discovery, allowing him to use heavier leaders without spooking the fish.

Ted pioneered fly fishing for summer-run steelhead in Idaho's Salmon and Clearwater rivers and in the Grande Ronde in southeast Washington in the late 1950s and early '60s. He also religiously taught other fly fishers of all ages how to cast. He declared regularly that "most fishermen can't cast" and viewed casting as the most basic and important aspect of catching fish. He also popularized the idea of keeping fishing notebooks and explained how important good records were to his success as a fisherman.

By the early 1960s, Ted Trueblood was at the peak of his career, writing extensively, lobbying for environmental issues, and hunting and fishing more than 140 days a year. His national popularity soared even higher in 1962 after a colleague at *Field & Stream*, Ed Zern, titled one of his "Exit, Laughing" columns "Is There Really a Ted Trueblood?" With a name so perfect, Zern suggested, Ted was "simply a creation of the collective imagination of *Field & Stream* editors." Ted sent a letter to the editor claiming he really did exist and mailed a signed black-and-white photograph of himself to Zern in friendly rebuttal. Numerous newspapers around the country ran the story.

Trueblood and other fly-fishing notables, including Zern and Lee Wulff,

gathered in Eugene, Oregon, in June 1965 to found the Federation of Fly Fishers. Three years later, in February 1968, at the age of 55, Ted suffered a heart attack. Upon reflection, he said, "I think it was aggravation that brought it on. . . . So I'm going to cut down on things I don't enjoy—like public speaking—and concentrate more on just being outdoors whenever possible."

As Ted spent more and more time hunting and fishing, he continued to witness the deterioration of the natural environment he loved so much. Accordingly, he slowly transformed from an outdoorsman to a conservationist to a preservationist. He continually reminded his readers of their role in conserving and perpetuating America's wildlife and other natural resources, and repeatedly led the way by his own example. By the time of *Field & Stream*'s 75th anniversary, in 1970, Trueblood was beginning to gain a national reputation for his environmental work. He worked directly with Idaho U.S. Senator Frank Church and Idaho Governor Cecil Andrus (later secretary of the interior) on many conservation issues and pushed hard for wilderness protection in his home state.

Ted's friend Peter Barrett used *Field & Stream*'s anniversary to publish his own rebuttal to the earlier Zern hoax, titled "The Real Ted Trueblood." Barrett, an associate editor, told the readership that Ted was "a skilled writer, photographer, hunter, fisherman, camp cook, woodsman, conservationist, and jack-of-all-outdoors. What's more, that really is his name." In 1972 Ted started the River of No Return Wilderness Council and presided over it through 1980, when Congress set aside about 2.2. million acres around the Salmon River in central Idaho as a preserve. That same year he founded Save Our Public Lands,

*"Ted Trueblood taught
valuable lessons about
how to fish but, far more
memorably, he taught
generations how to think
about fishing, about the
fish, and the fish's habitat."*
*—Ted Trueblood Chapter
of Trout Unlimited, 1991*

an Idaho-based group opposing the sale or disposal of federal public lands.

Trueblood received numerous awards and honors in the later years of his life, testimony to his impact on the outdoor world. He received the Idaho Wildlife Federation's Conservationist of the Year Award in 1974, which was followed the next year by the U.S. Department of the Interior Conservation Service Award, the Outdoor Writers Association of America Outdoorsman of the Year Award, and the Winchester Western Outdoorsman of the Year Award. He received a special citation from Trout Unlimited in 1977, the National Audubon Society Golden Eagle Conservation Award in 1979, and the Boise State University President's Award for Western Life and Letters in 1980. The following year he became the Coors Western Outdoorsman of the Year. None, however, was more important to him than the "Ted Trueblood Night" in his hometown of Nampa, Idaho, on February 14, 1978. The three-hour testimonial was attended by Senator Frank Church and Governor John Evans along with numerous other notables, relatives, and friends. Secretary of the Interior Cecil Andrus, unable to attend, sent Ted a laudatory letter stating that he was "one of America's foremost outdoorsmen and conservationists."

The first signs of cancer appeared in Trueblood's body in 1978, and his physical condition declined fairly quickly. In 1980, he spent a total of just 38 days hunting and fishing, and, after surgery and chemotherapy, things got even worse. No longer able to enjoy the things that were central to his life, Trueblood died in his Nampa home on Sunday, September 12, 1982, from a self-inflicted gunshot wound. Two days later, in a short interview on Nampa's *Channel 6 News*, Ted's son Jack said his "father had told him that when Eskimos are too old to be of use to their tribe, they go out on the ice and end their life." Jack added that his "father just couldn't find any ice in Nampa." The front page of the *Idaho Statesman* featured a photograph of Ted along with a lengthy obituary titled "Ted Trueblood: Dean of Outdoor Writers Dies at 69" in its September 14 issue. He was survived by his wife, Ellen; sons Jack and Dan; stepdaughter, Mary Michaelson; brother, Burtt; five grandchildren; and five great-grandchildren. His ashes were spread over his favorite area in Owyhee County, Idaho.

Several important developments have kept the memory of Ted Trueblood alive. At Boise State University, the Ted Trueblood Memorial Conservation Fund was established, as well as the Ted Trueblood Scholarship in the Department of Communications. In 1987 a 300-acre public hunting area in Idaho was named the Ted Trueblood Wildlife Area, and in 1989 the Idaho Conservation League's conference on Idaho wild lands was dedicated to Ted's memory and he was honored with a poster bearing his photo and the words "WILD IDAHO." That same year, Ellen Trueblood donated all of her late husband's papers to Albertsons Library at Boise State. In 1991 members of the Boise chapter of Trout Unlimited renamed it the Ted Trueblood Chapter, pointing out that "Ted Trueblood taught valuable lessons about how to fish but, far more memorably, he taught generations how to think about fishing, about the fish, and the fish's habitat." Also during the 1990s, *Fly Tyer, Flyfishing, American Angler*, and *Fly Fisherman* each published articles specifically referring to Trueblood's contributions to nymph fishing. Most recently, in 2000, librarians Mary Carter-Hepworth, Sarah Davis, and Alan Virta published *The Ted Trueblood Collection at Boise State University—A Guide to the Papers of One of America's Foremost Outdoor Writers and Conservationists*.

Part Four:

Montana

FRANZ POTT POSING WITH THREE TROUT ALONG A MONTANA RIVER, CIRCA 1918. (PHOTOGRAPH COURTESY OF MIKE WILKERSON, POTT FLY COMPANY, MISSOULA, MONTANA)

"No fly of mine has gone on the market unless I have excellent success with the brand and am assured of its quality myself." —Franz Pott

Chapter 10

Franz B. "Frank" Pott (circa 1890–1955):

COMMERCIAL FLY TIER AND DESIGNER OF THE
WOVEN-HAIR SERIES OF POTT FLIES

Franz B. "Frank" Pott, a German immigrant, owned and operated a barbershop on Main Street in Missoula, Montana, as early as 1918. Pott brought the crafts of barbering and wig making with him from his native country. He was also an avid fly fisherman and frequented Montana streams on a regular basis. It did not take long before Pott realized that he could make better and cheaper flies than those he could buy on the market. Soon thereafter, his friends started asking him to make flies for them as well.

Pott began experimenting with fly patterns and tying techniques in his barbershop in the early 1920s, and applied his knowledge of weaving hair used in the wig-making trade to attaching hair to a hook shank. From this early work, Pott began to develop a series of woven-hair flies. Due to continued interest in his flies, a result of word of mouth among anglers, and worsening varicose veins that forced him to stop barbering, Pott opened the Pott Fly Company in Missoula in 1924. Once he began to tie commercially, his innovative and meticulously woven and cross-woven badger-hair creations began to appear in fly shops and fly boxes throughout his home state.

At the time, Montana was entering its "golden age" of trout fishing, and Pott was one of the leaders in this movement. Fly-fishing historian Paul Schullery remarked that in the 1920s and 1930s "new flies and new ideas were everywhere, as western anglers came into their own with patterns and techniques suited to the waters. No longer did they simply order flies from back east." Pott's contemporaries included Jack Boehme, also of Missoula, who first tied

AN ORIGINAL POTT FLY CARD BEARING POTT'S REGISTERED TRADEMARK AND HIS TWO PATENTS. EACH FLY WAS SNELLED ON A SHORT, FAIRLY HEAVY LEADER AND PLACED UNDER TWO SLITS IN THE CARD. (ORIGINAL COURTESY OF MIKE WILKERSON, POTT FLY COMPANY, MISSOULA, MONTANA).

his Picket Pin with a stiff wing made from gopher-tail hair in 1915; Wilbur "Bill" Beaty of Butte, who started to produce woven-hair flies commercially in 1920; Norman Means ("Paul Bunyan") of Missoula, who made his Bunyan Bugs out of cork and horsehair around 1927; George Grant from Butte, who first tied his Black Creeper in 1931 and began to weave flies similar to Pott's in that decade; and Dan Bailey, who began to tie western patterns, such as his Mossback series, in the 1930s and opened his famed fly shop in Livingston in 1938. Schullery also observed that "most of the flies tied by Pott, Boehme, Grant, and the rest were large, for use in heavy, swift water. Some may have inadvertently imitated stonefly nymphs, many just looked like something the trout wanted to eat." And, with a cavalier disregard for tradition, this group of Montana fly tiers used flies that found no acceptance in other parts of the world. In fact, as Schullery has argued, they "divorced themselves from the mainstream on angling thought and found their own way, and they caught as many fish as anybody else."

The style of fly tied by Pott and his followers was, in fact, unique in the 1920s. The woven-hair bodies made from coarse badger or ox-ear hair were harder than most flies, and the stiff hair hackles did not move in the water as individual fibers, as was the case for most feathers. Of course, there were detractors who argued that hard-bodied flies with coarse hackles would not catch trout, but the fly weavers proved them wrong in Montana.

Not only did these flies catch fish, but they had several other notable advantages over traditionally tied flies. In fast water, the stiff hackle remained extended and did not conceal the body of the fly. The hard woven bodies tended to withstand repeated fish-catching, and, in fact, as trout teeth frayed them, most anglers believed the flies became more effective. Additionally, the hand-woven style utilized a narrow stripe of thread interwoven on the underside of the fly. Its main purpose was to strengthen the body and prevent unraveling, but because it was usually orange or yellow, the stripe also added color and gave the flies a nymph-like appearance. And while the flies were not designed to match any particular insect, the very nature of the woven technique presented a very "buggy" look. Pott especially took great pride in the durability and craftsmanship of his flies and often remarked, "No fly of mine has gone on the market unless I have excellent success with the brand and am assured of its quality myself."

Pott's flies were popular and effective enough to demand a higher price than other commercially tied flies. For years his flies retailed at 35 cents each or three for a dollar. Bud Lilly, famous Montana fly-shop proprietor and a pioneer in his own right, remembered, "The staple of our fly patterns was the series of flies developed by F. B. Pott." He also remembered losing them in trees or rocks and hearing his mother ask, "Can't you find something cheaper to lose?" Schullery, in his own research on the history of fly fishing, discovered that records kept by Sax & Fryer's, a small Livingston store that sold flies in the 1920s and '30s, showed that most of the larger trout caught in the Yellowstone River (those that

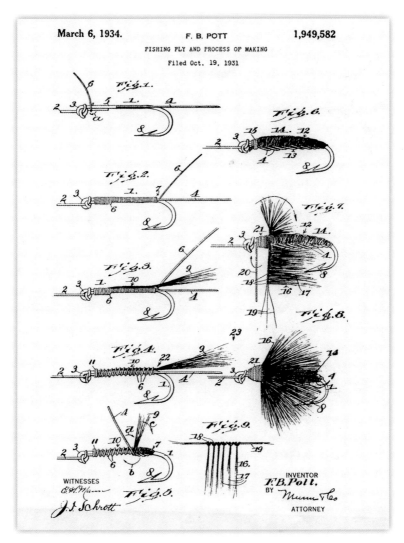

March 6, 1934.

F. B. POTT

1,949,582

FISHING FLY AND PROCESS OF MAKING

Filed Oct. 19, 1931

F. B. Pott's "Fishing Fly and Process of Making" patent, filed on October 19, 1931, and awarded March 6, 1934

were not caught on bait or hardware) were caught on Pott flies.

At the peak of production in the 1930s and '40s, Pott hired female students from the University of Montana to weave the fly bodies, but he insisted on weaving all of the hackles himself so he could maintain uniformity and quality and serve as his own final inspector. The Pott Fly Company produced 30 different patterns in all, but was most known for its Mite series of flies—Sandy Mite, Lady Mite, Buddy Mite, Mr. Mite, and Dina Mite. George Grant, Montana's leading fly-fishing historian and the most avid follower of the Pott tradition, believed that "Mite" came from "hellgrammite," the common but inaccurate local term for the large stonefly nymphs found in Montana streams. Another of Pott's early flies, the Rock Worm, was the subject of his first patent (number 1,523,895), secured in 1925. The other flies in the Pott collection were Orange Badger, Green Badger, Yellow Badger, Red Badger, Peacock Badger, Pinto Badger, Black Fibber, Yellow Fibber, Orange Fibber, AT Special, Yellow Cliff Special, Red Cliff Special, Orange Cliff Special, Royal Coachman, Coachman, Peacock Fizzle, Orange Fizzle, Red Fizzle, BT Special, Black Jack, Sandy Ant, Black Ant, and Maggot.

The description of the Mite series from a Pott brochure noted that when "submerged the fly has the effect of the helgramite [sic] going up stream." The Badger group comprised wet flies "made for larger streams," especially the Yellowstone. Fibber flies, so named perhaps because all anglers were assumed to be liars, were made from badger hair and had a "heavy nylon" body. The Fizzles were surface flies "with a motion of a fly or bug darting across the top of the water" and were named in honor of Fort Fizzle, near Lolo, Montana. The Cliff Specials and the AT and BT Specials were originally made by Pott for a group of regular veteran Montana anglers and then added to his collection. His Black Jack pattern was "especially designed for late evening fishing." All of the Pott patterns were tied on the Mustad 9485 regular-shank hook with an offset bend, almost exclusively in sizes 8 and 10. Although the hook is not easily found today, and is perhaps not even made any longer, Grant suggested that it was used "for so many years that it was considered to be part of the pattern." Pott secured another patent (number 1,949,582) in 1934 to protect both the method of making his fly bodies as well as the process of combining the body and the woven hackle to make the finished fly.

Grant, who has written extensively about Pott, especially in his two books, *The Master Fly Weaver* (1980) and *Montana Trout Flies* (1981), freely admitted that his "system of flytying [sic] is based to a great extent on a method of weaving hair into the form of a hackle devised by Franz B. Pott." He noted that Pott's Sandy Mite was Montana's most successful wet fly for 50 years and, from his experience as a retailer and wholesaler of trout flies for 40 years, he knew that "the Sandy Mite outsold its closest competitor by at least five to one."

Pott's Black Jack was Grant's favorite fly when he first started to fish the Big Hole River in the 1920s. Consequently, based upon his own direct experience and his vast knowledge of fly fishing, Grant argued that "the Pott hand-woven hair hackle was one of the most important contributions to the construction of artificial trout flies for western big-river fly fishing occurring in the past half-century." Further, Grant believed, "Pott contributed more [than] anyone else to the sport of fly fishing in Montana by creating flies that were especially suitable to the waters in which they were intended to be used, and thereby gave an unschooled fishing public the confidence they needed to convince them that trout could be readily taken by a more interesting, imaginative and humane method than using a snelled hook and a worm."

Grant's reverence for Pott was quite evident in his "Author's Comment" at the beginning of *The Master Fly Weaver*—"To me, there will always be only one 'master weaver,' and that is Franz B. Pott of Missoula, Montana. . . . I should like to have my readers look upon the title as being a tribute to this man."

The Pott Fly Company continued to prosper during the 1940s, and in 1942 Pott was issued an official trademark (number 392,730) by the U.S. Patent Office for display on each of his packaged flies. It consisted of a facsimile signature of F. B. Pott and the words "The Original and Genuine have my Signature." Pott indicated that it had been used in his business since May 1, 1940, and was "applied by affixing the goods in a slotted card on which the trade-mark is shown." "Hair Trout Flies," "The Mite Family," and the following fly names also appeared on the cards: "Sandy, Mr. Mite, Lady Mite, Buddy, Fizzle, Dina, Black Jack, Maggot, and Fibber."

Shortly after receiving the trademark, Pott leased his business to the Finline Tackle Company in Denver, but the deal did not last long. Pott was dissatisfied with their workmanship, and, because he had put a clause in the contract relating to maintaining "high quality," he was able to abrogate the lease and move the operation back to Missoula. His flies were still popular in the late 1940s, and Syl Macdowell, in his popular book *Western Trout* (1948), discussed Pott's Mite series and stated that his "choice of these for wet fly angling is Sandy Mite on [a] Number 10 hook." Macdowell also noted that the fly was "a leading number in my fly-box anywhere" and that he had used it "more universally than any other trout fly except Coachman."

Pott continued his commercial fly-making operation in Missoula into the early 1950s and then sold the entire operation to an individual in the Bitterroot area who kept the company alive for a few more years. Pott died in 1955; the business was eventually sold to Gene Snyder, who operated out of his Angler's Roost fly shop near Hamilton. In 1986 Dwain Wright of Missoula purchased all of the rights and patents from Snyder. Wright produced all of Pott's original patterns by employing three people to weave the hair hackles and three more to tie the bodies and add the hackles. He estimated that he sold about 1,000 dozen flies a year up until 1990, when he stopped production and put the business up for sale.

The Pott Fly Company was acquired by its fifth round of owners in 1991, when Ray Prill, John Satre, and Mike Wilkerson purchased the company from Wright "so that it would be kept alive" in Montana. Wilkerson refers to the Pott flies as "an important part of Montana and Montana fly fishing—the heritage" and focuses present production on eight of the "old favorites": Sandy Mite, Lady Mite, Buddy Mite, Mr. Mite, Dina Mite, Orange Badger, Rock Worm, and Olive Badger. They make the Pott flies using the "patented methods of creating woven bodies and woven hackles from high quality natural materials." Wilkerson adds that the majority of their flies are sold in the West, namely Montana, Idaho, Wyoming, and Utah.

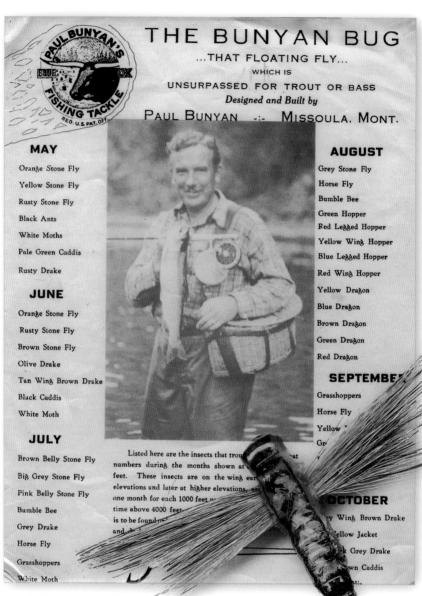

THE BUNYAN BUG

...THAT FLOATING FLY...

WHICH IS

UNSURPASSED FOR TROUT OR BASS

Designed and Built by

PAUL BUNYAN -:- MISSOULA. MONT.

MAY

Orange Stone Fly
Yellow Stone Fly
Rusty Stone Fly
Black Ants
White Moths
Pale Green Caddis
Rusty Drake

JUNE

Orange Stone Fly
Rusty Stone Fly
Brown Stone Fly
Olive Drake
Tan Wing Brown Drake
Black Caddis
White Moth

JULY

Brown Belly Stone Fly
Big Grey Stone Fly
Pink Belly Stone Fly
Bumble Bee
Grey Drake
Horse Fly
Grasshoppers
White Moth

AUGUST

Grey Stone Fly
Horse Fly
Bumble Bee
Green Hopper
Red Legged Hopper
Yellow Wing Hopper
Blue Legged Hopper
Red Wing Hopper
Yellow Dragon
Blue Dragon
Brown Dragon
Green Dragon
Red Dragon

SEPTEMBER

Grasshoppers
Horse Fly
Yellow ~
Gr~

OCTOBER

~y Wing Brown Drake
~ellow Jacket
~k Grey Drake
~wn Caddis

Listed here are the insects that trou~ ~at
numbers during the months shown at ~
feet. These insects are on the wing ear~
elevations and later at higher elevations, an~
one month for each 1000 feet ~
time above 4000 fee~
is to be found ~
and ~

A BUNYAN BUG ADVERTISEMENT AND "HATCH CHART" FROM THE 1940's; NOTICE THE PAUL BUNYAN'S FISHING TACKLE PATENTED LOGO IN THE UPPER LEFT (ABOVE). WITH IT IS A LARGE FEMALE "SALMONFLY" (THE GIANT STONEFLY, PTERONARCYS CALIFORNICA). MOST ARE BRIGHT ORANGE AND YELLOW AND CAN BE AS LONG AS 2 INCHES. THE BLACK TIP ON THE BODY REPRESENTS THE EGG SAC. (ORIGINAL FLY COURTESY OF MIKE WILKERSON OF MISSOULA, MONTANA).

Chapter 11

Norman Edward Lee Means (1899–circa 1984):

AKA PAUL BUNYAN, INVENTOR OF THE BUNYAN BUG SERIES OF FLIES

Norman Edward Lee Means was born in Davis, West Virginia, on October 11, 1899. During his youth, he loved to fish in the numerous lakes and streams in this mountainous region. He was fishing dry flies for trout by the age of 10 and experimented with making his own flies during his public school days. In the fall of 1921, Means traveled to Missoula, Montana, to begin his studies in forestry at the University of Montana. He purchased his first Montana fishing license the following spring and began to explore the local rivers, primarily Rock Creek and the Blackfoot River. He soon became a professional forester and acquired the nickname "Paul Bunyan," for the legendary lumberjack of the north woods of the United States and Canada. The name stuck with Means until his death. He signed his personal checks using the Bunyan name, and most of his acquaintances never knew his true name.

Means resided in Missoula the remainder of his life and was the father of six children. Here, around 1927, he began tying his "bugs." His education and curiosity as an amateur naturalist helped him to become very knowledgeable about most of the terrestrial and aquatic insects of western Montana. Accordingly, he developed a series of patterns to imitate the most important food for trout. At one time, his series of Bunyan Bugs consisted of about 35 distinct artificials. He gave each insect a name anglers could pronounce and remember (Orange Stone Fly, White Moth, Black Ant, Olive Drake, Bumble Bee, Brown Caddis, Yellow Jacket, Big Grey Stone Fly, etc.) and provided hatch charts showing which of his flies were best for specific months. All were floating flies composed of cork bodies and a variety of animal hair, generally available in sizes 10 to 2.

Although Means was establishing quite a local reputation for himself and his flies by the late 1920s, he never received much national attention. An exception came in August 1929 when a young writer from Michigan by the name of Enos Bradner fished with Means and published an article about the experience the following year in *Forest and Stream*. Titled "The Bugs of Bunyan" and appearing in the July issue, the article was a detailed description of fly fishing with Paul Bunyan on his home rivers around Missoula. Bradner described Means as "heavy set with a ready smile, as wide as the river, he is an expert angler thoroughly conversant with local streams. Although well versed in the wiles of the dry fly, he will use nothing but his own 'Bugs' which he varies in pattern to suit the season." As Bradner sat in Means's workshop, Means told him to "leave your fly books at home tomorrow. . . . You won't

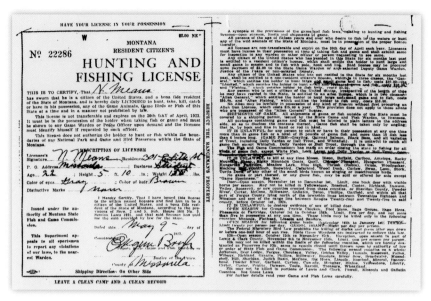

A COPY OF NORMAN MEANS'S FIRST MONTANA FISHING LICENSE, IN 1922
(COURTESY OF MIKE WILKERSON)

need flies when you fish with me." At that point, Means held up "a torpedo shaped bit of cork about one half inch long with a hook sticking from one end and Badger hairs slanting from the other. It was wound in a pattern of black silk and painted a dull tan to resemble a salmon fly." He informed Bradner that "it's the baby that gets 'em. The big ones can't resist it." After a very successful day of fishing, Bradner said to Means, "Well, your Bugs sort of do the trick, don't they?" and Means replied, "They should, I've worked over them for a long time."

During the 1930s and '40s, Means and his Bunyan Bugs became very famous in his home state. He patented the name of his company, Paul Bunyan's Fishing Tackle, and was known throughout Montana as "Mr. Fishin'." He was an expert fly fisherman and superb roll caster, and put on demonstrations at local sportsmen's shows. One such show, called Fisherman's Fiesta, advertised, "Presenting on our stage, Paul Bunyan, Montana's beloved sportsman, displaying the art of roll casting and the best way to catch mammoth trout." Besides his expertise as a fly tier, Means was also a skilled maker of split-bamboo fly rods. In fact, in his book *Montana Trout Flies* (1981), George Grant noted that those "fortunate enough to own one would not have traded it for a Leonard or a Thomas." Means also had a reputation as a rugged outdoorsman who oftentimes waded the cold Montana rivers in shorts and tennis shoes and regularly swam from one side of the river to the other holding his fly rod in one hand above his head.

Means's most familiar "bug" was his imitation of the giant female stone-fly, *Pteronarcys californica*, commonly called a salmonfly. He developed it for use on Rock Creek, where flights of thousands of these bright orange-bodied adults would begin to appear at the mouth of the creek in early June and hatch farther and farther upriver as the days progressed. Means used a ferrule die to cut the cylindrical cork bodies, further shaped them by hand, and made a belly slit to hold the hook. He used bent-shank Herters hooks, usually size 4 or 2, with a 1.5-inch-long shank. The wings were made from horse mane

> *"They floated beautifully, and the fish couldn't get enough of them."* —Bud Lilly

hair, usually sandy colored, and inserted into the slit in the cork body near the eye of the hook so that they would lie flat. The bodies were originally hand-painted with different colors and lifelike designs, but later Means switched to stenciled designs on tissue paper. The paper was affixed to the body like a decal and varnished. The hook was glued in the underbody slit and the body was wrapped with nylon thread. Another coat of varnish then finished the fly. By the early 1950s Means had begun to use a curve cut for the hair-wing placement, and he secured a patent (No. 2,754,612) for this new technique. This gave the wings an upward swing and a more lifelike appearance. These time-consuming flies were unique in construction and had no parallel among other Montana or western trout flies. Bud Lilly, a pioneer angler himself in

BUNYAN BUG PATTERNS COURTESY OF MIKE WILKERSON OF MISSOULA, MONTANA.

Montana and former operator of the world-famous Trout Shop in West Yellowstone, remembered fishing with Bunyan Bugs in the early 1940s: "They floated beautifully, and the fish couldn't get enough of them."

Bunyan's large salmonfly pattern was most widely used on the Blackfoot River and Rock Creek, but its fame spread via fly shops such as Dan Bailey's in Livingston, Fran Johnson's in Butte, and Bob Ward's in Missoula. Soon anglers were using it during the hatch on the Big Hole, Madison, and Yellowstone rivers. George Grant, in *Montana Trout Flies*, noted that it was the "No. 1 fly of boat fishermen during the 'salmon fly' season. It always floats, it lies flat on the water like a natural, and it presents an outline to the trout much like the fly it represents." And, he further noted, it "made up in effectiveness . . . what [it] lacked in classic design." Paul Schullery, noted fly-fishing historian, reported in *American Fly Fishing: A History* (1987) that the Bunyan Bugs "were constantly in demand on Montana streams" and that Bunyan's use of horsehair wings as early as 1927 preceded that of Lee Wulff, who has been credited by others as the first to use animal hair in a dry fly, in 1929.

Means turned over the Bunyan Bug business to his son, Norman Means, Jr., in the early 1970s. The younger Means continued to make several of the more popular patterns in the family shop in Missoula as his father began to grow weaker and weaker from complications arising from diabetes. Then, in 1976, as the popularity of Bunyan Bugs was beginning to wane, the University of Chicago Press published a book by Norman Maclean titled *A River Runs Through It and Other Stories*. The novel, set in Maclean's home state of Montana in the 1920s, featured several fishing excursions made by Norman, his father, and his brother, Paul. On one particular day on the Blackfoot, after Paul had just chided Norman for carrying too many flies, Norman studied a hatch and proclaimed:

> The fly that would work now had to be a big fly, it had to have a yellow, black banded body, and it had to ride high in the water with extended wings, something like a butterfly that has had an accident and can't dry its wings by fluttering in the water.

Maclean continued his story:

> It was so big and flashy it was the first fly I saw when I opened my box. It was called a Bunyan Bug, tied by a fly tyer in Missoula named Norman Means, who ties a line of big flashy flies all called Bunyan Bugs. They are tied on big hooks, No. 2's and No. 4's, have cork bodies with stiff horse-hair tied crosswise so they ride high in the water like dragonflies on their backs. . . . Probably the biggest and flashiest of the hundred flies my brother made fun of was the Bunyan Bug No. 2 Yellow Stone Fly. I took one look at it and felt perfect.

Indeed, it was the perfect fly. Norman landed a huge rainbow and exclaimed, "So on this wonderful afternoon when all things came together it took me one cast, one fish, and some reluctantly accepted advice to attain perfection." Maclean alluded to his Bunyan Bugs several other times in the book, and artist R. Williams drew a large salmonfly replica as one of the book's illustrations. As more and more readers enjoyed the book, which sold more than 160,000 copies and narrowly missed winning the Pulitzer Prize for fiction in 1977, the Bunyan Bug experienced a rebirth.

In the early 1980s, the Bunyan Bug Company moved to Greenough, Montana, and was taken over by Means's grandson Richard Rose. Rose's son Daniel also began to learn the trade, and together they sell the Salmon Fly No. 4 to anglers and collectors worldwide. These handcrafted pieces of art require about 13 different steps and two to three hours to complete the intricate assembly and finishing touches.

Norman Edward Lee Means died in Missoula in the mid-1980s.

His Bunyan Bug had one final bout of fame in 1992, when the motion picture *A River Runs Through It* became a box-office bonanza. Produced and directed by Robert Redford and Patrick Markey, the film stayed true to Maclean's original story. With Paul Maclean played by Brad Pitt and Norman by Craig Sheffer, and several Bunyan Bugs tied by Ron Brown in Bailey's Fly Shop, the big trout scene was played out on the silver screen. Not only did this film help popularize fly fishing throughout the United States, but it also became a lasting tribute to the ingenuity of Norman Means and his Bunyan Bugs.

Perhaps George Grant said it best in *Montana Trout Flies*: "Paul Bunyan is a true pioneer in the art of flytying in Montana and must be recognized and honored as an individual who contributed substantially to the sport of fly fishing in the West."

Don Martinez in his Los Angeles home circa 1947.
Note that he is holding his famous "pin vise" (photograph courtesy of Robert Wethern and *The Creel*).
Woolly Worm fly popularized by Don Martinez, tied
by Jon Luke (inset)

Chapter 12

Donald S. Martinez (circa 1900–1955):

POPULARIZER OF THE WOOLLY WORM, EARLY WEST YELLOWSTONE FLY-SHOP OWNER, AND PIONEER IN WESTERN DRY FLIES

Donald Skillman Martinez spent his younger years in Connecticut and possibly attended Cornell University for a few years. His father, of Spanish descent, was from New Orleans, and his mother, whose maiden name was Skillman, was from Princeton, New Jersey. Much of his early life is sketchy, but it is known that he lived in Chicago for a time and later in Michigan, where he began to perfect his trout-fishing and fly-tying skills. In his late 20s Martinez moved to Los Angeles and married his wife, Mary. He established a commercial fly-tying operation in his home and became one of several professional fly tiers in the United States, shipping flies throughout North America for $1.50 to $4.20 per dozen.

During his travels Martinez had discovered the spectacular trout fishing in Montana and Wyoming, and in 1932 he opened Don's Tackle Shop in the corner of the old Totem Café in West Yellowstone, Montana. He sold all types of fishing equipment, including his flies; guided fly fishers; and printed his famous *Fishing Guide*, noted for its detailed maps and directions for finding the best fishing in the Yellowstone region. He catered to summer anglers, mostly fly fishers from the East Coast, and returned home to Los Angeles every winter. He continued to spend time in both places until 1943 or 1944, when his business partner, Rae Servatius, took over the shop. It eventually changed hands and evolved into Bud Lilly's Trout Shop in 1950.

Martinez was "the first West Yellowstone fisherman to really establish himself as an important fly tier and authority. For many years he ruled the fly-fishing scene there, especially as that business concerned wealthy and influential visiting fishermen." —Bud Lilly

Lilly knew Martinez well and remembered that he was "the first West Yellowstone fisherman to really establish himself as an important fly tier and authority. For many years he ruled the fly-fishing scene there, especially as that business concerned wealthy and influential visiting fishermen." Martinez also had quite a reputation as an amateur entomologist, and Lilly reaffirmed that he was "one of the top fly tiers and fly-tying theorists of his time" and noted that "his flies were excellent and his knowledge of the insect life of the Yellowstone area was extraordinary." The other legendary Montana fly fisherman and historian of flies of the West, George Grant, remembered Martinez as "one of the world's finest fly dressers" and as the "Western dry-fly master." Grant said Martinez was a "versatile artist" and that every fly he tied "had the unmistakable touch of a master craftsman."

Because he tied for a living, Martinez developed an interesting and labor-saving vise style. His "pin vise" was made by attaching the head part of a Thompson table vise to about 18 inches of an old cane rod. Then he nailed a small tin can to the arm of a wooden lawn chair and placed the cane handle in it so he could spin the vise and roll his tying materials onto the hook. Later, Thompson manufactured this type of vise with a chrome shaft. Martinez also improvised by using a section of car antenna. Ray Bergman, noted writer and author of several fishing books, including his most famous, *Trout* (1938), noted that Martinez was an advocate of the "hand vise" and went on to explain that "tiers who use this vise need no other tool than a pair of scissors, and they produce flies faster than tiers using any other method." Bergman, who was a regular fishing companion of Martinez, also explained that with this vise "you can sit relaxed and comfortable in an arm-chair while tying, thus avoiding the fatigue attending tying flies at a vise where you must sit at a desk, table or bench."

Martinez is probably remembered most as the popularizer of the Woolly Worm, which originally had a thick, black chenille body palmered with a grizzly hackle and a short red floss or wool tag. Initially, in the mid-1930s, Martinez admitted that the fly "was not original with me" and told of its earlier history as a Missouri bass fly. But, in fact, it probably dates back to the Palmer, a fly intended to imitate a "woolly bear" caterpillar described in Thomas Barker's book, *Barker's Delight, or, The Art of Angling* (1651). Martinez told Bergman that his Woolly Worm was "probably the most popular number that was ever commercialized" and took credit as being "the first to make them commercially as a trout fly, or, to be more accurate, trout lure."

Martinez always tied the Woolly Worm by fastening the hackle feather at the bend of the hook by the butt and then winding it dull side forward so that the hackle fibers would slant forward toward the eye. In this way, the soft fibers would pulse and undulate as the fly was retrieved rather than flatten back against the chenille. Black was his favorite color for the fly, and in a letter to Preston Jennings, author of *A Book of Trout Flies, Containing a List of the Most Important American Stream Insects & Their Imitations* (1935), Martinez referred to his "Wooley-worm" as a "horrible looking grub," but admitted that when "properly fished it is murderous all season long." Martinez explained to Jennings that it "should be used only in still or very slow water, fished deep, with a twitching of the line" and believed that "the movement of the hackle is what gets 'em, suggesting perhaps the waving breathing apparatus of the May-fly nymphs and others." The Woolly Worm quickly became a staple

FRONT COVER OF DON MARTINEZ'S FAMOUS *FISHING GUIDE*, WHICH WAS AVAILABLE FREE OF CHARGE TO PATRONS OF DON'S TACKLE SHOP IN WEST YELLOWSTONE, MONTANA (PHOTOGRAPH COURTESY OF ROBERT WETHERN AND *THE CREEL*)

attractor wet pattern and one of the most popular flies in the West, used as an imitator of giant stonefly nymphs, riffle beetle larvae, dragonfly nymphs, and cranefly larvae in larger sizes, and, tied in smaller sizes, used to imitate damselfly nymphs, caddisfly pupae, mayfly nymphs, and caterpillars. Its fame spread worldwide as well, and it was used in New Zealand to imitate "creepers" and in Europe as a good stonefly larva imitation.

Although most would agree with Bud Lilly's assertion that Martinez's popularization of the Woolly Worm "should entitle him to a front-row seat among angling history's luminaries," George Grant said Martinez's real love was "for the quill-bodied, sparsely-hackled, bunch-wing dry flies" compared to "those produced by the Darbees, the Dettes, and other eastern experts." As a commercial tier, Martinez tied what fly fishers wanted, but overall he did not believe pattern was the most important thing for dry flies. He did admit that "the Adams, and similar flies combining brown and Plymouth Rock hackles, will get my vote every time." His favorite fly, which he called a Quill Adams, was known as a Whitcraft in the Jackson Hole, Wyoming, area in honor of Tom Whitcraft, superintendent of Grand Teton National Park in the 1940s and an expert dry-fly fisherman. Martinez also popularized tying Western dry flies as "variants" of traditional patterns such as the Whitcraft, the Hairwing Variant, and the Multi-colored Variant, generally in sizes 16 and 18. Some of his other famous dries were his Pictorial mayfly series, Chocolate Dun, Birch's Favorite, Reversed Caddis, Teton Special, and Bradley M. In *Trout*, Bergman

SIX MARTINEZ TROUT FLY PATTERNS ON THE COVER OF HIS 1941 *FISHING GUIDE* BOOK
OF MAPS (PHOTOGRAPH COURTESY OF THE AMERICAN MUSEUM OF FLY FISHING)

discusses other Martinez flies, such as his Golden Quail, Dunham, and Rough
Water Series of blue, yellow, and white bulky-bodied composites of Cligan
Bass Bugs, Emidas, and Irresistibles.

Martinez was at the peak of his career in the early 1940s and was becoming
well known throughout the United States for his fly shop and his innovative
flies. He had begun to collect and classify natural trout-stream insects from the
Madison River as early as 1938 and became good friends with Preston Jennings
and other luminaries in the fly-fishing world. When several members of the elite
New York Anglers Club traveled to Montana in 1943, they visited Martinez
and his shop because "no one has a better knowledge than he of where to fish,
what flies will be on the water, and all the other minutiae of fishing lore of the
first-class angler." The same fisherman also noted that "Don has studied the
natural flies of the region and he ties imitations which are mighty good."

Martinez's famous *Fishing Guide* was in its third printing by 1941, and in
it one could see the early stages of the modern conservation movement in his
opinions of killing large trout and fishing contests. In fact, he deplored "contests
and competitions based on size or numbers of fish caught" and informed his
clients to "please return surplus trout to the water." He admitted that it was
"harder at first to put back a good fish than it is to catch it, but returning good
fish can be made a habit like anything else." This was at a time when anyone
who caught and released a fish was seen as a "show-off," and it was certainly
a questionable practice for a guide and fly-shop owner to advocate.

Some of Martinez's more innovative dry-fly accomplishments occurred after
he left West Yellowstone and teamed up for a few years during World War II

with Bob Carmichael, a guide and fly-shop owner in Moose, Wyoming, near Jackson Hole. Here, in addition to natural grizzly, Martinez dyed some necks light blue, which he combined with brown, dark furnace, and ginger. While he preferred "a fly with a scanty hackle," Martinez told Jennings that he had to change "in order to please the majority of the people I work for" and, accordingly, he began using caribou hair. His fame had spread to the point that in 1946, in *Fortune* magazine, he was singled out as one of "eleven of the finest U.S. flytiers from coast to coast."

Much of the Martinez philosophy of dry-fly fishing was contained in his article "The Right Dry Fly," published in *Field & Stream* in 1953. He began by suggesting that "when fish are not rising or the stream is deep and wide, a rather bulky fly with plenty of hackle is needed. It takes a fairly large fly to lure a fish up from the bottom in deep, rough water." He went on to discuss the importance of good stiff hackle, hackle length, hook weight, and body material, and explained that "any dry fly worthy of the name will support itself on tail and hackle with the hook clear of the table." Martinez said he "hoped that fishermen will come to regard fly quality as more important than conformity with certain color combinations." For actual hatch conditions, he argued that "smaller flies with sparse hackle and slim bodies will come closer to approximating the natural insects" and urged anglers to "try to match the size of the natural first, then the general shape or outline, and lastly the tone and color." He also reported on his tests looking up at flies in the water and happily noted that it "is certainly fortunate that an artificial fly floating along on the surface of running water cannot be seen very well by trout," further suggesting that "this may explain in part the success of very imperfect imitations."

Martinez died in 1955 in Los Angeles, but his contributions to fly tying and fly fishing have continued to be remembered. George Grant wrote affectionately about Martinez in *The American Fly Fisher* in 1982 and concluded with the fact that he was "fondly remembered in Montana and Wyoming . . . as an exceptional fly tier, a skillful fly fisherman, and an individual who loved our great rivers and wanted to preserve them for others." Bud Lilly's Trout Shop continued to use Martinez's maps and guides during the 1950s, and Lilly thought they were the "biggest and most effective promotional effort in those early years." Lilly also remembered reprinting "Don Martinez's little fishing map for the Yellowstone area and distribut[ing] it by the thousands." And, in *American Fly Fishing: A History* (1987), Paul Schullery put the Woolly Worm in the company of "Leonard Halladay's Adams, Lee Wulff's series, and Don Gapen's Muddler Minnow" as the most "popular among modern fly fishermen." Schullery also identified Martinez as a key player in the "dynamic national evolution" and "cross-pollination process" of fly patterns in different regions of the United States. Some original Martinez vises and flies are housed in the Museum of American Fly Fishing in Manchester, Vermont, and the International Fly Fishing Center in Livingston, Montana.

An early photograph of Dan Bailey from *Fortune* magazine in 1946. The caption read, "His clublike shop magnetizes fly-fishers around Livingston." Dan Bailey's Marabou Muddler, tied by Jon Luke (inset)

"[A]s long as a dry fly floats well and comes fairly close to imitating a large group of insects it does the trick." —Dan Bailey

Chapter 13

Dan Bailey (1904–1982):

an Bailey was born March 26, 1904, on a farm near Russellville, Kentucky, and spent his public-school years in that area. By the age of 7, he was fishing for crappies and smallmouth bass with his uncle. Soon thereafter he traded his bobber and worms for a fly rod and began dressing his own flies. Bailey left his hometown in 1922 to attend college at The Citadel in Charleston, South Carolina, where he was graduated in 1926. Next he enrolled in the University of Kentucky, where he earned a master's degree in physics, and then took his first teaching job, at Jefferson City Junior College in Missouri. Here he became interested in fly fishing for trout and spent many days angling in Bennett Spring State Park in the Ozarks. Bailey's next job was at Lehigh University in Bethlehem, Pennsylvania, in the heart of trout country, where he was introduced to some of the most technical fishing on the East Coast.

In the fall of 1929, Bailey changed jobs again, this time taking a teaching position at Brooklyn Polytechnic Institute. While in the area, he started work on a Ph.D. in physics at New York University. While teaching and attending his own doctoral-level classes, Bailey found time to begin exploring the excellent trout fishing in the surrounding Adirondack and Catskill mountains. He also befriended a local commercial artist by the name of Lee Wulff, who, like Bailey, was an avid fisherman. Together, Bailey at 25 and Wulff at 24, they began to fish the Esopus, Beaver Kill, Neversink, Willowemoc, Ausable, and Saranac rivers, among others, where they experimented with flies, techniques, and equipment. During this time Bailey became acquainted with many of the great fly tiers and experts on trout fishing in "the cradle of American fly fishing," a meaningful experience for a neophyte angler.

It was on the Esopus, fishing with Wulff, that Bailey convinced his friend not to name his newly perfected flies the Ausable Gray, Coffin May, or Royal Bucktail. "Call them all Wulffs," Bailey said. The two also started a fly-tying class in Greenwich Village in the early 1930s. They had just a few students, but two were John McDonald and Ray Camp, a writer for *Fortune* magazine and the rod and gun editor of *The New York Times*, respectively. Bailey and McDonald fished together after that, and it was in their shared cabin on a tributary of New York's Rondout Creek that Bailey first outlined on the wall a large brown trout he had caught. Dated July 14, 1935, this began the tradition of "wall fish" that Bailey reinstituted later out West.

In 1936, Bailey married Helen Hesslein, a public-health nurse and long-time friend of McDonald's wife, Dorothy. For their honeymoon, they took an extended camping and fishing trip to Montana and Wyoming. They were accompanied by another of Bailey's trout-fishing friends, Preston Jennings, who had just published his highly acclaimed *A Book of Trout Flies* the year before, and his wife, Adele. Bailey fished the Madison and Gallatin, among others, and was simply enthralled with the region and its trout. He developed both the Black Wulff and Grizzly Wulff on this trip and also started to advertise his flies and a mail-order business in *Outdoor Life*. He and Helen returned to the area the following summer, and at that point Bailey decided to drop out of his doctoral program in atomic physics and try to make a living tying and selling flies.

Dan and Helen Bailey moved to Livingston, Montana, in 1938 and opened a small fly shop and shooting gallery in the old Albemarle Hotel. Since there was not much local business, they put most of their efforts into the wholesale and mail-order side of things and supplemented their income as commercial dealers in whitefish. Dan also worked as a substitute teacher and Helen went back and forth to New York with her nursing career. It was during these early years that Red Monical and Gilbert Meloche were hired as young teenage fly tiers and Bailey began to hire the first female tiers. Bailey also started his famous "Wall of Fame" with Meloche's large brown trout caught on August 5, 1938, by tracing the fish on paper and hanging the silhouette on the fly-shop wall.

In 1939 Bailey began selling his Mossback Nymph, a woven-bodied fly made originally from horsehair, similar to Pott flies, and also a light-colored mayfly imitation he named the Meloche, since it was responsible for that first "wall fish." He also modified the Wulff dry flies based upon western conditions by reversing the hackles so they would bend toward the eye and stay at a 90-degree or greater angle to the fly body to improve floatation. The addition of hair tails added further buoyancy, and medium-weight hooks held trout better in the fast water. These flies, as well as Bi-Visibles, Fan Wings, Spiders, and Variants were included in Bailey's first catalog in 1941. It was 4 by 6 inches and totaled 12 pages. Standard dries were $2.40 a dozen, Wulffs were $3 a dozen, and wet flies sold at two for 25 cents.

After World War II, Monical became a junior partner in the business and the entire Montana/Yellowstone region began to become a popular fly-fishing destination, mainly because of endorsements from national fishing writers such as Ray Bergman, Ed Zern, and Joe Brooks. As trout-fishing opportunities disappeared on the East Coast and a large middle class made use of better cars, roads, and air travel, anglers flocked to Montana in search of trout and to pay a visit to Dan Bailey's Fly Shop. Outdoor writer Charles Waterman, another Bailey friend for more than 30 years, observed that "Dan became accepted as an angling authority" who was featured in magazine and newspaper articles and provided personal attention to anglers throughout the world via typed letters and telephone conversations. Bailey also continued his innovative fly designs,

DAN BAILEY TIES FLIES WITH HIS COMMERCIAL FLY TIERS IN HIS LIVINGSTON
SHOP IN THE EARLY 1940S. NOTE THE FAMOUS "WALL FISH" IN THE BACK-
GROUND (PHOTOGRAPH COURTESY OF JOHN BAILEY)

introducing his Grayback, Red Variant, Bi-Fly, Pop-Eye Sawtooth Orange, Dan's
Hopper, Fuzzy Bear Yellow and Brown, and Mossy Creeper (also the Orange,
Olive, and Yellow Creepers) during the 1940s. It was at this time, too, that Bailey
began modifying Don Gapen's original Muddler Minnow (1937) into his own
versions, most notably the Bailey Muddler and Marabou Muddler.

The fly shop moved to a new location on Park Street in the early 1950s, and the Baileys bought a ranch south of Livingston where they raised their two children, Susan and John. Business really took off, and Dan Bailey and his fly shop gained national and international renown. Joe Brooks began writing for *Outdoor Life* in 1953, and he and his wife, Mary, made their summer home in Livingston. Waterman, who also summered in Livingston, realized that Brooks "became a constant asset to Bailey's" and remembered that "he was literally followed to Montana and to Bailey's by dozens of fly fishermen. . . . They bought summer homes and they headquartered at the Bailey store, which acquired a clublike atmosphere." Brooks and Bailey began to popularize big streamers and long casts for western trout fishing and added the double haul and weight-forward lines to the trout fisher's arsenal. Along with this type of fishing, Brooks highlighted Bailey's variants of the Muddler Minnow. "It was this fly," said Waterman, "that got Dan Bailey's Fly Shop as much recognition as anything else ever produced."

A GROUP OF BAILEY'S FLY TIERS IN HIS LIVINGSTON SHOP IN FRONT OF THE FAMOUS
"WALL FISH" WALL IN THE EARLY 1950S (PHOTOGRAPH COURTESY OF JOHN BAILEY)

Also during the 1950s, Red Monical's wife, Louise, began to direct the fly-tying department, which consisted of a staff of about 12 female production fly tiers. Bailey added more flies to his list of innovations during this time, including the Blond Goofus Bug, Green Drake, and Yellow-Stone Nymph.

Bailey's old New York friend John McDonald, who had recently written *The Origins of Angling* (1953), contributed an article titled "The Best Vacation Trout Fishing" for the inaugural issue of a magazine called *Sports Illustrated* in August 1954. He reported that "the best fly fishing in America is in progress right now in a magic 100-mile circle of the Yellowstone National Park area" and urged anglers to visit Dan Bailey's Fly Shop and to view the "Wall of Fame." Both were pictured in the article.

It was in this same year that Bailey made his theories on fly construction known to his old friend Preston Jennings, who was a well-known imitationist. In a letter to Jennings, Bailey told him that he saw "little value in working from the naturals" and went on to explain that "as long as a dry fly floats well and comes fairly close to imitating a large group of insects it does the trick." Bailey went on to say that the changes he made to flies "have been based on the trout's acceptance. That being the case, my patterns might look less like the natural than English or Eastern flies."

Bailey was also an avid big-game and bird hunter, but he told his friend Waterman that "the main thing about hunting is to get meat in the locker so we can go fishing." Whatever he did, he would generally be smoking his pipe and be accompanied by at least one black Labrador retriever. Joe Brooks further popularized Dan Bailey, his flies, and his shop in his highly regarded *The Complete Book of Fly Fishing* (1958), and soon thereafter Bailey began an involvement with Trout Unlimited (TU), an organization that had missions very similar to his own. He met with others in Bud Lilly's Fly Shop in West Yellowstone, and Lilly became president and Bailey vice president of Montana's first TU chapter. He went on to serve on the board of directors of TU for more than 10 years.

During the 1960s, Bailey and his shop gained additional fame through his friend and fishing companion Ted Trueblood, a nationally known fishing editor for *Field & Stream*. Bailey himself gained entry to the "Wall of Fame" in 1965 for a 6-pound brown trout he caught in the Yellowstone River on one of his other innovative flies, a White Muddler, also known as a Missoulian Spook. He and Monical developed their popular Spuddler pattern around this time, and the fly shop expanded to accommodate more tiers and customers. As the '60s concluded, Bailey realized that there was an increasing interest in more delicate fly fishing on the smaller western streams and that anglers were becoming more sophisticated. In fact, he remarked to Waterman that things were really changing, as "they come through the door talking Latin now."

By the 1970s, Dan Bailey was beginning to be recognized for his numerous achievements in the world of fly fishing, by his fellow Montana residents and by others throughout the world. Novelist William Hjortsberg called the fly shop an "American institution" in an article in *Esquire*, and George Grant argued in *Montana Trout Flies* (1972) that Bailey's influence "will be the most dominant, the most remembered, because his fame extends far beyond the borders of Montana into all of the fly fishing regions of the world." By the time Tom Wendelburg visited Bailey for a feature article on his flies and shop for *Fly Fisherman* in 1976, the operation employed around 45 tiers who produced more than 750,000 flies annually. Bailey noted at the time that he

DAN BAILEY SELECTING A FLY FOR HIS FAVORITE RIVER, THE YELLOWSTONE (PHOTOGRAPH BY THE LATE CHARLES WATERMAN, CIRCA EARLY 1970S, AND COURTESY OF DEBBIE WATERMAN)

believed his contributions to fly design were "mainly in the modification or further development of existing patterns" and suggested that "all we would like to be known for is that we feel we tie the best flies which are produced in large enough quantity to keep many fishermen supplied."

In addition to Bailey's long-lasting relationship with TU, he was also actively involved in numerous other conservation groups, including the Izaac Walton League, Nature Conservancy, Wilderness Society, Sierra Club, Montana Wildlife Federation, Federation of Fly Fishers, and Montana Trout Foundation. He was also outspoken in his support for the Wild and Scenic Rivers Act and testified for TU against the proposed damming of his beloved Yellowstone River, saying, "May these ideas be laid to rest for all time and the Yellowstone, longest free-flowing river and greatest trout stream in the contiguous states, flow on in its present splendor for generations to follow." Bailey had great faith that, through human intervention and nature's own work, America's waterways could become "blue ribbon" rivers full of trout, all the while arguing for preserving wilderness areas and the public's right to use the outdoors.

Dan Bailey's Fly Shop was at its peak in 1981, when Jim Merritt devoted a special article to it in *Rod & Reel*. The shop had more than 50,000 mail-order customers in all 50 states and 36 foreign countries, and produced more than 750,000 flies a year for both wholesale and retail. The "Wall of Fame" totaled more than 300 plaques of fly-caught trout more than 4 pounds, and Bailey's was clearly the largest manufacturer of flies in the United States. Bailey, Monical, and Bailey's son, John, were the three company stockholders, and John had become president of the corporation. Bailey himself was 77 and lived by the motto inscribed on all of the red fishing-license holders given free to his customers: "FISH MORE—LIVE BETTER—LIVE LONGER." He died from a heart attack the following year, in 1982, and his wife, Helen, died soon thereafter.

The Bailey family asked that remembrances of Dan be sent to the Joe Brooks Chapter of Trout Unlimited in Livingston, and the fly shop established a Dan and Helen Bailey Memorial Award in their honor. Montana Governor Ted Schwinden proclaimed August 14, 1982, Dan Bailey Fishing Day in the state of Montana as a further honor to his legacy. Major obituaries appeared in *Rod & Reel, Trout, Fly Fisherman,* and *The Flyfisher,* among others, and Lee Wulff, his friend of more than 50 years, remembered Bailey as "a hard and avid fly fisherman, yet a very friendly and gentle man. He had great warmth and charm and a deep integrity. And a fierceness for what was right." More recent tributes include a book about Bailey's life by Charles Waterman, *Mist on the River: Remembrances of Dan Bailey* (1986), and a good survey of Bailey's flies in *Trout Country Flies from Greater Yellowstone Area Masters* by Bruce Staples (2002). Certainly, though, the greatest compliment to the life and contributions of Dan Bailey is the fact that his son, John, continues to operate the fly shop and that fly fishers not even born when Dan passed away still hear and see his name on a regular basis through catalogs, waders, flies, and more still bearing his name.

Part Five:

Oregon

Maurice "Mooch" Abraham, circa 1910. (photograph courtesy of Robert Wethern and *The Creel*, 1971)

"He was recognized as one of the most accomplished fly casters and fly makers in the United States." —The Oregonian, September 30, 1936

Chapter 14

Maurice "Mooch" Abraham (1867–1936):

PORTLAND FLY TIER, FLY-FISHING MENTOR, AND ORIGINATOR OF THE DOUBLE-HAUL TECHNIQUE

Maurice Abraham was born March 1, 1867, in Canyonville, Oregon, the son of well-known Jewish merchant Solomon Abraham and his wife, Julia. He had a brother, Albert, and a sister, Mollie. Solomon Abraham was born in Poland, emigrated to the United States in the 1840s, and opened a general store in Roseburg, Oregon, in 1853. He married Julia Hinkle, a Roseburg resident, in 1861.

Solomon began the Abraham & Brother Company in 1854 and operated it until 1875. From 1877 through 1887, when he retired from business, he was a partner in Abraham, Wheeler and Company. In 1882, while Solomon was an agent for the Oregon & California Railroad, he purchased extensive tracts of land, including a town site in Cow Creek Canyon where he built a sawmill and other buildings. He named the town Julia after his wife, but in 1883 the name was changed to its present Glendale. Overall, Solomon and his wife owned stores in several towns near Roseburg; significant real estate, including most of Glendale; and large tracts of timber.

Young Maurice lived in several locations between Glendale and Roseburg, including his birthplace of Canyonville, during the first 20 years of his life. He fished, hunted, and trapped with some of the local Umpqua Indians, who had a difficult time pronouncing his name, Maurice. Consequently, he acquired the nickname "Mooch," which stayed with him the remainder of his life. He roamed the territory around the North and South Umpqua; hunted deer, elk, and ducks; and learned to fish for salmon, steelhead, and sea-run cutthroat trout. Mooch also established a reputation as an expert hunter, woodsman, and crack shot. He attended Bishop Scott Academy and took business classes for a short time in San Francisco and at the University of Oregon in Eugene.

Around the time Mooch turned 21, in 1888, he moved to Portland and took a job with the Fleischner-Mayer Company. Already balding, he was slight of build, quiet, and had a polite manner. His sister, Mollie, lived in Portland too, and was married to county commissioner J. G. Mack. Their mother died in 1897 and father Solomon followed in 1901, leaving an estate valued at about $150,000. Shortly thereafter, Mooch married former Roseburg resident Madge Carlon, who was 16 years younger than he was. They had one child, a daughter named Julia after Mooch's mother, in 1908. Around this time, Mooch joined with his brother-in-law J. G. Mack to start a furniture and carpet business in

Portland. Madge was an avid horsewoman and belonged to the Portland Hunt Club. Mooch still fished and hunted, but excelled at fly tying, fly casting, and trap shooting.

During the first decade of the 20th century, Mooch and Madge were one of the most stunning outdoor-oriented couples in the greater Portland area. Mooch was associated with the Multnomah Anglers' Club, taught pistol shooting for the Portland Police Department, was a member of the Portland Gun Club, trained and raised English springer spaniels, and fished regularly throughout most of the state. He was a good friend of William F. Backus, who joined with James C. Morris to open Backus & Morris Sporting Goods in 1909. Mooch also fished with Walter Honeyman, the owner of Honeyman Hardware, who hired William C. Block as a salesman in 1914. In addition, Dick Carlon, Mooch's other brother-in-law, was the sporting goods manager for Honeyman. It was during these early years that Mooch, who was several years older than many of his friends, became their outdoor mentor.

Mooch and his fishing partners traveled regularly to Seaside, where his family had a cabin, and to Meadow Lake and the Nestucca River, mostly to fish for cutthroat, his favorite fish. He and others relied heavily on railroads and electric streetcars to reach their fishing destinations. Some companies even ran "Fishermen Special" trains. Mooch rode the Salmonberry Line to the Nehalem area; the Astoria and Clifton Division of the Spokane, Portland and Seattle Railway to Necanicum; the Bull Run Line to the Sandy River; the Estacada electric car to Boring; and another electric car line from downtown Portland to the Clackamas River.

Block and Mooch were both friends with Frank, Bert, and Milo Godfrey, the brothers who ran Godfrey Brothers Hardware in Seaside, on Necanicum Bay, as early as 1915. Here, about three years later, Bert began tying his Godfrey Special or Godfrey Badger Hackle, which became known later as the Spruce Fly. Another of Mooch's Portland fly-casting friends, W. E. Carlson, served as a vice president in 1916–1917 for the National Association of Scientific Angling Clubs (NASAC). It was also in 1916 that Backus published an article on Rogue River steelhead fly fishing in *Field & Stream*.

While Mooch and his close circle of outdoor enthusiasts were gaining both regional and national attention, his business was suffering from a series of financial setbacks. Finally, in 1917, the J. G. Mack Company filed for bankruptcy. Mooch, Mack, and Mooch's sister, Mollie, owned all of the stock, valued at $100,000. In a short time, Mooch, his brother-in-law, and his sister lost all of their money as well as land in Portland and stock in the Oregon Land Company, which was part of their inheritance. Soon thereafter, Mooch and Madge began the Abraham Fly Tying Company and started to supply flies to Backus & Morris Sporting Goods, Honeyman Hardware, and Meier & Frank Sporting Goods. Before this, Mooch had just tied flies for himself and a few of his friends in the Multnomah Anglers' Club and the Meadow Lake Club. Now,

KALAMA SPECIAL, DESIGNED BY "MOOCH" ABRAHAM AND TIED BY JON LUKE

out of necessity, he resorted to his hobby to earn a living to support his family. Madge became an expert tier as well, and Honeyman Hardware advertised Mooch as their "great expert." Flies from their commercial enterprise were delivered in cigar boxes on a regular basis to retailers in the greater Portland area. Mooch was best known for his coastal cutthroat patterns, generally fairly bushy creations featuring badger and grizzly hackle on bodies of red, orange, yellow, and purple chenille.

William Backus and Mooch helped form Portland's first casting club in the teens; in 1919, Backus achieved national distinction for Portland by winning the National Dry Fly Accuracy Championship held by the NASAC in Chicago. Backus also served as a vice president of the NASAC in 1919, 1920, and 1926, and was successful in drawing its 15th annual international tournament to Portland in 1921. Backus was elected to the presidency of the Multnomah Anglers' Club in 1920, and two of Mooch's other fishing and casting friends were elected officers: William L. Kinzer, Jr., became a director, and Jack Herman was the unanimous choice for secretary-treasurer. Herman also served as a NASAC vice president in the early 1920s, and Kinzer won the Dry Fly Accuracy Championship in 1921. This was a major turning point in Oregon fishing and hunting, since Backus and his followers, including Mooch, represented the "Harmony Slate," which stood behind the newly reorganized Oregon Fish and Game Commission. Three years later, their club was renamed the Multnomah Anglers' and Hunters' Club.

Mooch continued his active involvement in a variety of Portland-area outdoor activities, but was most well known for his fly tying, fly casting, and his strong angling ethic, long before it became popular. The Oregon Fish and Game Commission recognized these accomplishments and qualities in Mooch and honored him with one of the first "Oregon Pioneer" fishing licenses, in 1926. Recipients had to have been a state resident for 60 or more years and shown a special interest in Oregon fish and wildlife conservation. Mooch was also an active member of the Royal Rosarian Band and the local Elks Club. He was a respected citizen of the state of Oregon as well as the city of Portland, and kept abreast of numerous community activities.

As Mooch began the 1930s in his early 60s, he was in a position to pass on to younger generations his expertise in a variety of outdoor pursuits. He taught fly tying to many young men and a few women in the Portland area and continued to operate, with his wife, Madge, their Abraham Fly Tying Company. When the Portland Casting Club reorganized in 1931, Mooch became its first honorary life member and was identified as the club's principal coach. It was at this time, because of a shoulder injury from a previous automobile accident, that Mooch began practicing what became the "double-haul" technique in fly casting. He introduced this method to his fellow anglers and casting club members, but especially to Marvin Hedge, whom he coached for the 1934 national casting competition in St. Louis. It was here that Hedge first introduced Mooch's double haul into competitive casting. The following year, taking advantage of Hedge's victory and the Portland civic pride that it generated, Mooch and his old friend Bill Block were instrumental in getting the Works Project Administration to use federal funds to construct one of the finest casting pools in the United States. In 1936 the Portland Casting Club, with its new facility, hosted the 28th international tournament of the NASAC. Hedge continued his casting accomplishments in the 1940s and remained committed to fly casting and fly fishing the remainder of his life.

Another famous Oregonian mentored by Mooch was Jay Winfield "Mike" Kennedy, one of the Northwest's premier steelhead fly fishermen and a pioneer in his own right. In 1932, when Kennedy was 22 years old, he was hired in the sporting goods department of Honeyman Hardware. He had caught his first steelhead on a fly when he was 15, had done some apprenticeship work with rod maker Harry Hobson, and called the North Umpqua one of his favorite rivers, but he had much to learn about fly fishing and flies. Mooch taught Kennedy fly casting and fly tying, and Kennedy remembered him as a "generous" and "patient" tutor. Even though the Kalama Special has been associated with Kennedy, he credited Mooch with tying that pattern first. Kennedy also remembered Mooch for his early stand on catch-and-release and noted that "Mooch was a nut on releasing fish unharmed." Similarly, Block remembered in a 1971 interview that his old friend Mooch had "an attitude toward fishing [that] was entirely on the quality side. . . . He'd transplant easy, today."

Unfortunately, Mooch died in September 1936, just after the Portland Casting Club hosted the national championships. He never had the opportunity to follow the exploits of his star casting pupil, Marvin Hedge, or the delightful career of Mike Kennedy. However, they and countless others in the Portland area who were touched in some way by the unique talents of Mooch Abraham carried his knowledge and philosophy of fly fishing, fly tying, and fly casting and passed it on to other men and women in distant places. Perhaps his obituary said it best: "He was recognized as one of the most accomplished fly casters and fly makers in the United States."

Mooch Abraham was remembered by most as "Mooch Abrams" and in fact was often referred to in that way during his life. But, thanks to Tom McAllister, an outdoor writer for the *Oregon Journal*, some of Mooch's accomplishments were recognized in a 1971 article published in *The Creel* (The Bulletin of the Flyfisher's Club of Oregon). Madge had died six years earlier and his daughter in 1938, but McAllister was able to interview a few relatives and some of his old friends to acquire an accurate overview of his life. Trey Combs also came to respect Mooch after talking with Mike Kennedy and others during his prolific research on the history of steelhead fly fishing in the early 1970s. Accordingly, whether he is remembered as Abrams or Abraham, he will always be known as Mooch.

MAURICE ABRAHAM DIES IN PORTLAND

Maurice ("Mooch") Abraham, Roseburg resident in days of his early manhood, died last Monday in Portland at the age of 69. He was a son of the late Sol Abraham, pioneer merchant and capitalist of Roseburg and Canyonville, and was born at the latter place. He was prominent in sports circles and for many years was in business in Portland. Surviving are his widow, Madge Y. Abraham; a daughter, Mrs. Julia Allen, and a sister, Mrs. J. G. Mack. The widow, nee Madge Carlon, is a native of Roseburg. Her father, the late Joseph Carlon, was a pioneer liveryman and stage line operator of this city. Mr. Abraham was an uncle of "Deb" Abraham, well-known automobile salesman of Roseburg.

Mr. Abraham was educated at Bishop Scott academy, attended business school in San Francisco and the University of Oregon. He was employed for a number of years by the Fleischner-Mayer firm in Portland, and later associated with J. G. Mack in the carpet and furniture business. Of late years he operated the Abraham Fly Tying company.

He played in the Royal Rosarian band, was a member of the Elks lodge and the Oregon national guard.

MAJOR JORDAN LAWRENCE MOTT, III WITH A MORNING'S CATCH OF STEELHEAD, SUPERIMPOSED ON A PHOTOGRAPH OF THE "GLORIOUS RUN" ON THE UMPQUA RIVER AS IT APPEARED IN THE JULY 1930 ISSUE OF *FOREST AND STREAM* MAGAZINE

"Gad man—did you ever see anything so wholly beautiful? Now then—take a quick look, as the little fly in the tough part of the upper jaw has done no harm and this chap goes back to his freedom."
—*Jordan Lawrence Mott III*

Chapter 15

Jordan Lawrence Mott III (1881–1931):

NOVELIST AND PIONEER ON THE NORTH UMPQUA RIVER

Jordan Lawrence Mott III was born on August 15, 1881, in New York City. He was the only child of Jordan Lawrence Mott, Jr., and the grandson of Jordan Lawrence Mott, Sr. His father and grandfather owned and operated the J. L. Mott Iron Works, a large manufacturer of plumbing fixtures and other iron products in Trenton, New Jersey. His grandfather was also president of the North American Iron Works, the Star Foundry Company, and the North River Bridge Company, and vice president of the New River Mineral Company, all in New York.

Mott Sr. and Mott Jr. were both avid outdoorsmen who traveled extensively throughout the world, hunting and fishing. By the time Mott III reached the age of 10, he had begun to accompany his father and grandfather on their adventures. They were particularly fond of the Canadian wilderness, but also hunted and fished throughout Europe, Asia, Africa, and all parts of North America. When Mott graduated from high school, he was highly skilled with guns, bird dogs, and fishing rods. He also had fly fished extensively for Atlantic salmon in England, Scotland, Newfoundland, Ireland, Labrador, and Nova Scotia, and was a superb fly caster.

He entered Harvard College in 1901 and shortly after married Caroline Pitkin from Braintree, Massachusetts. Two years later they had a son, Jordan Lawrence Mott IV. While still an undergraduate student, Mott began to write short stories and accounts of some of his adventures, simply for his own enjoyment. However, just before his graduation in 1905, his writings were shown to the editor of New York's *Century* magazine, who liked them and accepted them for publication. This was such a rare occurrence that a writer for *The Critic and Literary World* noted that young Mott had written "a batch of stories with the wilderness for a background" and they were accepted immediately by a major national magazine. He went on to say that "I cannot recall any other man or woman whose talent has been so quick to gain recognition. Mr. Mott's manuscripts have never been rejected."

Beginning with the June 1905 issue and continuing through September, *Century Magazine* published four of his stories. Another story was published in *Outing* magazine in October. Mott was working at the time at a New York City newspaper and was dubbed "the millionaire reporter" by those who knew his family background. Later in 1905 the Century Company published his first novel, *Jules of the Great Heart: "Free" Trapper and Outlaw in the Hudson Bay Region in the Early Days.* By year's end, his portrait appeared in *The Critic and Literary World*. He was pictured at his desk with hunting trophies, gun cases, fishing rods, angling and hunting photographs, and guns all around him. The story about Mott suggested that his photograph "shows the tastes of the young author, who is as enthusiastic a sportsman as he is a writer" and that "the trophies of the chase by which he is surrounded in the picture are of his own getting."

Mott's writing career developed substantially between 1906 and 1910. Several of his articles were published in *Harper's Weekly*, *Century*, and *Lippincott's Monthly Magazine* in 1906, and that same year "Salmon Fishing on the Forteau, Labrador" and "Love in the Wilderness" were published in *Outing's* June and November issues, respectively. The following year, short stories by Mott appeared in *Outing*, *Harper's*, and *Lippincott's*, and he published his second and third novels. His second book, *The White Darkness, and Other Stories of the Great Northwest*, was published by the Outing Publishing Company; his third book, *To the Credit of the Sea*, was published by Harper Brothers. Other short stories, as well as poems, appeared in *Harper's* and *Century* in 1909. His fourth novel, *Prairie, Sea, and Snow*, was published in 1910.

In 1911, Mott met and befriended Frances Bowne, a Broadway musical comedy star and wife of New York attorney Walter Bowne. Despite the best efforts of Mr. Bowne and Mott's grandfather to stop the relationship, Mott and Mrs. Bowne eloped to Japan and resided in Tokyo from 1912 until 1914. The affair made sensational news in New York City, with several articles appearing in *The New York Times*, and interrupted his literary career.

Mott was commissioned a major in the U.S. Army Signal Corps during World War I and wrote sporadically after that for *Collier's*, *Harper's*, and *Sunset*. He and Mrs. Bowne moved to Catalina Island, California, in the 1920s, and he finally divorced his first wife in 1927. Mott and Mrs. Bowne were married in October the following year.

Throughout the 1920s, with his home on the West Coast, Mott continued to fish and hunt. He was a contemporary of, and friends with, two other famous novelists of this period who wrote about the wilderness, outdoor life, and hunting and fishing—Jack London (*The Call of the Wild*) and Zane Grey (*Riders of the Purple Sage* and *Tales of Fresh Water Fishing*, among many others). Grey lived near Mott in California and trolled for swordfish off Catalina Island. It was Grey who first fished Oregon's Rogue River in 1916 and was joined there later by London. Mott loved to fish for salmon and steelhead, and fished the Klamath, the McKenzie, and the Eel, among others. He eventually spent several weeks on the Rogue in October and November 1928, just after Joe Wharton's article "Game Fish of Rogue River" appeared in the June issue of *Forest and Stream*. He returned home and sold a radio station he owned in Avalon, California, and began making plans to return to Oregon the following year.

Instead of going back to the Rogue, Mott, his wife, and Captain Frank

Winch of *Forest and Stream* magazine drove Mott's red Cadillac to Roseburg, Oregon, pulling a skiff on a trailer behind it. The next morning they drove up a newly completed dirt road along the North Umpqua River. Mott noted that the road took "a decided bit of 'doing' to negotiate . . . as it is entirely a dirt way, very narrow, for the most part, with an uncomfortable lot of sharp turns." Upon reaching the Steamboat Ranger Station on the upper river, they stayed in one of a few rustic cabins built by John Ewell, a motel operator from Roseburg, where Canton Creek joins Steamboat Creek. Mott was so impressed with the steelhead fly fishing that he stayed for six weeks, obtained a permit from the U.S. Forest Service, and set up a fly-fishing camp on the south side of the North Umpqua, overlooking the pools just below the entrance of Steamboat Creek. He constructed tents on wooden platforms and hired a local guide, Zeke Allen, to be his assistant. Mott returned home with a great appreciation for the North Umpqua and the anticipation of operating his new fishing camp the next summer and fall.

With the memories of his first trip to the North Umpqua in 1929 still fresh in his mind, Mott wrote three articles for publication in *Forest and Stream*. Signing each Major Lawrence Mott, he published "Steelheads on 2.5 Ounces of Bamboo" in the January 1930 issue, "Umpqua Salmon" in the April issue, and "Umpqua Steelheads" in the July issue. In the first article, Mott told of his battle with a 6-pound steelhead on a very light rod and described the Steamboat pool as "a delicious run of water to lay fly over, and as it is at the head of a very steep rapid, there are always steelhead resting in its swift, though smooth-flowing depths. When the light is right . . . the great fish can be easily seen." In his second article, on salmon, Mott says he actually spent four months on the North Umpqua in 1929, but fished for salmon in late April and May on the lower river. He had heard that "the salmon of the Pacific Coast will not take a fly," but, still not believing it, reported that "all these negatives notwithstanding I simply had to whip the magnificent pools of the Oregon stream with almost every salmon fly ever tied, while grand fish rolled and played all about me—ere I would definitely admit the puzzling truth!" He finally caught a 40-pound chinook on a spoon using a fly rod of 8.5 ounces. The battle lasted one hour and 49 minutes.

Mott's article "Umpqua Steelheads" immediately attracted national attention to the North Umpqua. He described the river as being "gorgeous" and having no "equal for charm of exquisite scenery." And, unlike several other notable western rivers, it was not crowded. He said it was on the North Umpqua that he "had the finest sport with the great steelhead, in all my years of fishing experiences," and that it "is the ONLY unspoiled river that is left on the whole of the American Pacific slope!" Mott described the river as "mile after mile of enchanting pools, riffles and deep runs," but warned that for an angler to do well, he must be able "to wade deep in the swift current" and "cast a long line." He recommended heavy felt soles for maneuvering over the slippery rocks and the use of a wading staff. For flies, Mott used Atlantic salmon flies such as a Jock Scott in a size 6, a Black Dose or Brown Fairy in a size 8, or a size 6 Durham Ranger. He was particularly enthralled with the beauty and magnificence of the steelhead and remarked that he knew of "no fish whose sheer loveliness of delicate hues and shadings surpass those of the famous Steelhead." Before he released a fish of 9.5 pounds, Mott asked, "Gad man—did you ever see anything so wholly beautiful? Now then—take a quick look, as the little fly in the tough part of the upper jaw has done no harm and this chap goes back to his freedom."

Mott's fishing camp on the North Umpqua had its first full summer of operation in 1930. He and Zeke Allen entertained guests from as far away as New York and Pennsylvania. Fishermen were transported up the dirt road along the river, and once they reached Steamboat Creek they were ferried across the river just below the confluence. With his strategically placed camp, Mott and his guests fished the best water on a daily basis.

After the very successful 1930 season, Mott again returned to his home in California. On a radio lecture tour that fall for the Sportsmen's Association of California, he became ill. It was soon discovered that Mott had leukemia, and there was no possible cure. Instead of resting for his remaining days, he returned to his beloved North Umpqua fishing camp and died there beside the river on June 3, 1931, at the age of 50. Mott left his camp to his partner, Zeke Allen, and gave away most of his fishing equipment to the friends he had met on the river. Most went to his closest friend, Fred Asam, the district forest ranger at Steamboat, and to Asam's four children. Zeke Allen eventually sold the old Mott campsite to Clarence Gordon, another Southern Californian, in 1934. Gordon built his famous North Umpqua Lodge there. In the early 1950s, Gordon moved across the river, opened the Steamboat Store, and sold the old lodge and site to the U.S. Forest Service to become the Steamboat Ranger Station. The Steamboat Store eventually became today's Steamboat Inn.

Mott's legacy on the North Umpqua has never been forgotten. A new bridge across the river built just upstream from Steamboat Creek in 1936 was named the Mott Bridge, and the part of the North Umpqua Trail on the south side of the river below the Mott Bridge was named the Mott Trail. In addition, several of the best pools and runs that make up the famous Camp Water from the Mott Bridge downstream past the confluence with Steamboat Creek bear names directly related to Mott. Upper Boat and Lower Boat below Steamboat Creek were so named because of Mott's boat that ferried his guests across the river at that spot. Upper Kitchen and Kitchen got their names because they were visible from Mott's kitchen tent. And Upper Mott, Middle Mott, and Lower Mott were named to honor the early pioneer on the North Umpqua. A landmark plaque was placed near the Mott Bridge in 1988, naming it an Oregon Historic Civil Engineering Landmark.

MAJOR JORDAN LAWRENCE MOTT, III WITH THREE STEELHEAD CAUGHT
ON HIS 2.5 OUNCE FLY ROD IN THE NORTH UMPQUA RIVER IN 1929.
(PHOTOGRAPH FROM *FOREST AND STREAM,* JANUARY 1930)

THE MOTT BRIDGE AND THE HISTORIC LANDMARK PLAQUE. (PHOTOGRAPH BY
JOHN SHEWEY)

It was not long after Mott's death that the North Umpqua gained more and
more national recognition. Zane Grey began fishing there and writing about
it in 1932, and wrote "North Umpqua Steelheads" for the September 1935
issue of *Sports Afield*. In 1938, Ray Bergman wrote a chapter on "Steelhead
of the Umpqua" in *Trout* and caught his first steelhead in Mott Pool. Claude
Krieder's *Steelhead* (1948) included a photograph of Mott, and when Krieder
fished the North Umpqua, he said, "I sought the famous Mott Pool and the
Kitchen Pool, waters in which many tremendous steelhead had been taken over
the years." Three years later, in *Steelhead to a Fly*, in his chapter "The North
Umpqua," Clark Van Fleet talked about Mott Pool and the rest of the Camp
Water, and concluded, "Before you is the best piece of flywater for really large
summer steelhead that remains in the United States."

In 1952 a 34-mile stretch of the river, including the famous Camp Water,
was designated for fly fishing only. Since then, still others, including Trey
Combs, Michael Baughman, John Shewey, and Michael Checchio, have written about Mott and his wonderful contributions to Northwest fly fishing. In
fact, in *Steelhead Fly Fishing* (1991), Combs referred to the North Umpqua's
Camp Water as "the most celebrated waters in all of steelhead fly fishing."
What could be a better tribute to Major Mott than a cold, clean, fast-moving
river filled with wild steelhead?

ZANE GREY WITH THREE STEELHEAD FROM THE NORTH UMPQUA RIVER, OREGON, IN 1935. ON THE BACK OF THE PHOTO, ZANE WROTE, "SOME-THING TO GLOAT ABOUT!" (PHOTOGRAPH COURTESY OF DR. LOREN GREY AND ZANE GREY, INC.) THE GOLDEN DEMON, TIED BY JOHN SHEWEY (INSET)

Chapter 16

Zane Grey (1872–1939):

LEGENDARY AUTHOR, ANGLER, NORTHWEST FLY FISHERMAN, AND DEVOUT CONSERVATIONIST

Pearl Zane Gray was born January 31, 1872, to Lewis M. Gray, a minister turned dentist, and Alice Josephine (Zane) Gray in Zanesville, Ohio. He was named for the color "pearl gray," popularized at the time by Queen Victoria, and was descended from Colonel Ebenezer Zane of Revolutionary War fame. Pearl was the fourth of five children and was raised in a strict home atmosphere: his parents forbade drinking, smoking, and chewing tobacco. His younger brother, Romer Carl (R.C., or "Reddy"), became his best friend, and they traveled and worked together until R.C.'s untimely death in 1934.

Young Pearl loved the outdoors, especially hunting and fishing, but his father viewed these activities as a waste of time. However, Pearl was greatly influenced by "Old Muddy Miser," a local angler on the Muskingum River, who told him, "You must make fishing a study, a labor of love, no matter what your vocation will be. You must make time for your fishing. Whatever you do, you will do it all the better for the time and thought you give to fishing."

Gray moved with his family to Columbus, Ohio, after he was graduated from high school in 1890. By then, Pearl had established himself as a star baseball pitcher and knew that his "heart was in writing stories."

Because of his baseball prowess, Pearl was awarded an athletic scholarship to the University of Pennsylvania in Philadelphia; he was graduated in 1896 with a degree in dentistry. He spent his weekends camping, canoeing, and fly fishing for smallmouth bass in the nearby Delaware River. The following year, Gray moved to New York City and set up a dental practice under the name "P. Zane Grey." He changed the spelling of his surname because he felt Grey was more dignified than Gray. While residing in New York, he and his brother R.C. played semiprofessional baseball for the East Orange, New Jersey, Athletic Club, and he completed his first novel, *Betty Zane*. His first published article about a fishing adventure, "A Day on the Delaware," appeared in *Recreation* in 1902, and that same year Grey became the youngest member of the Camp-Fire Club of America, composed of some of the country's leading conservationists and outdoorsmen, including Gifford Pinchot, William Hornaday, and Theodore Roosevelt.

In 1903 Grey turned over his dental practice to R.C. and moved to Lackawaxen, Pennsylvania, at the confluence of the Lackawaxen and Delaware rivers, where he devoted his time to writing. In 1905 he married Lina Elise Roth, a young woman he had met while canoeing on the Delaware five years earlier. Zane nicknamed her "Dolly," and after she earned a master's degree at Columbia University she became his business manager and editor. Their honeymoon took them to the Grand Canyon, San Diego, San Francisco, and Catalina Island, destinations to which Grey would return later during his travels.

Grey labored intensely at writing several novels and magazine articles about hunting, fishing, and camping, and published another novel, *The Spirit of the Border*, in 1906. In the book's dedication to his brother R.C., Zane expressed a sentiment that would motivate and guide him and his writing for the rest of his life: ". . . with fond recollections of days spent in the solitude of the forests where only can be satisfied that wild fever of freedom . . . and know a happiness that dwells in the wilderness alone." He followed with two more novels, *The Last of the Plainsmen* and *The Last Trail*. By 1910, Grey had a son, named Romer after his brother, and had published two more novels, both for juvenile readers, titled *The Short Stop* and *The Young Forester*. He was now acquiring a reputation as a noted author, and began earning enough royalties to permit travel to distant places to hunt and fish.

Long Key, Florida, was the site of Zane's first full-fledged fishing excursion. Here, in 1910, he popularized light-tackle fishing for sailfish, permit, tarpon, and bonefish, and eventually became president of the Long Key Fishing Club. That same year, he published the first of his Western novels, *The Heritage of the Desert*, and began writing fishing articles for *Field & Stream*, the official publication of the Camp-Fire Club. Grey also published numerous angling articles in *Outing*.

Grey casting to steelhead in Washington's Deer Creek in 1918 (photograph courtesy of Dr. Loren Grey and Zane Grey, Inc.)

Grey became even more famous—and wealthy—in 1912 after his most famous Western novel, *Riders of the Purple Sage*, sold more than a million copies. His daughter, Elizabeth was born that same year, and he continued to write more and more books and articles. As his notoriety and bank account grew, Grey used his time to travel to distant and remote places seeking big game, big fish, and solitude. He sought the most remote waters and wilderness areas for his sport. "All my life," he would explain, "I have envied country boys, backwoodsmen, native fishermen, and the hardy men who eke out a living from the deep. For they see nature's wonders. They are always there, daybreak and sunset, and they catch the most and biggest fish."

His journeys took him to Mexico, Arizona, Utah, Colorado, and Catalina Island. Eventually he built a home near Arizona's Tonto Basin, and another overlooking Avalon Bay at Catalina Island so he could be closer to his quarry. At Catalina he set records catching tuna, marlin, and swordfish, and also became honorary vice president of the famous Tuna Club on the island.

Grey's third child, a son named Loren, was born in 1915, and the following year Grey visited Oregon's Rogue River for his first attempt at catching a steelhead, a fish he had just learned about from a fishing acquaintance at Long Key. He also started traveling to British Columbia's Vancouver Island and the Campbell River in search of giant chinook, or "tyee," salmon, and, while en route to B.C. in August 1918, he fished Washington's Deer Creek, a tributary of the North Fork of the Stillaguamish River near Oso. Here he caught his first steelhead—on a fly rod, gut leader, sinker, small hook, and "a small ball of fresh salmon eggs rolled on the bottom with the current."

This method of steelheading involved "stripping off the reel a goodly length of line, which fell in coils into the basket" strapped on his waist. Grey noted that "not only was this the first steelhead we had ever captured, but the first we had ever seen. It was a strikingly beautiful fish, graceful, symmetrical, powerfully built, with great broad tail and blunt, pugnacious nose. The faint pinkish color, almost a glow, shone from a background of silver and green."

Traveling with him on this trip, and most others after that, were his brother R.C. and Dr. J. Auburn Wiborn (known as "Lone Angler"), a former Penn classmate and track star whom Zane met again in Avalon.

By 1919 Grey was earning more than $100,000 a year and was beginning his love affair with the Pacific Northwest. After moving permanently to Altadena, California, he fished regularly in Oregon, Washington, and British Columbia, and made deep-sea excursions to Catalina Island, Nova Scotia, New Zealand, Tahiti, and Australia, mostly on his private 146-foot yacht, *Fisherman*. The first of his eight books documenting his worldwide fishing exploits, *Tales of Fishes*, was published in 1919, and in it Grey remarked, "In my experience as a fisherman the greatest pleasure has been the certainty of something new to learn, to feel, to anticipate, to thrill over. . . . As a man, and a writer who is forever learning, fishing is still a passion, stronger with all the years."

ZANE GREY WITH A 57-POUND CHINOOK SALMON LANDED AT THE
MOUTH OF CALIFORNIA'S KLAMATH RIVER IN 1919 (PHOTOGRAPH
COURTESY OF DR. LOREN GREY AND ZANE GREY, INC.)

Also in *Tales of Fishes*, Zane explained that he and his companions released bonefish, tarpon, marlin, and swordfish, along with several other species caught, "inaugurating a sportsman-like example never before done." In another statement indicating his strong belief in, and commitment to, conservation, he warns, "Let every angler who loves to fish think what it would mean to him to find the fish were gone."

In the summer of 1919, Grey fished in Pelican Bay on Oregon's Upper Klamath Lake, and also fished nearby Crater Lake; he ventured to the Campbell River, the mouth of the Klamath at Requa, California, and made his second trip to the Rogue, although "its incomparable steelhead had captivated us and utterly defeated us."

Details of these trips were soon published in national magazines, including *Country Gentleman* and *Izaak Walton League Monthly*, later retitled *Outdoor America*. Grey made other trips to the same region in the early 1920s and caught his first steelhead on a fly on the Rogue in September 1922. He got his fishing supplies and much-needed local expertise from Joe Wharton and his store in Grants Pass, and was guided by Wharton and by other notable fly fishermen, including Fred Burnham from California, Joe DeBernardi, and "Mr. Carlon" from Portland. Grey used a 9.5-foot Kosmic fly rod and relied on size 4 and 6 Royal Coachmen, Professors, and Brown Hackles. His regular companions, R.C. and "Lone Angler," also began to publish articles in national magazines about their exploits with Zane, and in 1923 Grey himself published "Steelhead" and "Fishing the Rogue" in *Country Gentleman*. He became so enamored with fly fishing for steelhead that he regularly practiced fly casting at home in Altadena. And once R.C. caught his first steelhead on a fly, Zane noted that "he devoted himself solely to fly-fishing. He became charmed, intoxicated with the sport."

In 1925, with guide Claude Bardon and a contingent of friends, family, and his regular cook, George Takahashi, Grey set out to float the Rogue from Graves Creek to Illahe in a flotilla of what became known as "McKenzie-style

ZANE GREY ON THE OARS OF A "MCKENZIE-STYLE" DRIFT BOAT WHILE FLOATING OREGON'S ROGUE RIVER IN 1925. (PHOTOGRAPH COURTESY OF DR. LOREN GREY AND ZANE GREY, INC.)

WITH THE HELP OF "MR. CALHOUN, THE PORTLAND EXPERT" (SEATED), ZANE GREY RAISED HIS FIRST STEELHEAD TO A FLY ON OREGON'S ROGUE RIVER IN 1922 (PHOTO-GRAPH COURTESY OF DR. LOREN GREY AND ZANE GREY, INC.)

drift boats." The following year he published a seven-part series in *Field & Stream* called "Rocky Riffle on the Rogue," and also penned "Shooting the Rogue" in *Country Gentleman*. Grey discovered fly fishing for New Zealand trout that same year, especially in the Tongariro River, where he used a fly called the Gold Demon. He told of his New Zealand exploits in *Tales of the Angler's Eldorado: New Zealand* (1926).

Zane had become so enamored with the Rogue and one special spot, Winkle Bar, that he bought the property and helped build a cabin there to serve as a base camp for his fishing adventures. In 1927 he took his entire family to the Winkle Bar camp for a nine-day fishing trip, and the following year R.C. helped to further his famous brother's angling reputation by authoring "A Klamath River Salmon" and "Salmon of the Pacific" for *Field & Stream*. Both featured photographs of Zane holding large chinook salmon. In 1928 Grey published *Tales of Fresh-Water Fishing*, a compilation of most of his previ-

ously published articles on salmon, trout, and steelhead fishing in the Northwest. It was this book, along with his and his brother's articles in national fishing magazines, that first introduced a large, nationwide audience to the spectacular fresh- and saltwater game fish inhabiting the Pacific Northwest.

During the late 1920s Grey wrote his only novel with a North-west fishing theme. "Rustlers of Silver River" appeared first in a serialized version in *Country Gentle-man* in 1929 before being published in book form as *Rogue River Feud* (1948). Therein he wrote about the destructive logging and commer-cial fishing practices in the Rogue region. He lamented the fact that a few men could net vast numbers of steelhead and salmon when a much greater economic value for them could come from fly anglers: "Then take the fly-fishermen. They're too many to count. They come and go. They spend money. They advertise the Rogue. And it is the most beautiful and wonderful trout stream in the West, perhaps in the world. Are a few men to be allowed to kill the food value and the sport value of this river?"

Grey's friend and guide Fred Burnham had fished another Oregon river, the North Umpqua, in 1927, and Zane's old friend from Avalon, Major Jordan Mott, fished it in 1929. After both spoke of its ruggedness and its magnificent

"I have given up the Rogue, and the fishing lodges I own at Winkle Bar . . . to camp and fish and dream and rest beside the green-rushing, singing Umpqua." —Zane Grey

wild steelhead in glowing terms and Mott had written so eloquently about it in three articles published in *Forest & Stream* in 1930, Grey stopped to fish it in the fall of 1932 on a return trip from British Columbia. He was instantly impressed and announced that "I have given up the Rogue, and the fishing lodges I own at Winkle Bar . . . to camp and fish and dream and rest beside the green-rushing, singing Umpqua."

Grey and his regular fishing partners fished the North Umpqua every year thereafter, and his son Loren made his first trip there in 1935, when they spent three months camped along the river. By then, Grey had concluded that "outside of Canada there is no stream in the United States that can hold a candle to the Umpqua for wet or dry fly-fishing." Loren landed 100 steelhead during that trip. Grey, then 64, used the Parmachene Belle and Hair Coachman in June and July and switched to the Turkey-and-Red, Turkey-and-Gold, and Gold Demon, all size 4, in September. Grey had his flies custom-tied, and ordered them directly from Clarence Shoff in Kent, Washington, but he also purchased some from Joe Wharton, noting, "I had Wharton make a pattern after the New Zealand Gold Demon, adding hair and jungle cock." Grey's detailed account of this trip was published in "North Umpqua Steelhead" in the September 1935 issue of *Sports Afield* and instantly brought national attention to the river and its wild steelhead.

While Grey continued his pursuit of big-game fish—he visited New Zealand, Tahiti, and Australia in the early 1930s—fly fishing for North Umpqua steelhead was constantly on his mind. He became the unofficial spokesman

> *"[O]utside of Canada there is no stream in the United States that can hold a candle to the Umpqua for wet or dry fly-fishing." —Zane Grey*

for the river and its fish, warning Oregonians about the dangers of logging, dam building, and fish hatcheries: "Unless strong measures are adopted by the people of Oregon, this grand river will go the way of the Rogue. And it will be a pity because the value of the Umpqua, with its wonderful steelhead, is inestimable." Grey and his angling friends, including sons Romer and Loren, spent two months on the North Umpqua in 1936, camped at Williams Creek, downstream from Steamboat Creek. They fished the hallowed "Camp Water" on a daily basis and named some of the more popular pools. The ZG pool has become Upper Mott, but some of the lower pools are still named Takahashi (after Grey's cook), Ledges, and Divide.

Grey returned to the North Umpqua in 1937 and fished with his son Romer and a guide in mid-July. Here, on the banks of his favorite river, Zane suffered a near-fatal stroke at the age of 65. He recuperated at his Altadena home and, after losing the use of his right hand, rehabilitated himself to the point that he could write and fish again. After trips to Tahiti and Australia, Grey returned to the North Umpqua for a brief visit in 1938 and for the last time in 1939. He suffered a massive rupture of his heart on October 23, 1939, and died at his home. His body was transported back to Pennsylvania to be buried in a small cemetery overlooking the Delaware River at Lackawaxen.

Zane Grey was one of the most prolific writers of all time, with his novels selling more than 130 million copies and being translated into more than 23 languages. He also wrote eight fishing books and more than 250 shorter works, including novelettes, short stories, and magazine articles on hunting, fishing, and conservation. Most of his writing was done in fishing camps, on ocean liners on his way to go fishing, or on his own boat. His writing played a major role in defining America's perception of the West, and between his frontier fiction and his angling nonfiction he presented epic heroes in epic situations displaying strength, loyalty, and courage. In fact, some of these characters were his friends, family, and himself. Grey was always searching for wild and primitive things to test his mettle and found some of them in the Pacific Northwest.

In his *Profiles in Saltwater Angling* (1973), George Reiger called Grey the "most celebrated blue water fisherman of his generation" and documented his 10 all-tackle world records. Ed Zern, in *Zane Grey's Adventures in Fishing* (1952), argued that no other man "has devoted so much of his fortune, nor so large a share of his time and energy, to the catching of fish for the sport of it," and concluded that "no other man will ever challenge his right to be known as the greatest fisherman America has ever produced." In turn, ships were named after him; Hardy named rods, reels, and hooks after him; Pflueger carried a "Zane Grey Teaser" for marlin fishing, along with Zane Grey hooks; Coxe sold a Zane Grey reel; Everol also produced a Zane Grey reel; the Ashaway Line Company used his name in a variety of promotions; the Pacific sailfish, *Istiophorus greyi*, was named for him (it is now known as *I. platypterus*); the Horrocks-Ibbotson Company invited him to write the introduction to their catalog "Fly Fishing." A few museums and "special collections" at libraries hold his artifacts and papers. Real estate agents along the Rogue River still call their region "Zane Grey Country," and visitors can still see Grey's cabin and one of his drift boats at Winkle Bar.

MARVIN K. HEDGE WARMS UP FOR A NATIONAL CASTING EVENT, CIRCA THE 1940s.
(PHOTOGRAPH COURTESY OF ROBERT WETHERN AND *THE CREEL*, JULY 1964)

Chapter 17

Marvin K. Hedge (1896–1969):

CHAMPION CASTER AND DESIGNER OF FLY LINES AND RODS

arvin K. Hedge was born in 1896 and grew up in Portland, Oregon. He was an avid fisherman during his youth, using bait to entice rainbow trout in Johnson Creek and the Clackamas River. One day, while on a picnic at nearby Lake Oswego, he happened upon a group of fly casters practicing their craft. After some careful observation, Hedge announced to one of the men, "I know I could cast like that."

Indeed he could! Hedge gave up bait fishing and became an instant convert to catching fish with a fly. He went on to break several distance fly-casting records during the 1930s and '40s in both national and international competition. He is also credited with perfecting and introducing the double haul into tournament casting. In addition, he designed his own fly lines, provided significant research for the rod making of fellow Oregonian John Wilson, helped Portland get its own world-class casting pool, and was personally responsible for bringing a great deal of civic pride to the Northwest area. Hedge was also one of the first Westerners to break into the world of tournament casting and was a recognizable sporting hero.

> *"[T]here wasn't a soul in St. Louis that had ever seen [a double haul]. They took motion pictures of it and, after that, they asked me questions about it until two in the morning." —Marvin Hedge*

During the early years of the 20th century in Portland, Hedge was befriended by and learned from one of the area's most respected sportsmen—Walter F. Backus (1882–1927). In fact, Backus was one of the men Hedge had seen casting on Lake Oswego and was himself a top cutthroat and steelhead fisherman as well as an accomplished fly caster. Backus, who owned Backus and Morris Sporting Goods in Portland, won the National Dry Fly Accuracy Casting Championship in 1919 at Washington Park in Chicago and tied for first in the same event in 1921 at the Multnomah Angler's Club in Portland. He also served as first vice president for the National Association of Scientific Angling Clubs for a few years in the early 1920s. In addition, he helped introduce Rogue River steelheading to the rest of the world. His 1916 article "Steelhead Trout on the Rogue River," published in *Field & Stream*, along with the Rogue River tales told by Zane Grey in *Tales of Fresh-Water Fishing* (1928), began to attract fly anglers from distant locales in search of the storied "sea-run rainbow trout."

The equipment, techniques, and especially the long casts used in steelheading captivated and motivated Hedge and his Portland-area friends. Hedge was also tutored by another local sportsman, Maurice "Mooch" Abraham (1867–1936). Abraham was a commercial fly tier who supplied flies for several local sporting goods stores, including Backus and Morris as well as Honeyman Hardware Company. (Hedge was also in the sporting goods and hardware business.) It was Honeyman Hardware that hired Bill Block (in 1914) and Mike Kennedy (in 1932), both important fly-fishing pioneers in their own right. Abraham began practicing a double-haul technique on the Willamette River after hurting his shoulder in an automobile accident. He then introduced the technique to his fellow steelheaders and "coached" Hedge in the technique in the early 1930s.

Casting contests began as early as 1864 in New York, but became popular in the Midwest by the 1880s through the invention and perfection of bamboo rods and silk lines. Tournament casters were reaching 80 feet or more in the "Single-handed Light Trout Fly" category by the end of the 19th century and generally hailed from New York or Chicago. San Francisco, with the formation of the San Francisco Fly Casting Club in 1894, also had some early champions. During the first two decades of the 20th century, distances increased to 125 feet for the longest cast in the "Trout Fly Distance—Light Tackle" category. This feat was accomplished in both 1923 and 1925 by George C. Chatt from Chicago. And before the "Trout Fly Distance—Heavy Tackle" category was eliminated in 1919, San Francisco Fly Casting Club president Walter Mansfield cast 134 feet in 1902 and 1915.

Angling historian Charles F. Waterman observed that "distance fly events were especially strong along the Pacific coast, partly because of the interest in steelheading, which placed a premium on long throws." He also correctly noted that fishermen sometimes forget that it was "competition that developed tackle and fishing methods and has aided research." Edwin C. Powell began to make rods in Red Bluff and then later in Marysville, California, about 1910; Robert Winther and Lew Stoner started their Winston rod-making operation in San Francisco in 1929; and Portland's John Wilson began making rods at about the same time. It is no coincidence that Western casters "came on strongly," as Waterman suggested, during the 1920s and '30s. In this respect, Waterman concluded, "tackle development very often begins on the casting platform—a place where results are measurable. . . . Nearly all of the innovations in casting method are competition born."

During the early 1930s, Marvin Hedge experimented with splicing his own lines with as many as seven different sections, matched them with his favorite Wilson rods, practiced the double haul, and developed skills and strategies

New York Times, August 24, 1934, page 20.

SETS FLY CASTING MARK.

Hedge Averages 141 Feet to Break 11-Year-Old Record.

ST. LOUIS, Aug. 23 (/P).—Marvin Hedge of Portland, Ore., today set a new world record with an average cast of 141 feet in the distance fly event of the national casting tournament at Forest Park.

The best of Hedge's three casts was 147 feet. His average exceeded the eleven-year-old record by eighteen feet.

Ralph Lyttaker of Seattle, with an average of 128 feet, and Eddie Robinson of Chicago, with 125 feet, both exceeded the old record of 123 feet established by George C. Chatt of Chicago in Denver in 1923.

for casting with the wind, against the wind, and in the calm. He also polished his lines with graphite dust. As he practiced at the local Sellwood pool before his many friends, he broke the world record by at least 7 feet in four successive casts. Casting with a Wilson rod, Hedge told John Wilson, "I'm afraid it'll fold up." "Well, go ahead anyhow," Wilson said, "and let her break if she will." The rod did break, but Wilson built Hedge another, stouter rod, "with a little more kick in the butt of it," according to Wilson. Hedge was indeed an imposing caster, standing 6 feet even and weighing about 217 pounds.

Hedge left Portland for his first national casting competition in August 1934, with great expectations. He participated in the 26th International Casting Tournament, held at Forest Park in St. Louis under the auspices of the National Association of Scientific Angling Clubs. Here, he set a new world's record with his longest cast of 147 feet and his three-cast average of more than 141 feet. This was in the "Light Distance Fly" category (rod limit 5.5 ounces and 11 feet 6 inches). Hedge beat the old mark of 125 feet, set in 1925, by 22 feet. *The New York Times* reported the record-breaking event, and a St. Louis newspaper report exclaimed, "The Westerner went into action with powerful rhythmic movements. . . . The gallery went wild!" It was at this event that Hedge introduced the double haul into competitive casting. With his special timing, and using techniques for converting line speed into distance, Hedge showed his competitors what he had learned on the Northwest rivers. Hedge proclaimed that "there wasn't a soul in St. Louis that had ever seen it. They took motion pictures of it and, after that, they asked me questions about it until two in the morning." In fact, the "Anglers Fly Distance" category at national tournaments has been often referred to as "the steelhead event."

In 1935, taking advantage of the excitement surrounding Hedge's victory, the Portland civic pride it generated, and the influence of community leader

Bill Block, the Works Project Administration (WPA) built one of the finest casting pools in the country. Hedge designed the facility, and it served as the home grounds for the Portland Casting Club. With Northwest casting talent beginning to rival that of the San Francisco Fly Casting Club and the Golden Gate Angling and Casting Club (founded in 1933), Portland set its sights on hosting a national casting event and training future national champions. It did not take long. The following year, the Portland Casting Club hosted the 28th International Casting Championships. Hedge, casting in the professional division, because he was a designer of fishing tackle, won the "Light Distance Fly" category with a cast of 142 feet.

Because of his growing reputation, Hedge was invited to compete in France and England in 1937. He defeated the reigning European champion, Albert Godart, by 9 feet in Paris, and in London he surpassed the previous record of 123 feet with a cast of 151 feet. Hedge was also awarded the Professional All-Round Championship with three firsts, two seconds, one third, and one fourth. His hometown paper, *The Oregonian*, kept fellow Northwesterners up-to-date on his exploits, and in an article titled "The Longest Cast on Record" spoke of Portland's "genuine pride" because "it may be accounted no small honor to claim as a neighbor the ablest fly caster in the world, whose method had revolutionized an art." Shortly thereafter, casting instructors in both America and Europe began to teach "the Marvin Hedge system of casting."

Hedge made international news once again when he won the International Professional All-Round Championships in 1938 in Paris. He set European records in the "Under 6-ounce Rod Trout Fly Distance" category with a cast of 146 feet 4 inches. Later, in London, Hedge set a new British and European record in the "Unlimited Rod Trout Fly Distance" category with a cast of 150 feet using a line limited to .052 inch in diameter. The S.A. Jones Line Company, which sponsored Hedge as a professional, thought the United States should be represented in this event by an amateur caster as well. After considerable deliberation, Hedge selected 18-year-old Milton James "Jimmy" Green of San Francisco to join him. They traveled together via steamer to Belgium and then through France and England, practicing along the way. Once at Paris for the competition, Green won the International Amateur All-Round Championships, thus making a clean sweep for America and its West Coast casters. Green went on to be a champion caster and rod designer for Fenwick in California and Washington, and was a pioneer in his own right.

In 1940, the S.A. Jones Line Company name was dropped in favor of Norwich Line Company. They began marketing their "top of the line" Hedge fly-line series and, as part of the advertising plan, adopted a theme of "the line of champions." Their top seller was the Norwich Hedge Taper series.

A NORWICH LINE ADVERTISEMENT THAT INCLUDES THE HEDGE TAPER FLY LINE, "THE CHOICE OF ALL AMERICAN AND EUROPEAN FLY CASTING CHAMPIONS," IN *FIELD & STREAM* MAGAZINE, 1940

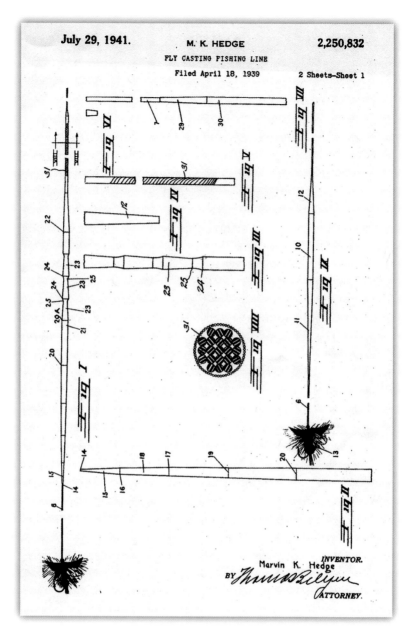

July 29, 1941.   M. K. HEDGE   2,250,832

FLY CASTING FISHING LINE

Filed April 18, 1939   2 Sheets—Sheet 1

U.S. patent for "Fly Casting Fishing Line," filed by M. K.
Hedge on April 18, 1939, and awarded July 29, 1941

Hedge continued to cast competitively through World War II and won
national "Trout Fly Distance" events in 1944, 1945, and 1947. Green won
in 1946. A. J. McClane from *Field & Stream*, who saw Hedge cast in Paris
in 1947, referred to "the underwear-ripping motions . . . that [he] used so

effectively." Hedge also had success developing, manufacturing, and selling his own specialized fly lines, prized mostly by Northwest steelheaders. His Marvin Hedge Silk Fly Line was composed of multiple-diameter lines and is remembered fondly by some of the early steelheaders. Both Trey Combs and Bob Wethern remember their Hedge 7 Taper. It was developed and filed in 1939 and finally patented in 1941. Walt Johnson loved to fish Hedge 10 lines on his small "midge" rod. Johnson remembered that the Hedge lines "had a patented camouflage finish, five front tapers, two back tapers, and a reinforced holding line with a colored section denoting the proper pickup or casting position." Johnson also noted that Hedge cataloged his lines by number rather than the customary lettering designation of that era since he believed "the action of the rod determined the size and weight of the line used, not its length or weight." Another early steelheader, Robert Arnold, also credits Hedge with the early innovations in compound tapers that fishermen tried to emulate in constructing their own lines. Hedge worked for Rain-Beau Lines after World War II and also made his design available to Hardy Brothers of England.

Hedge remained active in Northwest fly-fishing circles into the '60s as a member of the venerable Fly Fisher's Club of Oregon and authored a small 40-page book, *Accurate Fishing and Long Distance Fly Casting Made Easy*. He was also present when the Federation of Fly Fishers was founded in 1965 in Eugene, and despite his competitive casting involvement, he never lost interest in fishing. In one of his many interviews, Hedge acknowledged his devotion to "the tournament work," but stated, "I never have permitted it to interfere with my fishing." His favorite waters included the Rogue, Umpqua, and Deschutes rivers, where he and his friends would return most of the trout they caught, long before catch-and-release had become understood. Marvin Hedge died in Portland in 1969.

MARVIN HEDGE DEMONSTRATES THE DOUBLE-HAUL TECHNIQUE USING ONLY A BAMBOO STICK AND STRING IN THE LATE 1930's (PHOTOGRAPH COURTESY OF ROBERT WETHERN AND *THE CREEL*)

E. H. "Polly" Rosborough poses with a nice catch of
Williamson River rainbows, circa 1965, when he was 63.
(photograph by Peter MacFarland from Robert Wethern and *The Creel*). E. H. "Polly" Rosborough's Red
Phantom Streamer, tied by Jon Luke (inset)

*"[T]he more vibrating action
a nymph produces, the better
my chances of success are."
—Polly Rosborough*

Chapter 18

Ernest H. "Polly" Rosborough (1902–1997):

ORIGINATOR OF WESTERN NYMPH PATTERNS AND NYMPHING TECHNIQUES, AUTHOR, AND COMMERCIAL FLY TIER

Ernest H. Rosborough was born September 13, 1902, in Mammoth Spring, Arkansas, deep in the Ozarks, and at age 3½ caught his first fish with his father and uncle. The following year his family moved to Oklahoma and then on to western Kansas, where from 1908 through 1915 he fished for sunfish, perch, and catfish. The family moved back to Oklahoma in 1916, and then to central Alberta, Canada, where Rosborough finished high school.

In 1921, at the age of 19, Rosborough acquired a job in a box factory in the small Northern California town of Bray, and was soon nicknamed "Polly" by his coworkers because he talked so much like "Polly the Parrot." He began fishing for trout in nearby Butte Creek, known for its brown trout, and, after catching many on worms, he started experimenting with flies. His favorite patterns included the Blue Upright, March Brown, and Black Gnat, all snelled flies he purchased three to a card. Polly also began reading all of the outdoor magazines he could find. By 1922, he remembered, he was "innoculated [sic] with trout fever—and nothing has ever cured it." With very little money for fishing equipment, he began repairing and rewinding rods for himself and friends.

Rosborough had several chances to fish new water during his early 20s, when he and a friend did several different "booms" (moving from one box factory to another, hoping for a better job) to Weed, Calpine, Loyalton, Oroville, and Susanville. His favorite waters included the Susan River, Truckee River, and the Middle Fork of the Feather River, as well as numerous alpine lakes. In 1926 he relocated to Klamath Falls, Oregon, and soon thereafter to Chiloquin, where he resided off and on for the remainder of his life. There he discovered the Williamson River and its main tributary, the Sprague River, and bought his first dry fly (his first fly tied on an eyed hook rather than a snelled hook).

After complaining to his barber in 1928 that he could not buy durable flies or flies that imitated local insects, Polly began to tie his own. Not able to find fly-tying equipment, he made his own vise, using wood as clamps. During that same year he took a four-day pack trip into the Trinity Mountains, where he studied the aquatic insect life in the alpine lakes. Polly was rapidly becoming an amateur entomologist, or "bugologist," as he fondly called it, and he fell in love with the Williamson to the degree that he admitted, "No other river has ever taken me to its heart such as this superb trout water."

On August 29, 1929, Rosborough married Goldie, a 5-foot 2-inch "hunting, fishing, and fly-tying companion," who accompanied him into the outdoors and became such an accomplished fly tier that she sold flies for extra money. He authored his first magazine article that same year for *Hunter Trader Trapper* and began trapping marten in the winters.

Just as America was moving into the Depression years, Polly began to cough and lose weight. The company doctor informed him that breathing sawdust on a daily basis for several years had led to chronic asthma and the only cure would be to "get outside for a few years." Consequently, Polly and Goldie moved back to Bray, where they earned a living by tying flies and trapping. In 1933 Polly worked briefly for the U.S. Forest Service under the National Recovery Act, but was kept busy with fly orders from dealers in Dorris, Klamath Falls, and other towns. He viewed the area around Bray as "a ready-made laboratory for future research into my first love—the furtherance of improved methods in tying [the] dry fly, as well as studying out and putting into effect methods of presentation."

In 1933 Rosborough saw a Willmarth Company (Roosevelt, New York) catalog and from it purchased his first real vise. He began ordering fly-tying materials from Willmarth, and for the first time saw the firm's black-and-white illustrations of several different types of nymphs. He was immediately intrigued and began trying to imitate the insects. He also took his first fly-caught steelhead in the Klamath River and began tying steelhead flies as well. Mostly a self-taught tier, Rosborough tied left-handed, used no bobbin, and added half-hitches to his flies in as many places as possible. His first nymph was a Light Caddis larva, and his Black Drake Nymph female was so lifelike that a male Black Drake tried to mate with the artificial attached to his wife's line. Polly found the commercially available nymphs of the time to be lifeless (they were molded-plastic "hard shells" or "hard backs"), so he began experimenting with fur materials, "which resulted in nymphs that come alive in the water." His dubbing noodle was a mixture of hair and glue that was wrapped and anchored on the hook shank.

In 1936, Polly and Goldie moved back to Chiloquin, where he resumed his work at the box factory and continued his fly-tying business. He pioneered the use of marabou on the West Coast at this time and invented his famous Silver Garland Marabou Streamer. He also resumed fishing and research on the Williamson, where he "regularly ran out the stomachs of fish caught" and used a wire screen to collect aquatic insects. As he remembered, it was at this time that he "turned more and more to the development of nymphs that would give their users more and more chances of success on the local streams." In fact, the goal of his first series of nymphs was to "anticipate the emergence of all known aquatic insects native to the Upper Klamath watershed."

During World War II, Polly served as an instructor in the maintenance of aircraft machine guns for the Air Corps at Denver's Lowry Field, and eventually ended up as a shipwright in the Oregon Shipyards in Portland. He and Goldie divorced during this time, and he began a six-year relationship with the Meier & Frank Department Store in Portland as their full-time fly tier. Rosborough moved back to Chiloquin after the war and began fishing and tying more streamer patterns. Fly-fishing notables such as Jack Horner of San Francisco and Pete Schwab of Klamath River fame came to visit and fish the Williamson with him. During the late 1940s, Polly invented his Red Phantom Streamer, Copper Colonel, and Polly's Pride, and experienced what he described as "a revolution . . . in my tying." By accident, Rosborough had discovered that he could easily separate fur mat or felt by spinning it in soapy water.

Rosborough continued to run his trap lines, specializing in marten, during the 1950s and early 1960s, while earning his principal income as a commercial fly tier. Around 1960 he began to think about writing a book that would include "a truly representative group of nymphs indigenous to the Western States" and started to assemble his thoughts. Finally, in 1965, Rosborough self-published an 88-page paperback titled *Tying and Fishing the Fuzzy Nymphs.* The book sold well, featured 15 of Polly's nymphs, and brought him national recognition in the fly-fishing world. He was a featured fly tier at the founding meeting of the Federation of Fly Fishers (FFF) in Eugene, Oregon, in June 1965, and was pictured with an accompanying article in *Field & Stream* magazine the following year. He argued that "the more vibrating action a nymph produces, the better my chances of success are," and called his Black Drake Nymph the "greatest and most consistent killer of them all." Polly's notoriety directly influenced his business to the point where he taught 15 to 20 high school and college girls "to tie under my rules" in order to dress flies by the dozen on a contract basis.

In 1969 Orvis published a greatly expanded edition of *Tying and Fishing the Fuzzy Nymphs,* and to it Polly added five more nymphs and a new chapter, "Dyeing, Bleaching and Blending Procedures." In his introduction to the book, Ted Trueblood called Rosborough a "pioneer," and in the text Polly preached "simulation" rather than "imitation." He suggested that anglers did not need "learned technical jargon." Instead, they needed clear and precise information on the "size, shape, and true colors of all parts of each and every species of aquatic insect that may be considered as food by all gamefish."

Rosborough, who had been highly conservation-minded all of his life, helped start the Klamath Country Flycasters in 1971, a group "dedicated to improving fishing that had been lost." Soon he became chairman of the club's Conservation, Environmental and Habitat Committee, and he noted that "we seem to have come to the realization that fishing can no longer be just a means to augment the butcher's bill, to keep the freezer full of trout." Also in 1971, he published his first article in *Fly Fisherman* magazine and began writing chapters for "an autobiography covering some 50 years in quest of trout, steelhead and salmon on the fly." Polly's career and popularity blossomed even more after he reached 70 in 1972. He was a featured tier and panelist at the eighth FFF Conclave in Sun Valley, Idaho, with Dave Whitlock, Art Flick, Carl Richards, Doug Swisher, and George Grant, and in 1975 he received the FFF's Buz Buszek Memorial Award honoring "that person who has made significant contributions to the arts of fly tying."

Upon reflection, when asked about his innovative nymphs and unconventional presentation (shallow rather than deep), Rosborough said, "It now seems I was just lucky in not reading Hewett [sic][Edward R. Hewitt's *Handbook of Fly Fishing*, 1933], Bergman [Ray Bergman, *Trout*, 1938] and Quick [Jim Quick, *Fishing the Nymph*, 1960] until I had explored my own original new ideas and had ample time to prove them." He was also a popular guest fly tier at clubs, shows, and stores, and did a five-day fly-tying show at Abercrombie & Fitch in San Francisco in 1976. Tackle manufacturers sought his advice. Accordingly, Rosborough urged Scientific Anglers to develop its Wet Tip lines and encouraged Wright & McGill to manufacture its 1197 line of steelhead hooks and later the 1206 heavy streamer hooks.

A third and further enlarged edition of *Tying and Fishing the Fuzzy Nymphs* was published in 1978 by Stackpole Books, and during that same year Rosborough began writing a regular fly-tying column in *Fly Tyer* magazine. He continued to do so until 1987. The new edition of his popular book listed 46 flies, of which 19 were new dry patterns, and covered the emergence of aquatic insects from larvae, pupae, and nymphs through to adults, duns, and spinners. Polly also realized that the use of new synthetic materials negated the blending and felting of natural furs "to get a winning fly" and succumbed to the use of Latin names for insects since doing so had finally been brought into "fly fishing language." In a 1978 article Polly wrote for *Flyfishing the West* titled "Rosborough on Rosborough," the editor referred to Polly as "the uncompromising master of fly design and vigilante of Western rivers."

*"[Rosborough was the] first real student of Western aquatic insects and the angling and fly-tying pioneer who convinced Western fly fishers to start looking—and fishing—beneath the water's surface." —*Fly Rod & Reel, *1997.*

In 1982, at the age of 80, Rosborough self-published *Reminiscences from 50 Years of Flyrodding*, and the following year he self-published a limited-edition book called *Marten I Have Known*, a how-to book on trapping techniques. This also marked the end of running his trap line on an annual basis. That same year, fellow Oregon author and fly tier Dave Hughes honored Polly with an article in *Fly Fisherman* on "The Importance of Polly Rosborough." Hughes paid tribute to Polly's "vision"—his way of looking at insects wherein he observed, matched, and figured out how to properly fish the imitations.

"Polly" Rosborough tying one of his "fuzzy nymphs" for the attendees at
the initial Fly Fishers Conclave in Eugene, Oregon, in June 1965, hosted by
the McKenzie Flyfishers (Ralph E. Wahl Photographic Collection, Center
for Pacific Northwest Studies, Western Washington University)

POLLY ROSBOROUGH FISHING HIS BELOVED WILLIAMSON RIVER IN 1974 AT THE AGE OF 72. (PHOTOGRAPH BY DAVID CHILDERS FROM ROBERT WETHERN AND *THE CREEL*)

In fact, Hughes said that Polly's "formula—collecting, studying, matching, fishing—more than the flies, is the true importance of Polly Rosborough."

In 1984 another award was bestowed on Polly, this one by the Washington Fly Fishing Club, which honored him with the Letcher Lambuth Angling Craftsman Award "for his long lifetime of contributions to the fly-tying arts."

Stackpole reissued *Tying and Fishing the Fuzzy Nymphs* in 1988 as Rosborough's health was beginning to wane. Polly was admitted to a nursing home in Medford, Oregon, in 1995 and died there on December 18, 1997. Friends spread his ashes in Spring Creek, a short tributary of his beloved Williamson River near his Chiloquin home. Obituaries appeared in every major fly-fishing magazine. Ernest Schwiebert suggested that "Rosborough and his original research are perhaps the first major contribution to the theory and techniques of American nymph fishing since Leisenring [James E. Leisenring, *The Art of Tying the Wet Fly*, 1941]," and *Fly Rod & Reel* credited Polly as being the "first real student of Western aquatic insects and the angling and fly-tying pioneer who convinced Western fly fishers to start looking—and fishing—beneath the water's surface." Finally, Randall Kaufmann, owner of Kaufmann's Streamborn, Inc., and one who had tied flies for Rosborough before opening his own stores, remembered that Polly "was an originator, [and] didn't worry about what the angler downstream was doing. He was too busy creating."

Part Six:
Washington

LETCHER LAMBUTH AT WORK IN HIS BASEMENT WORKSHOP IN THE EARLY 1940s. HE IS EXAMINING FLY LINES IN THE DRAWERS OF THE WOODEN CASE HE DESIGNED AND BUILT TO STORE AND ORGANIZE HIS LINES. (PHOTOGRAPH COURTESY OF ROBERT WETHERN AND *THE CREEL*, 1971). LAMBUTH CANDLEFISH, TIED BY JON LUKE (INSET)

"He is a man of gentle precision, extremely skillful with his hands and with a mind that sorts detail into place and forces meaning from it; he has a scientist's touch, a scientist's objective honesty, a scientist's devotion to inquiry and experiment. Yet he is also a man of intense and glowing enthusiasms, and in a quiet, disarming way he carries almost everyone else along on his enthusiasms."
—*Roderick Haig-Brown*

Chapter 19

Benjamin Letcher Lambuth (1890–1974):

INNOVATOR, MASTER ROD BUILDER, AND AMATEUR ENTOMOLOGIST

enjamin Letcher Lambuth was born in 1890 in Washington, D.C., but moved shortly thereafter with his family to Seattle. There, choosing to use his middle name (after John Letcher, Civil War governor of Virginia and a distant relative), Lambuth attended public school and graduated from Broadway High School. He went on to college at Centre College in Kentucky and also attended Princeton and the University of Washington during his undergraduate years. Lambuth's father was an attorney, and perhaps at his suggestion, young Letcher attended the University of Washington Law School. In the early 1920s, Lambuth chose a career in real estate and moved his family to Longview, Washington. He was hired by the Long-Bell Lumber Company, founders of that city, to plan its layout and to manage the sale of their real estate. Upon completion of that large assignment in 1928, Lambuth and his family moved back to Seattle, where he began the industrial real estate firm of Lambuth, Sill and Sprague. With offices in the Hogue Building, his firm represented many of Seattle's large businesses, including the Boeing Company.

As a young man, Lambuth explored the nearby waters of Lake Washington in a rowboat and began to cultivate an interest in fly fishing. By the 1920s and '30s, he was actively fishing the rivers, lakes, and saltwater bays of Washington as well as Oregon and British Columbia. Lambuth, an inquisitive man with the meticulous talents of a scientist, was driven to discover new things about his favorite pastime—fly fishing for trout and salmon. He was also a talented craftsman, especially doing woodwork, and had a well-fitted basement workshop where he spent countless hours doing research and making fishing-related items. In addition, as is characteristic of those doing systematic research, Lambuth kept detailed records in a number of different notebooks. For every new question and for any problem that needed to be answered or solved, Lambuth started a "project." And most of his projects involved various fly-fishing implements.

One of Lambuth's first challenges was making his own cane rods. During the 1930s, when he began this task, all fly rods were made from bamboo by a handful of very skilled professional craftsmen and were quite expensive. Lambuth studied George P. Holden's *The Idyll of the Split Bamboo* (1920) for guidance and began to develop his own rod-building techniques. While his friend Harold Stimson helped fabricate steel planing forms, Lambuth researched and collected various types of bamboo, and he contacted the Devine

Rod Company in Utica, New York, holders of a patented spiral construction method that interested him. With permission from Fred Devine, he began to construct his own six-strip (hexagonal) spiral bamboo fly rods. They were unique, with the rod shaft twisted one-sixth of a turn between each guide. For a rod with 11 guides, the cane would have nearly two full 360-degree twists over the length of the rod. Letcher always inscribed "Stimson-Lambuth" on these rods, to pay tribute to his friend, although Stimson did none of the construction. In all, Lambuth made about 30 rods, most of which were given to friends.

Lambuth's other projects during the 1930s included making landing nets, designing and crocheting a zippered twine "breathing" creel, assembling a wooden outboard motor stand, making wooden fly boxes, building a set of wood drawers to store fly lines, making a line dryer and swift, and designing and sewing a tying apron as well as one of the first fishing vests. Letcher noted that there were "a considerable number of anglers who have some measure of manual skill and a spirit of inquiry which leads them to carry the problems of the stream side into the home workshop," and explained that "I have adopted this plan and have found many enjoyable projects." Simply put, Lambuth believed that "making and building things is good for the soul."

An important event in the life of Letcher Lambuth came in 1935 with the publication of Preston J. Jennings's landmark book, *A Book of Trout Flies;*

LETCHER LAMBUTH BUILDING A PIECE OF FURNITURE IN THE BASEMENT WORKSHOP OF HIS SEATTLE HOME IN THE LATE 1930S. NOTICE HIS NOTEBOOKS AND FISHING PHOTOGRAPHS ON THE LEFT SIDE AND THE CANE RODS AND BAMBOO STOCK ALONG THE BACK WALL. (PHOTOGRAPH COURTESY OF ROBERT WETHERN)

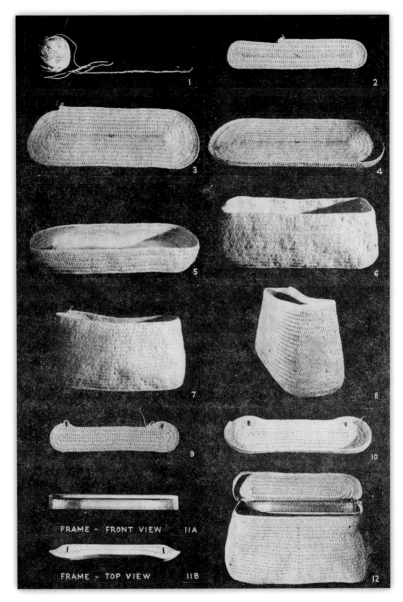

STEP-BY-STEP PROCESS SHOWING THE CONSTRUCTION OF LAMBUTH'S CRO-
CHETED COTTON CREEL, FROM HIS BOOK *THE ANGLER'S WORKSHOP*, 1979

*Containing a List of the Most Important American Stream Insects & Their Imi-
tations,* by New York's Derrydale Press. Jennings had contacted Lambuth to
collect insects for him and asked him for a list of his favorite fly patterns, and
they began corresponding on a regular basis. Lambuth also became friends
with Eugene V. Connett, Derrydale's publisher, and began negotiations to

publish his own book-in-progress. Because many of the insects in Jennings's book were of East Coast origin and fishing was so different in the Northwest, Lambuth began another project to collect, preserve, photograph, and catalog many of the insects inhabiting Northwest lakes and streams. As an amateur entomologist, he compiled an impressive and comprehensive list of hatches

"[O]ne of the West Coast's pioneer angling entomologists."
—*Paul Schullery,* American Fly Fishing: A History*, 1987*

and matching fly patterns, beginning around 1936 and continuing into the early 1960s. In his usual style, he built a wooden attachment for his camera that held insects at the correct distance from the lens for a photograph. For this early work, Paul Schullery in *American Fly Fishing: A History* (1987) called Lambuth "one of the West Coast's pioneer angling entomologists." Later in his life, Lambuth donated his entire collection to Professor N. H. Anderson, an aquatic entomologist at Oregon State University, who proclaimed in 1975 that "Lambuth's study stands as perhaps the most complete one of its kind ever to be done for this region by scientist or layman alike."

Because Lambuth also spent considerable time fly fishing for Pacific salmon in the salt water of both Washington and British Columbia, he experimented with fly patterns to represent the two most common baitfish in the region—candlefish and herring. After consulting about light refraction with Professor C. L. Utterback of the University of Washington's Physics Department, Lambuth set up an aquarium in his workshop, filled it with Puget Sound water and a dozen candlefish, and began experimenting with light and coloration as he simulated different water depths with filters. It became obvious that the fish looked much different in the water than in his hand, so Lambuth set out to imitate these colors and textures in his flies. As a result, two of the most enduring saltwater fly patterns ever developed—the Lambuth Candlefish and the Lambuth Herring—took the shape of a fairly simple silver-bodied hair-wing streamer utilizing polar bear hair layered in French blue, red, and a mixture of blue and pale green from top to bottom for the candlefish, and, for the herring, polar bear hair in three layers with the top bright green with a few strands of olive, the median line gray, and the bottom pale green mixed with white. Lambuth, his experiments, and his two flies were credited with starting the "systematic fly development" for Pacific salmon by Bruce Ferguson, Les Johnson, and Pat Trotter in their groundbreaking book, *Fly Fishing for Pacific Salmon* (1985), and Lambuth patterns are still used today by avid coho fishermen.

In 1939 Lambuth became one of the eight founding fathers of the Washington Fly Fishing Club (WFFC), an organization that he helped in many ways, and, in turn, the club introduced Lambuth, his talents, and his wonderful gentlemanly demeanor to fly anglers throughout the Northwest. In his book on the history of the WFFC, *Backcasts* (1989), Steve Raymond credits Lambuth with writing letters to recruit new members, visiting other towns to recruit members and discuss conservation plans, organizing the campaign to get Pass Lake and the North Fork of the Stillaguamish River designated as the state's first fly-fishing-only waters in 1940, organizing fly-tying classes, and keeping detailed records of most club activities. He was also a regular attendee at the weekly WFFC luncheons held in the Fly Room of Seattle's Camlin Hotel.

By the early 1940s, as a result of diabetes, Lambuth began to lose his eyesight. However, he stayed active, continued to fish, and never lost the congenial and sincere personality that was his trademark. He completed the book manuscript he had been working on for several years, calling it *The Angler's Workshop*, but despite his friendship with Connett and his interest in Derrydale Press, Lambuth withdrew the manuscript because he disliked the proposed limited-edition publishing plan.

In 1940, as a close friend of both Preston J. Jennings and Roderick Haig-Brown, Lambuth passed along one of Jennings's Iris series flies to his friend on Vancouver Island. Haig-Brown went on to popularize the Lord Iris for Northwest steelheading, and it made its debut in his classic *A River Never Sleeps* (1946), in the chapter "January," in which he is deciding what fly to use and says, "It stared up at me from the first box I opened, Preston Jennings's Lord Iris . . ."

A portrait of Lambuth from the 1960s (photograph courtesy of Robert Wethern and *The Creel*)

Haig-Brown also devoted a chapter in *Fisherman's Spring* (1951) to "The New Rod." Here, Haig-Brown began, "My friend Letcher Lambuth made me a rod. Not because I had asked for one or because he knew I had desperate need of one, but rather because he believed I was a fit person to own a Lambuth rod." And it was in *Fisherman's Spring* that Haig-Brown acknowledged, for all to read, the talents, skills, and spirit of Letcher Lambuth: "If Letcher's rods were far less good than they are, I should still value this one above all my other rods because of Letcher's quality as a fisherman. He is a man of gentle precision, extremely skillful with his hands and with a mind that sorts detail into place and forces meaning from it; he has a scientist's touch, a scientist's objective honesty, a scientist's devotion to inquiry and experiment. Yet he is also a man of intense and glowing enthusiasms, and in a quiet, disarming way he carries almost everyone else along on his enthusiasms."

Other notables who received a Lambuth rod as a gift included Connett, Jennings, and Clark Van Fleet, who in his book *Steelhead to a Fly* (1954) concluded that his Lambuth rod was "the most perfect I have ever wielded." At the urging of Haig-Brown, as Lambuth was losing his sight, he taught his rod-building skills to British Columbia angling artist Tommy Brayshaw, who built his own Lambuth rod.

As has been the case for many notable men and women throughout time, their contributions and pioneering efforts were not noted and appreciated until after their death. This was not entirely true for Lambuth, since Steve Raymond published two chapters of Lambuth's book manuscript in 1973. As editor of *The Flyfisher*, Steve published "Tonkin Rod Bamboo" and "Devising a Streamer Fly Pattern." Unfortunately, on January 14 of the following year, Letcher Lambuth died at the age of 84, leaving behind his wife, Olive, a son and a daughter, and a legion of friends and fly-fishing acquaintances.

Soon after his death, Lambuth's friends were quick to pay their respects and to make certain that many of his contributions were preserved for future generations. Raymond authored an obituary published in the Fall 1974 issue of *The American Fly Fisher*, Bob Wethern organized and published a commemorative issue of *The Creel* (The Bulletin of the Flyfisher's Club of Oregon) in December 1974 (Lambuth was on the cover), and Olive Lambuth donated his rod-building equipment and many other fly-fishing items to the Museum of American Fly Fishing in Manchester, Vermont. The following year, Pat Trotter published a thorough testimonial in *Salmon Trout Steelheader* titled "Matching the Pacific Northwest Hatch—Letcher Lambuth: The Pacific Northwest's Answer to Jennings, Flick and Marinaro," and *The American Fly Fisher* published Lambuth's "Salt Water Fly Fishing," another previously unpublished chapter from his book. Fittingly, the Washington Fly Fishing Club established the Letcher Lambuth Angling Craftsman Award that year to honor one of its most admired and respected members. The first winner was Roderick Haig-Brown, and those who followed have been a virtual who's who of Northwest fly fishing.

In 1979 Steve Raymond was able to convince Oregon's Champoeg Press to publish *The Angler's Workshop*. Ironically, it appeared in a limited edition of 1,250 copies, something Lambuth would not have liked, but his pioneering work in its entirety finally became available to the angling public. Since then, Pat Trotter has written about Lambuth's trout-fly contributions several times and also acknowledged Lambuth's pioneering salmon streamers, all in articles published in *Salmon Trout Steelheader*. In 1998, thanks to the publication of Steve Raymond's *Rivers of the Heart: A Fly-Fishing Memoir*, Lambuth's early work in rod building was surveyed in a chapter aptly titled "Raising Cane." And, in 2000, some of Letcher's rod-building tools were displayed beside those of Hiram Leonard and Hiram Hawes in the "Angler's All: Humanity in Midstream" traveling exhibit of the Museum of American Fly Fishing. The museum now has a fairly extensive Letcher Lambuth collection, including 107 books from Lambuth's library donated by his son, Alan, in 1993. The Washington Fly Fishing Club also has some Lambuth materials.

One can only speculate about the additional contributions Letcher Lambuth would have surely made to Northwest fly fishing if his writings had been published in a timely manner and had he not lost his eyesight when he was in his 50s, at the peak of his career. Nevertheless, Northwest fly fishers can still look back at the numerous inventions, innovations, and contributions of this fine man whom Steve Raymond referred to as "every inch a gentleman," and remember him as a true pioneer.

LETCHER LAMBUTH AT A WASHINGTON FLY FISHING CLUB LUNCHEON IN SEATTLE, CIRCA 1970. NOTE THE TOMMY BRAYSHAW ART ON THE WALL IN THE BACKGROUND (PHOTOGRAPH BY ROBERT WETHERN).

Enos Bradner tying Brad's Brat, circa 1949 (MSCUA, University of Washington Libraries, UW 21519). Brad's Brat, tied by John Luke (inset)

"I decided to try to publicize the sport of fly fishing within the state." —Enos Bradner

Chapter 20

Enos Bradner (1892–1984):

OUTDOOR WRITER, FLY-FISHING ADVOCATE, AND CONSERVATIONIST

Enos "Brad" Bradner was born October 7, 1892, in Powers, Michigan, on the Upper Peninsula. In this small hamlet of about 500, Bradner's family owned a country store. It was here that Bradner learned hunting and fishing from his uncle and spent days stalking animals and birds as well as catching native brook trout, rainbows, bass, pike, and pickerel. He spent his high school years with an aunt in Marinette, Wisconsin, where he graduated as the class valedictorian. From there he moved to Ann Arbor and graduated from the University of Michigan with a double major in literature and business. When World War I broke out, Bradner enlisted as a corporal in the 10th Field Artillery and fought in several major battles in France. After the war he returned to Michigan, where he operated a small store and a restaurant.

In 1929, at the age of 37, Bradner's life began to change. He ventured to the West Coast on a fishing trip and became instantly enamored with the Pacific Northwest. On that trip he fished the North Fork of the Stillaguamish, near the Deer Creek confluence, and was immediately drawn to all of its splendor. Shortly thereafter he moved to Seattle and opened Bradner's Bookshop at Broadway and Olive on Capitol Hill. This was his headquarters for the next 15 years and was the place he planned most of his hunting and fishing trips. Typically, Bradner would take off on Thursday for "weekend" jaunts throughout the state of Washington.

Bradner learned to tie his own flies in the early 1930s from Dan Conway of Seattle, a one-handed fly tier who was best known for his Conway Special, a variation of the popular Yellow Hammer. Because of his love of hunting, Bradner quickly stocked his own fly-tying boxes with a variety of furs, feathers, and hair.

Bradner raised his first steelhead to a fly in the Wind River Canyon, and summer-run steelhead fly fishing quickly became his passion. By the mid-1930s he was fishing the North Fork Stillaguamish and Deer Creek on a regular basis, and it was for these waters that he developed his most well-known fly, Brad's Brat. It was very effective for both winter and summer steelhead, as well as sea-run cutthroat trout. The front half of the body was red wool and the rear half was orange wool, both ribbed with gold tinsel. It had an orange-and-white bucktail tail and the same combination for the wing (one-third orange and two-thirds white, with the white on top). It was finished with a brown hackle.

Bradner always stocked his steelhead fly box with an array of Brats in sizes 6 to 2, dressed bushy for the early season and very sparse for what he called "low-water-late-summer-hard-to-interest steelhead." For higher water conditions, he tied the Brat on heavier hooks, from 1 to 2/0. For Bradner, the orange-and-white bucktail combination was the key ingredient for his fly: "when wet, [it] produces an illusive shade that sea-going trout find very desirable," he said. This fly continued to be one of the Northwest's most popular steelhead patterns through the 1980s and still appears in numerous books.

Bradner and one of his fishing companions, Ken McLeod, outdoor editor of the *Seattle Post-Intelligencer*, were both members of the Steelhead Trout Club of Washington in the 1930s and became frustrated that their club would not act on behalf of the interests of fly fishermen. So, in the late 1930s, Bradner, McLeod, and a few others started to hold meetings in Bradner's Bookshop to organize a club specifically for fly fishermen. As a result, Bradner became one of eight founders of the Washington Fly Fishing Club (WFFC) in 1939 and was its first president. The WFFC and Bradner set out immediately to convince the Washington State Game Commission that certain lakes and streams should be "set aside experimentally for fly fishing only during the regular trout season." After considerable "politicking," Pass Lake on Fidalgo Island, near the Deception Pass Bridge, and the North Fork of the Stillaguamish River were restricted to fly fishing only in 1944. These were the first such designations in Washington state and helped popularize fly fishing for both trout and steelhead. Bradner continued to be active in the WFFC over the next 40 years, teach-

BRADNER HOLDING A LARGE KISPIOX RIVER STEELHEAD CAUGHT ON ONE OF HIS SEVERAL TRIPS TO THAT FAMED BRITISH COLUMBIA RIVER IN THE 1960s (PHOTOGRAPH COURTESY OF THE WASHINGTON FLY FISHING CLUB)

Brad's Fly Of The Week

Today we list the first of a series of drawings and dressings of trout and salmon flies that will be continued each Sunday. These are patterns that have either been devised or developed by local fly-tiers for Northwest fly fishing. Clip each drawing so as to retain a complete listing of these "trout getters."

The Orange Shrimp is a steelhead pattern that has proved an effective fly both for winter-run fish and the elusive summer runs. The fly derives much of its "fish qualities" from the Jungle Cock shoulder. If this feather is not obtainable one can buy a synthetic one or use the eyed feather from a rooster quail touching it with a dot of orange enamel.

CONWAY SPECIAL

Hook: 6 or 8.
Tag: Gold tinsel or none (optional).
Tail: Red and white hackle fibers.
Ribs: Gold.
Body: Yellow wool palmered with yellow hackle.
Hackle: Red and yellow.
Wings: White goose, or swan, with strips of red on each side.

This fly was developed from the yellow hammer pattern by Dan Conway, the Irish fly-tier who is now deceased. Although having only one arm, Dan tied an almost perfect fly, and was responsible for many of the present day anglers taking up fly making.

The Conway Special was originated for sea-run cutthroats and has been an excellent fly to take these trout ever since. Wings made from the wing feathers of an adult snow goose are the best as their fibers stay put under incessant casting. A good idea is to dress one fly with a light yellow body and hackle, another with orange yellow and then alternate them in teasing out the "cuts" from underneath a snag. The wings should either be cupped or dressed at a slight angle so as to give them a fishy action when retrieved.

This fly is also a killer for trout in lakes and for kamloops in British Columbia. Dressed on number 4 hooks it is a taker for summer-run steelhead and may be varied by using white bucktail for wings.

ORANGE SHRIMP (WET FLY)

Hook: Summer-runs 4 to 6; winter runs 4 to 2/0.
Tag: Gold.
Tail: Red hackle fibers.
Ribs: None.
Body: Orange wool.
Hackle: Orange.
Wings: White bucktail or polar bear.
Shoulder: Jungle cock-eyed feathers.

ing fly tying, serving as librarian, and being active in almost every event and outing. In this role, Bradner and the WFFC greatly furthered fly-fishing concerns in the Northwest.

Because of Bradner's reputation as an accomplished outdoorsman, *The Seattle Times* invited him to join their staff as an outdoor columnist in 1943. So, at the age of 50, Bradner started a new career. In a *Times* release that April, he was introduced as "the *Times* reporter and commentator on fishing and hunting affairs." His column, "The Inside on the Outdoors," first appeared on April 25, 1943, and continued three times a week for the next 26 years. From the start, Bradner's heart was in fly fishing, and he remembered later that when he joined the *Times'* staff, "I decided to try to publicize the sport of fly fishing within the state." Between 1950 and 1951, he teamed up with *Times* artist and cartoonist Alan Pratt to produce "Brad's Fly of the Week," and once that stopped, he said, "each year before the opening of the fishing season I would run a column showing a few fly patterns that would be effective after opening day." Pratt, a favorite fishing companion and WFFC member, also illustrated these flies. Bradner's columns had a significant impact on an entire generation of fly fishers and, because of their frequency and longevity, were said to be the most widely read of any newspaper column in Washington state. Robert Wethern, fly-fishing historian and former editor of *The Creel*, argues that Bradner's "columns gave flyfishing an exposure in this area (and elsewhere) that was missing until Fenton Roskelley in Spokane and Tommy McAllister in Portland came along a bit later."

In 1945, Bradner and several other WFFC members convinced the Washington State Game Commission to trap Deer Creek summer-run steelhead and take their eggs to the Arlington Hatchery. These smolts were then adipose fin clipped, tagged, and released back into Deer Creek, where some were eventually caught in 1949. This first experiment to artificially propagate summer steelhead proved that summer stocks would return and not mingle, and led to the beginning of state-operated summer steelhead hatcheries on the Washougal, Skagit, and the North Fork of the Stillaguamish. It was also in 1945 that Bradner and fellow WFFC member Frank Headrick invented their Dandy Green Nymph fly pattern after examining the stomach contents of a brook trout caught on Price Lake.

The following year, Bradner spent some time doing research in Bikini Atoll on board the U.S.S. *Haven* as a member of the University of Washington team taking radiation samples for Operation Crossroads following the United States' atomic bomb tests. Dr. Lauren Donaldson, U.W. fisheries professor in charge of testing fish, recalled that Bradner was the "chief sampler." Whenever the scientists needed fish to test for radiation, Bradner caught them. Later that year, Bradner and Sanford (Sandy) Bacon purchased Bucktail Camp, a cabin near the confluence of Deer Creek and the North Fork of the Stillaguamish. With this purchase, Bradner became inextricably linked to the "Stilly" and continued to be one of its river keepers until his death.

Bradner's first book, *Northwest Angling*, published by A. S. Barnes in 1950, was one of the earliest to detail steelhead angling methods and included significant information on fly fishing. Specifically, he included chapters on "The Contemplative Fly-Tier" and "Taking Steelhead on a Fly," and long sections on fly fishing in chapters on "The Sea-Run Cutthroat as a Sport Fish" and "Boating the Leaping Cohoe [sic]." A second edition of this book was printed in 1969.

Bradner never went anywhere during the 1950s without his black Labrador, Rendarb (Bradner spelled backward) Jet of Bikini. Jet slept in the bathtub when Bradner stayed in motels and hotels, and became almost as famous as his owner after being featured in a prize-winning film by Howard Gray, a friend and fellow WFFC member. It was also during the 1950s, as a member of the Outdoor Writers Association of America, that Bradner began to publish articles in major outdoor magazines, beginning with *Outdoor Life* in 1953. He also continued his devotion to summer-run steelhead fly fishing and, when chided about devoting too many of his "Inside on the Outdoors" columns to it, Bradner admitted that "they are pretty well stacked in favor of taking summer-run steelhead on the feathered offering." In response to his critics, he said, "So what—that's what I liked to do and I wanted every other angler to learn about this superlative kind of angling." Later, he warned his readers, "Beware—Steelhead-on-Fly Virus" was spreading rapidly through the Northwest.

In the early 1960s, 50 of Bradner's favorite flies were compiled in a small, nine-page pamphlet titled "Brad's Fly of the Week," and he published articles on

Washington's success at planting trout in *Trout* magazine and "Fly Fishing for Silvers in the Pacific" in the *Atlantic Salmon Journal*. It was also about this time that Bradner invented his Puget Bug fly, a nymph designed for rainbow fishing in lakes when no recognizable nymph was present. *The Seattle Times* won several Excellence in Journalism awards presented by the Sigma Delta Chi professional journalism fraternity in 1963, and Bradner's column was one of the recipients. His recognition was based upon "his skill in translating his accumulated woodsman's wisdom into the printed word for the benefit of others."

In 1965 the charter conclave of the Federation of Fly Fishermen (FFF) met in Eugene, Oregon, and Bradner became charter vice president. Later, in a 1968 "Faces of the City" column by fellow *Times* reporter John Redden, Bradner was referred to as a "tough old rooster" who was "lean and rawhide-tough," the "dean of Northwest outdoor writers," and a "white-thatched preacher of conservation and sportsmanship."

In 1964 author Steve Raymond joined the staff of *The Seattle Times*, and he became a member of the WFFC the following year, with Alan Pratt as his sponsor. He also met Bradner and they instantly became friends and regular fishing companions. Raymond remembered that "Brad was in his seventies when I first met him but still an impressive physical specimen, lean and spare with ramrod posture and hair as white as the plumage of the snow geese he sometimes hunted." Until his death, Bradner played a significant role in Raymond's life. He wrote the foreword to Raymond's book *Kamloops* (1971), and Raymond wrote extensively about Bradner, Deer Creek, the WFFC, and

BRADNER HOOKS A TROUT AS HIS FAITHFUL FISHING COMPANION JET OF BIKINI JUMPS INTO THE LAKE AFTER THE FISH (PHOTOGRAPH COURTESY OF THE WASHINGTON FLY FISHING CLUB)

Bucktail Camp in several of his books. Steve dedicated his book *Steelhead Country* (1991) to Bradner and Ralph Wahl, another Northwest steelhead pioneer. In 1976 Raymond bought Bucktail Camp from Bradner and Bacon, and he devoted a chapter in *The Year of the Trout* (1985) to a history of the

cabin. Because of this, the North Fork "Stilly" became Raymond's home river, which enabled him to maintain Bradner's legacy in that watershed.

Bradner finally retired from *The Seattle Times* in 1969 at the age of 77 and continued to fish and hunt into his 80s. He authored *Fish On!* (*Everything You Should Know About Steelhead Including How to Catch 'Em*) in 1971 and included two long chapters on fly fishing: "Fly Time Is Fun Time, Once You Have Learned It" and "Tie Me a Lucky Steelhead Fly." That same year he gained national notoriety for Lake Lenice, Washington's first "quality lake," in a *Field & Stream* article titled "Sagebrush Rainbows." Bradner published his third book, *The Inside on the Outdoors*, a compilation of his past *Seattle Times* columns, in 1973, and in November of that year became one of nine founders of the Northwest Outdoor Writers Association (NOWA). In 1976 he won the WFFC's highly coveted Letcher Lambuth Angling Craftsman Award, and in 1979 he received the Order of the Lapis Lazuli award, the FFF's most prestigious honor. And, commencing in 1985, NOWA began recognizing talented Northwest outdoor writers with its Enos Bradner Award.

Bradner turned 85 in 1977, and he was still as thrilled about catching a steelhead as ever. He told *Seattle Post-Intelligencer* outdoor writer Greg Johnston that "you get a couple of steelhead and you get the fever and you just can't get over it. You've got it and that's it. There's nothing you can do about it. . . . I still get so dang excited when I get one on sometimes I don't know what I am doing." Bradner visited his beloved Bucktail Camp with Steve Raymond in 1983 and soon thereafter was put in a nursing home for constant care. Bradner passed away there on January 12, 1984, in his 92nd year. In *The Year of the Trout* (1985), Raymond wrote that in May 1984 a small group of Bradner's friends and relatives met at the edge of the Elbow Hole on the North Fork of the Stillaguamish and "scattered the old fisherman's ashes over the water he had fished so long and loved so well. When they had finished, they returned once more to Bucktail Camp and stood before the fire to drink a final toast to their relative and friend. And now he belongs to the river."

JUDGE RALPH OLSON WALKS A TRAIL ALONG THE SKAGIT RIVER
AFTER A SUCCESSFUL DAY OF STEELHEAD FISHING IN THE EARLY
1940's (RALPH E. WAHL PHOTOGRAPHIC COLLECTION, CENTER
FOR PACIFIC NORTHWEST STUDIES, WESTERN WASHINGTON UNI-
VERSITY). OLSON'S LADY GODIVA FLY, TIED BY JON LUKE (INSET)

Chapter 21

Ralph O. Olson (1902–1955):

JUDGE AND PIONEER WINTER-RUN STEELHEADER

Ralph Oliver Olson was born in Alden, Minnesota, on March 26, 1902, to Ralph O. and Genevieve (Larson) Olson. His father was a prominent banker in the region, and young Ralph grew up hunting and fishing with him and developed a love of the outdoors. Graduated by St. Cloud High School in 1918 when he was just 16, Olson began his college studies in Northfield, Minnesota, at Carleton College a year later. After two years he transferred to the University of Minnesota in Minneapolis, where he became a star lineman on the football team. By the time his athletic career ended in the early 1920s, he had been voted a second-team All-American. After earning his bachelor's degree, he remained at the university to earn his law degree, with honors, from the school of law in 1924.

With law degree in hand, Olson traveled up and down the West Coast looking for the ideal location to live and work. In 1924 he selected Bellingham, Washington, because there were few attorneys and because of "the climate and the fishing and hunting opportunities." He was admitted to the Washington State Bar on June 27, 1924, and started his own law practice. On November 27, 1924, he married Louise Moore of St. Cloud, Minnesota, who joined him in Bellingham. They had three children: daughter Phyllis and sons Charles and Dan.

In 1926 Olson won an election to become a part-time municipal court judge, justice of the peace, and police judge in Bellingham, positions he held for 10 years. During this time, he met Ralph Wahl, a Bellingham merchant who was four years his junior and living less than two blocks away. Wahl remembered that Olson's "secret love was fly fishing for trout which by coincidence was also mine. Through it we became close friends." Accordingly, in 1934, Olson and his wife invited Wahl to accompany them on their annual fishing trip to British Columbia, where Wahl was introduced "to the spectacular sea-run cutthroat trout fishing . . . along the wind swept beaches of big Harrison Lake." Thereafter, on the first weekend of March each year, through 1942, Wahl and the Olsons made this pilgrimage.

In 1936, Olson was elected state superior court judge for Whatcom and San Juan counties; he served in that role until 1951. He had a special interest in young people and organized summer youth programs and started a college scholarship fund with the University Club of Bellingham. Also in 1936, he and Wahl began tying flies together and Wahl started to fly fish for steelhead. Wahl caught two summer-run fish from the nearby Skagit River in September and excitedly reported his success to the judge. Finally, on August 13, 1939, Olson undertook his first steelhead fly-fishing trip with Wahl, and, as Wahl entered in his diary, promptly "hooked himself in the ear." Nevertheless, Wahl was impressed with Olson's "ability as an angler" and his stature, describing him as "a personable giant towering six feet five inches, [and] weighing two hundred twenty-five pounds." Wahl landed his first winter-run steelhead on a fly later that year, and in early 1940 he and Olson began a 10-year systematic and dedicated quest to catch winter-run steelhead on flies on their three "home rivers," the Skagit, Nooksack, and North Fork Stillaguamish. Olson caught his first winter-run on a fly on January 20, and a week later Wahl noted in his diary that "Ralph O. just returned from Vancouver with new flies, fly-tying vise, and a lot of hopes for Harrison Lake. What one steelhead does to a person!!"

Wahl's diary for 1941 was filled with entries describing numerous fishing excursions that always began with "Ralph O. and I to Skagit!" That January, Wahl named one of his new flies Lord Hamilton and soon thereafter said he had "a companion—I call it 'Lady Hamilton.'" Just two months later, Wahl wrote that "Ralph O. took a 5 lb. buck steelhead at Grandy Pool today on his new Lady Godiva fly—this I've got to see!" Another diary entry for March noted that "Judge and Mrs. Judge connected with eight steelhead." Later that month, Ken McLeod asked the readers of his popular outdoor column in the *Seattle Post-Intelligencer*, "how do you fellows compete on the smooth bars of the Skagit with the six-foot strides of Judge Olson?" The judge, using a "home-tied bucktail" on the Skagit, was rewarded for his pioneering efforts three days after Christmas with a 13-pound, 7-ounce steelhead that placed fourth in the annual *Field & Stream* Big Fish Contest, Western Rainbow Trout Division.

"Ralph's love for fishing was deep-seated and sincere. He enjoyed the solitude of lonely places and was fascinated with even the smallest things in nature. Marking the water-height of the river was a ritual with him, and a change, either up or down, provided unlimited speculative conversation." —Ralph Wahl

Olson and Wahl were becoming well-known figures to anglers in the Pacific Northwest by 1942, as reported by McLeod in the *Post-Intelligencer*: "We heard of two fishermen from Bellingham who caught fifty-three steelheads between them from December to March—and all were caught on flies—it looks like the days when steelheads wouldn't take flies in the winter months are gone forever."

Such accolades were not undeserved, however, as Wahl remembered many years later in a chapter titled "My Friend Judge Ralph Olson" in his book *One Man's Steelhead Shangri-La* (1989): "We tied our own flies, constructed our own leaders and built fly rods especially for steelhead fishing. We honed our

JUDGE RALPH OLSON LANDS A LARGE STEELHEAD ON WASHINGTON'S SKAGIT RIVER
IN THE EARLY 1940'S. (RALPH E. WAHL PHOTOGRAPHIC COLLECTION, CENTER FOR
PACIFIC NORTHWEST STUDIES, WESTERN WASHINGTON UNIVERSITY)

casting skills at a wading pool in the park . . . and we kept our local game officials on their toes by clamoring for improved fishing conditions." He wrote that fishing with the judge "was never dull. His dry humor and ability to take as well as give friendly badgering made our days together something special."

Olson and Wahl were at the peak of their winter-run steelhead fly fishing between 1942 and 1946, a five-year period Wahl called the "Golden Years." They discovered the great summer-run steelhead fishing in Mystery Lake; Olson landed a 16-pound, 10-ounce winter-run on the Skagit; and in his 1943 *Field & Stream* article titled "Winter Steelheads on Flies," Wahl talked about "the Judge" and featured him in several photographs. During World War II they rode the bus to work so they could save gas rationing coupons to fuel their Model A Fords to drive to the Skagit, Nooksack, and North Fork Stillaguamish. By 1944, so well known was their prowess that Wahl realized "we were marked men and we parked our cars in the trees" to try to keep favorite spots a secret. The judge place sixth in the 1945 *Field & Stream* contest with a 13-pound, 5-ounce fish caught on his Lady Godiva in the Skagit, and placed second the following year with a 15-pound, 5-ounce winter-run caught on the same fly. In May 1946 the *Bellingham Herald* featured Wahl and Olson, with a photograph of the two tying flies at Wahl's bench in his basement, in a story titled "2 of City's Most Ardent Fishermen Enjoy Fly-Tying."

The judge's Lady Godiva sported a tail of married red and yellow swan, a tag of embossed silver tinsel, body of spun yellow seal fur ribbed with embossed

JUDGE RALPH OLSON TIES HIS FAMOUS LADY GODIVA AS HIS FISHING PARTNER RALPH WAHL LOOKS ON. THIS PHOTOGRAPH APPEARED IN THE *BELLINGHAM HERALD* IN 1946. (RALPH E. WAHL PHOTOGRAPHIC COLLECTION, CENTER FOR PACIFIC NORTHWEST STUDIES, WESTERN WASHINGTON UNIVERSITY)

silver tinsel, butt of red chenille, and wing with a small amount of white polar bear overlaid with red bucktail. Olson also developed a fly he named Orange Wing, which he used on bright days. It had an orange tail, orange butt, silver tinsel rib over a yellow wool body, and wing of white and orange polar bear.

Olson was elected president of the Washington State Superior Court Judges Association in 1947 and that same year placed seventh in the *Field & Stream* contest with a 16-pound, 2-ounce Skagit River fish taken on a Lady Godiva. His wife placed 10th that year with a 15-pound, 2-ounce Skagit winter steelhead, also taken on a Lady Godiva. The judge's astounding record of large fly-caught Skagit River fish continued in 1948 and 1949, with a sixth-place 14-pound,

9-ounce fish and a massive second-place fish weighing 18 pounds, 4 ounces, respectively. Both were caught on Lady Godivas, and the latter fish was the 12th-largest steelhead in the *Field & Stream* Western Rainbow Trout Fly-Casting Division as reported in A. J. McClane's *The American Angler* (1954). The Skagit had become the top river for winter-run steelhead fly fishing in 1949, with Wes Drain's 20-pound, 7-ounce fish placing first in the *Field & Stream* contest, Olson's fish second, and Al Knudson's 15-pound, 13-ounce fish third. Wahl's records of steelhead he and Olson caught from 1940 through 1949, which he referred to as "the Winter Tally," showed they had hooked 232, landed 149, and lost 83, with those landed averaging 9.2 pounds.

The judge's personal and professional life began to change in the late 1940s and early 1950s. His son Charles ("Chuck") captained the University of Washington (U.W.) football team and went on to law school there. His other son, Dan, rowed for the U.W. crew team and also attended law school. Olson had less and less time to fish and did not get to fish with Wahl at all in 1950 or 1951, but still managed to land a 15-pound, 12-ounce winter-run on the Skagit that placed fourth in the *Field & Stream* contest for 1951. Then, in August of that year, when Judge Walter Beals retired from the Washington State Supreme Court, Governor Arthur Langlie appointed Olson to fill his vacancy. Olson subsequently moved to Olympia, the state capital, several hours away from the Skagit. In a letter to Wahl later that year, he said, "They say winter steelhead will not take a fly down here. Haven't done anything about it and may not get a chance to for a while." In the same letter, Olson told Wahl that he hoped "we can get out together some time. I will need some coaching badly after my long abstinence."

Judge Olson ran unopposed for his Supreme Court seat in the 1952 election and was elected to a full six-year term. One of his colleagues identified him as a "tall man with a friendly demeanor and without pretentiousness" who "was one of the hardest working members of the court." He averaged 35 opinions a year and, in keeping with his long history of working with young adults, always had several law clerks learning and helping him in his office, including his sons, both of whom went on to successful careers in law. In 1954 Olson was one of the Washington judges featured in *Eminent Judges and Lawyers of the Northwest, 1843–1955* by C. W. Taylor, Jr.

Although Olson enjoyed very little fishing time in the early 1950s, his past exploits were not going unnoticed. In his correspondence with Peter Schwab in 1952, Wahl ranked Olson's Lady Godiva as one of the top six Northwest winter-run steelhead patterns, provided the tying recipe, and told Schwab that the judge "likes 'em big—to 3/0." In other letters, Wahl referred to the Lady Godiva as a "hot pattern," a "fabulous" fly, and the "wonder bug." Finally, McClane's *The American Angler* confirmed that Olson had made his mark in steelhead fly fishing history. Between 1936 and 1955, Olson had seven prize-winning fish recorded in the annual *Field & Stream* contests and his wife had one. In comparison, Wahl

RALPH OLSON FISHING THE STAMP RIVER IN BRITISH COLUMBIA IN AUGUST 1935
(RALPH E. WAHL PHOTOGRAPHIC COLLECTION, CENTER FOR PACIFIC NORTH-
WEST STUDIES, WESTERN WASHINGTON UNIVERSITY)

had five, fellow Washingtonians Al Knudson and Enos Bradner had four
each, and Northern Californians Bill Schaadt and Harry Hornbrook had two
each. McClane's list of the top 50 fly-caught steelhead shows that—thanks
to Olson and Wahl especially—11 were caught in the Skagit (the famed Eel
in California produced nine, and both rivers were soon to be surpassed by
large steelhead from British Columbia's Bulkley and Kispiox rivers).

Misfortune struck Judge Olson on January 15, 1955, when he collapsed

at his Olympia home from a brain aneurysm. He died later that day at a nearby hospital at the age of 52. Shocked and surprised, since there had been no signs of illness in the judge's life, Chief Justice Frederick G. Hamley remarked, "We will miss him as an affectionately regarded friend and an able colleague, learned in the law." Hamley also noted that Olson "was held in highest esteem by the entire bar and judiciary" and declared that his passing was "a great loss to all of the people of our state."

Olson's fishing friends remembered and missed him too, but none more than Ralph Wahl. In a touching photographic tribute sent to the judge's widow a month after his death, Wahl remembered that "Ralph's love for fishing was deep-seated and sincere. He enjoyed the solitude of lonely places and was fascinated with even the smallest things in nature. Marking the water-height of the river was a ritual with him, and a change, either up or down, provided unlimited speculative conversation." Wahl also observed that Olson's "keenest delight was to catch a bigger fish than I, which he did many times. I believe his supreme fishing pleasure was to fish behind me through a riffle and to hook a steelhead."

Wahl published a short essay titled "The Judge and I" in the Fly Fisher's Club of Oregon's newsletter, *The Creel*, in 1962, and told the readers that "right above me is a picture of the Judge holding up two steelhead. Pipe in mouth, he smiles down in perfect agreement when I say, 'Yes, sir.' The Judge and I had quite a time together.'" Enos Bradner discussed Olson's Lady Godiva and Orange Wing in *Northwest Angling* (1969), and Trey Combs provided a short biographical sketch of Olson and his two flies in *Steelhead Fly Fishing and Flies* (1976). The significance of Olson's two steelhead flies was also discussed by Pat Trotter in "Evolution of the Steelhead Fly" in *Flyfishing the West* (1978) and "Winter Flies, Winter Water" in *Salmon Trout Steelheader* (1979). More recently, Robert Arnold recognized both Wahl and Olson in his article "Ralph Wahl's Shangri-La," published in *Flyfishing* (1988). Olson's brilliant career as a judge was detailed in Charles H. Sheldon's book *The Washington High Bench: A Biographical History of the State Supreme Court, 1889–1991* (1992), and Wahl published "Journey to Harrison Lake" in *Flyfishing* that same year, describing a trip to British Columbia he had made with his friend Judge Olson.

KEN MCLEOD WITH A DEER CREEK STEELHEAD CAUGHT ON A
DRY FLY IN THE SUMMER OF 1931. (PHOTOGRAPH FROM *THE
NORTHWEST SPORTSMAN*) KEN AND GEORGE MCLEOD'S SKY-
KOMISH SUNRISE, TIED BY JON LUKE (INSET)

Chapter 22

Ken McLeod (1898–1987):

EARLY STEELHEAD FLY FISHERMAN, OUTDOOR WRITER, INNOVATOR, AND ENVIRONMENTALIST

Ken McLeod was born August 6, 1898, in Seattle, near Lake Union; when he was 5, his family moved to the Ravenna neighborhood near the University of Washington and Lake Washington. From here, young Ken began to fish with his older brother, Norm, especially for perch in the lake and trout in some of the local small streams. By the age of 16, Ken was taking the Kirkland ferry across the lake and hiking to the Tolt River near Carnation to fish for trout and steelhead. On the North Fork of the Tolt, in 1915, he saw a steelhead for the first time when the fish chased McLeod's single-salmon-egg bait to the surface.

McLeod was graduated in 1916 by Lincoln High School, where he competed in track and basketball. He took a job as a stenographer and bookkeeper for a local wallboard company and continued to fish and explore nearby rivers. In his late teens he became a proficient sea-run cutthroat angler, concentrating his efforts on the lower Stillaguamish. He was called to military duty by the U.S. Army in 1918 and attended the Central Infantry Officers Training School at Camp McArthur, Texas. His stint was short, however, because World War I ended later that same year.

"Determination to stay with a fly and an unwavering confidence that the feathered counterfeits, when fished properly, can be just as deadly as any metal or plastic lure go hand in hand in making a successful steelhead fly fisherman." —Ken McLeod

During the early 1920s, McLeod married Evelyn Slater and they had two children—a son, George, and a daughter, Mary. He landed his first steelhead in the lower canyon of the Sultan River on a spinner in 1921, and during that same summer he began taking three-day hikes to Deer Creek and the North Fork of the Stillaguamish near Arlington. In 1922 he caught his first steelhead on a fly (a Western Bee) in Deer Creek and also began to bait-fish for winter-run steelhead. He landed a 10-pound, 8-ounce steelhead in August the following year, placing third in the annual *Field & Stream* contest for fly-caught trout. He told the story of the trophy in the August 1924 issue of *Field & Stream* in an article titled "The End of the Rainbow." The story included a photograph of McLeod holding the 31-inch- summer-run steelhead.

By the mid-1920s McLeod was a devoted steelhead fly fisherman and regularly fished Deer Creek with dry flies. It was at this time, too, that he designed and began using a canvas stripping basket, or "bucket," as a place to coil his line before casting. He referred to it as "a practical portable casting platform" similar to the platform used by tournament casters. This innovation allowed him to "shoot" line, achieve longer casts, and get much longer drifts. He published "Deer Creek—Home of the Rainbow" in *Outdoor Life* in 1926 and began teaching his young son to fish and to cast. He admitted that "there was something compelling, something haunting about that fascinating little stream" and called Deer Creek steelhead "veritable tackle smashers." Two years later McLeod and some other steelheaders founded the Steelhead Trout Club of Washington, and he became president in 1930. In the interim he and two friends purchased some land below the mouth of Deer Creek, where they camped and fished on what he declared was "the most beautiful rainbow stream in the whole Northwest." He built a cabin there in the early 1940s.

McLeod began to write the outdoor news for the *Seattle Post-Intelligencer* in early 1931 and authored hundreds of columns through 1950. In June of 1931 he began publishing and editing *The Northwest Sportsman*, a monthly magazine in the "interest of outdoor recreation and the conservation of natural resources of the Northwest." Therein he authored articles on "Fishing for Sea-Run Cutthroat," "Fly Fishing for Big Trout," and "Caught in the Act: A Steelhead Story of the Stillaguamish," and also offered "Instructive Lessons on Steelhead Fishing" on the stream for $10 per day or "fly casting lessons" for $2 per hour. He also used his new magazine as a tool to spon-

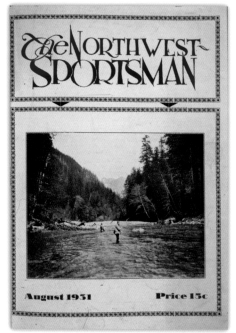

COVER OF THE AUGUST 1931 ISSUE OF *THE NORTHWEST SPORTSMAN*, WHICH MCLEOD EDITED AND PUBLISHED IN SEATTLE

sor and publicize a state initiative
to rid Washington of county game
control in favor of state control. By
late 1931 he had become secretary
of the newly formed Washington
State Conservation Association,
started "for the sole purpose of drafting, sponsoring and campaigning
for an initiative to submit to the
voters the next general election."
He also donated 10 percent of his
magazine's subscription income to
the cause. Initiative 62 passed in
1932, resulting in the formation of
separate state departments of fisheries and game.

Ken pioneered steelhead fly
fishing in the early 1930s on the Skykomish River, and, as members of the
Seattle Casting Club, he and his son, George, became champion fly casters.
McLeod also continued his political involvement in conservation issues in 1934,
working tirelessly to get Initiative 77 passed to outlaw fish traps, becoming
a founding member and secretary-treasurer of the Washington State Sports
Council, and serving as executive secretary of the Salmon Conservation League.
The following year, he helped get Deer Creek closed to fishing, served as an
adviser to the Washington State Legislative Fisheries Interim Committee, and
was responsible for getting $1 million from the federal government to screen

irrigation diversions in eastern Washington to protect steelhead and salmon on their downstream migrations. Some of this money was also used to build the Minter Creek Biological Station and the Issaquah Salmon Hatchery. Also in 1935, Washington officially designated steelhead as "game fish," thereby disallowing their sale in whole or in part and permitting only hook-and-line fishing.

The Skykomish Sunrise is "often used as a logo for the sport, very much analogous to the Royal Coachman and trout fishing . . . [and it] . . . is simply the most popular steelhead fly pattern in the history of the sport."
—*Trey Combs,* Steelhead Fly Fishing, *1991*

During the mid-1930s, Ken and George developed two of the most popular steelhead flies of all time. Since Ken did very little tying himself, son George and daughter Mary produced most of his flies. Accordingly, when George bought materials to tie a Montreal and got purple instead of claret, the Purple Peril was born. Originally tied as a dry fly, the wet version has since become the most popular dressing. It has a tail of purple hackle fibers, a body of purple floss, chenille or wool yarn, purple hackle, and a natural brown bucktail wing. The wet version also has a tag and rib of embossed silver tinsel. The Skykomish Sunrise resulted from observing the brilliant reds and oranges of a January sunrise as Ken and George drove to fish the Skykomish River for winter steelhead. George tied the fly with a tail of red and yellow hackle fibers, a red wool or chenille body ribbed with flat silver tinsel, red and yellow mixed hackle, and a white polar bear wing, all secured with red thread. Later, white bucktail was substituted for the polar bear. Trey Combs, in *Steelhead Fly Fishing* (1991), says the Skykomish Sunrise is "often used as a logo for the sport, very much analogous to the Royal Coachman and trout fishing," and that it "is simply the most popular steelhead fly pattern in the history of the sport."

Both Ken and George befriended Enos Bradner when he moved to Seattle and were members with him in the Steelhead Trout Club. After Ken and Enos tried to convince the membership to act more on behalf of the interests of fly anglers and got rebuked, they and a few others became charter members of the Washington Fly Fishing Club in 1939. It was this group, along with the eventual support of the Steelhead Trout Club and the Washington State Sports Council, that convinced the Washington State Department of Game to institute fly-only rules for the North Fork Stillaguamish and Pass Lake in 1941. This was accomplished through much hard work by Bradner, Letcher Lambuth, and Ken McLeod's "shrewd political knowledge," as described by Steve Raymond in *Backcasts: A History of the Washington Fly Fishing Club, 1939–1989.* McLeod still fished locally for rainbows, and after a trip to Lake

Ballinger, where the trout were feeding on tiny perch fry, he and George developed their Nylon Nymph in 1941.

It was during the 1940s that Ken fought several more battles for the good of the environment, especially speaking out against dams. After he heard that a dam was proposed for his beloved Deer Creek in the summer of 1941, he fired off a letter to the director of the U.S. Fish and Wildlife Service, saying, "My God, Fred, what a travesty this set-up is . . . if they destroy all of our migratory fish runs which provide recreation for hundreds of thousands of our citizens . . . we might as well sell our souls and submit like slaves to industrial serfdom, for that is where we are surely heading in this era of power and irrigation craze." In 1946 he fought against dams on the Nooksack and Skagit and was instrumental in getting the dam on the Green River moved from a planned site 6 miles above the town of Auburn upriver to Eagle Gorge, above the migratory fish range. Three years later, he and his sportsmen's groups fought against two proposed dams for the Cowlitz River, resulting in the establishment of the Lower Columbia River Sanctuary Act, affecting tributaries below Bonneville Dam.

Ken McLeod received national and international acclaim in the 1950s for his contributions to fly-line development and his exploits catching large steelhead on flies in British Columbia's Kispiox River. He had been making his own weighted shooting-heads with monofilament running line for several years before he was contacted in 1952 by Leon Martuch of Scientific Anglers to help his company design a sinking line. Scientific Anglers had pioneered with their Air Cel floating line; through the help of McLeod and a few others on the West Coast, the company began to produce Wet Cel lines and put them on the market in 1954. These lines revolutionized steelhead fly fishing, and anglers soon put them to good use on the Kispiox and other Northwest rivers. As a result of the new lines and the Skykomish Sunrise especially, larger and larger steelhead began to be entered in the *Field & Stream* contests from 1954 on.

For the Kispiox, the first-place fish in 1954 weighed 20 pounds, 8 ounces and was caught on a Skykomish Sunrise. George McLeod set a new world record the following year with his 29-pound, 2-ounce fish on a Skykomish Sunrise, and in 1957, using the same fly, he placed fourth with a 21-pound, 9-ounce fish. That same year, Ken placed second with his 23-pound, 14-ounce fish, also taken on a Skykomish Sunrise. Ken also took first place in 1959 for his 22-pound, 8.5-ounce steelhead, third in 1960 with a 17-pound, 3-ounce fish, and fourth in 1961 with a 17-pounder. While most of these record fish fell to the Skykomish Sunrise, a few were taken on a new fly called the McLeod Bucktail or McLeod Ugly. Art Lingren, in *Kispiox River Journal*, noted that it was "one of the first large black-bodied flies used for steelhead on the Kispiox." This fly continued to account for several more record steelhead in the Kispiox as well as other rivers in the 1960s and early '70s, including Ken's 27-pound third-place fish and Karl Mausser's first-place 27-pound, 8-ounce fish in 1970. In all, 17 of the 60 largest steelhead entered in the *Field & Stream* contest from

Ken McLeod fishing the famed Oso Pool on the North Fork Stillaguamish River in September 1970 (Ralph E. Wahl Photographic Collection, Center for Pacific Northwest Studies, Western Washington University)

the Kispiox between 1954 and 1975 were caught on a Skykomish Sunrise and four were caught on a McLeod Ugly.

McLeod had a lasting influence on many steelhead fly anglers through the authorship of a small Scientific Anglers booklet in 1962 titled *Steelhead on a Fly? Here's How*. It led many a novice to the sport and also helped convince others that it was possible to catch steelhead on flies. The booklet's preface stated, "Ken McLeod has long been recognized as a pioneering master. Many of the skills and techniques commonly used by steelhead fly fishermen are the results of his discoveries and developments." For encouragement, Ken told his readers, "Determination to stay with a fly and an unwavering confidence that the feathered counterfeits, when fished properly, can be just as deadly as any metal or plastic lure go hand in hand in making a successful steelhead fly fisherman." He explained also that the "truth is that some steelheads will hit a fly at any time under reasonable water conditions in any month of the year."

Ken kept active in state issues that related to fish and fishing, especially steelhead, in the late 1960s and 1970s. He was instrumental in the Washington State Legislature naming steelhead the state fish in 1969 and was one of several sportsmen leaders to fight the 1974 decision by Judge George Boldt that permitted more off-reservation netting of steelhead and salmon by Native Americans and made them comanagers of Washington's fish. He was still actively wading and fishing local rivers in the late 1970s when he was 80, and was pictured in a *Seattle Times* article in 1978, written to commemorate the 50th anniversary of the Steelhead Trout Club of Washington. For that anniversary, McLeod authored a 50-year history of the club and his old friend Enos Bradner wrote an article titled "Mr. Sportsman—Ken McLeod."

During the 1980s, Ken received several awards and recognition for a life of major achievements in outdoor writing, fly fishing, and conservation. In 1983, to celebrate the Washington Game Department's 50th anniversary, the Washington State Legislature commended him for 50 years of work with wildlife and natural resources, and the Department of Game honored him as "Founding Father." Two years later the National Wildlife Federation presented him a Special Achievement Conservation Award, and in 1986 the Washington Fly Fishing Club recognized McLeod for his "life-long work in conservation" with their Letcher Lambuth Angling Craftsman Award. Bob Arnold's tribute to Ken, "Homage to Ken McLeod," was published in the January/February 1986 issue of *Flyfishing* and referred to him as a "living history of steelhead fly fishing." The following year, on a Sunday in October, Ken McLeod died at his home from a massive stroke at the age of 89. His obituary in the *Seattle Post-Intelligencer* said he was an " 'environmentalist' before there even was such a word" and described him as "a tireless and fearless fighter for the state's fish and game." In the obituary published in *Flyfishing*, Arnold referred to McLeod as an "innovator and pioneer." His son, George, lives in Anacortes, Washington, and his grandson, Ken James McLeod, lives in the Seattle area and is actively involved in many outdoor-related clubs and organizations.

Ken McLeod ready to go fish the Kalama River in the 1970s (photograph courtesy of Robert L. Bettzig)

RALPH WAHL WITH A 15.5-POUND STEELHEAD CAUGHT IN SEPTEMBER 1956 IN BRITISH COLUMBIA'S KISPIOX RIVER. (RALPH E. WAHL PHOTOGRAPHIC COLLECTION, CENTER FOR PACIFIC NORTHWEST STUDIES, WESTERN WASHINGTON UNIVERSITY). RALPH WAHL'S LORD HAMILTON FLY, TIED BY JON LUKE (INSET)

Chapter 23

Ralph E. Wahl (1906–1996):

PHOTOGRAPHER AND PIONEER WINTER-RUN STEELHEADER

One of seven children, Ralph E. Wahl was the son of Joseph and Anna Wahl of Bellingham, Washington. Ralph was born on April 2, 1906, and attended public schools in his hometown. His father owned and operated the J. B. Wahl Department Store and the Grand Theatre, and young Ralph worked at both, sometimes making store deliveries on his bicycle. He began fishing at the age of 14 and started reading outdoor magazines. Cutthroat were his primary target, and he regularly used single salmon eggs to fish the local streams. By the time he graduated from high school in 1923, he had read about distant rivers like the Eel and Umpqua and begun an interest in photography.

After attending the University of Washington for one year, Wahl returned to Bellingham to work for his father. He also began shooting color slides and started to amass a large collection of rural scenes from Whatcom and Skagit counties, and photographs of local rivers, family life, animals, fish and fishing, and boats and ships. In 1925, while fishing on the nearby Samish River, Ralph saw two fly fishermen catch several cutthroat. He remembered that "it was a revelation to me" and began to try fly fishing. His first fish on a fly was a 3-pound cutthroat from Whatcom Creek, and after that he "gave up my bait and spinner ways for fly fishing." At the time, he "knew nothing about steelhead," but he began to learn fly fishing through trial and error, and explored new waters. He caught his first steelhead on a fly in Squalicum Creek in 1927. Since he had a six-day workweek, he devoted most of his Sundays to fishing. By the early 1930s, Wahl was tying his own flies and fishing for summer-run steelhead and cutthroat in the Skagit River and the North Fork of the Stillaguamish River. It was at this time that he began a lifelong fishing friendship with Les Townley, also from Bellingham. He also developed his first fly, Wahl's Cutthroat, at this time, and became aware of *Field & Stream's* annual fishing contests. He had read about the fabulous winter-run steelheading in California's Eel River and began to think that "maybe we could do something like that up here on the Skagit." In 1936 he and Townley began fishing the Skagit in earnest for winter-run steelhead, and he carried a camera on every trip.

It took a while to catch a winter steelhead, but Wahl's first two summer-run steelhead from the Skagit came in September 1936 from an area that would soon become his secret "Shangri-La." Here he caught what he described as "the most beautiful trout I had ever seen," and immediately thereafter he "bought an E. C. Powell cane rod, the largest size Medalist fly reel, 200 yards of 18-pound test white linen backing, a GBG silk casting line, some heavy silkworm gut tapered leaders, and a few home-tied bucktail flies." At that point in time, Wahl had become, in his own mind, "a full-fledged steelhead fly fisherman."

After his father died in 1937, Wahl took over management of the store and theater with two of his brothers and began running the movie projector in the evenings. This allowed him more time to fish on weekdays, and in 1939 he caught his first winter-run steelhead. He used a Cummings pattern he saw in Ray Bergman's *Trout* to hook the 16-pound, 9-ounce April fish. It placed second in the *Field & Stream* contest for Western Rainbow Trout—Fly Casting Division, and was the first Skagit River fish to place in the annual contests. At this same time, Wahl started his fishing diaries and also wrote letters to *Field & Stream* protesting the fact that their contest began on April 1 and ended December 31, thereby eliminating most of Washington's large winter-run fish from competition. He particularly noted that the Eel's "earlier winter runs had a decided advantage and consequently were able to dominate the earlier contests."

In early 1940, Wahl began to fish winter-run steelhead with Ralph Olson, a judge from Bellingham. They did a lot of experimentation with their own flies and fished on the Skagit at Grandy Creek, Hamilton Bar, and Jackman Creek, with the Shangri-La pool "pretty much a summer show," and as an "alternate to the splendid summer-run fishing available in the North Fork of the Stillaguamish River." In 1940 they hooked 16 winter-runs and landed nine, in 1941 they hooked 23 and landed nine, and the following year they hooked 52 and landed 28. It was in this year, too, that Wahl and Olson found "Mystery Lake," where they "took fresh-run summer steelhead," and Letcher Lambuth traveled to Bellingham to invite the two fly fishermen to join the Washington Fly Fishing Club. Here, Wahl met and became friends with Enos Bradner and Tommy Brayshaw, among other pioneers and legends.

> *"It's a comparatively new sport, this fly-fishing for winter steelheads. . . . Five years ago it was a downright rarity to meet a fisherman bent on taking a steelhead with nothing but an artificial fly during the dead of winter."*
> —*Ralph Wahl, 1943*

Wahl published "Winter Steelheads on Flies" in the February 1943 issue of *Field & Stream*, admitting, "It's a comparatively new sport, this fly-fishing for winter steelheads," and noting, "Five years ago it was a downright rarity to meet a fisherman bent on taking a steelhead with nothing but an artificial fly during the dead of winter." Yet, because of Wahl's pioneering efforts, he predicted in the article that "fly-fishing will soon become an accepted method of taking winter steelheads in most of the rivers that empty into the ocean."

RALPH WAHL'S FIRST SUMMER-RUN STEELHEAD FROM THE
SKAGIT RIVER, CAUGHT ON SEPTEMBER 20, 1936 (PHOTO-
GRAPH BY LES TOWNLEY; RALPH E. WAHL PHOTOGRAPHIC
COLLECTION, CENTER FOR PACIFIC NORTHWEST STUDIES,
WESTERN WASHINGTON UNIVERSITY)

The next year, on a business trip to New York City, Wahl visited the *Field
& Stream* offices and complained once more about the starting date of the
fishing contest for western rainbow trout/steelhead. In 1945, *Field & Stream*
changed the beginning date to January 1. Almost immediately, West Coast rivers
such as the Klamath, Rogue, Umpqua, Skagit, and Wilson began to show up in
the prize-winning categories. With January, February, and March now open for
contest entries, Wahl and Olson, as well as Townley and a few other Northwest
pioneers, including Wes Drain, Walt Johnson, and Al Knudson, began to place

"Ledge Pool," Grande Ronde River, October 15, 1964. (Ralph E. Wahl Photographic Collection, Center for Pacific Northwest Studies, Western Washington University)

regularly. As a result of this change, 11 of the top 50 largest steelhead in the *Field & Stream* contest between 1945 and 1954 were caught in the Skagit River. The second most productive river was the Eel, with nine on the list.

Wahl read steelhead fly-fishing articles by Peter Schwab in several issues of *Sports Afield* in 1946 and began to incorporate some of Schwab's ideas as well as those of Jim Pray into his own flies, equipment, and technique. In the early 1940s he named his first two steelhead flies Lord Hamilton and Lady Hamilton "after a little settlement on the Skagit River where a lot of steelhead history has been made." In a letter to Schwab in 1950, he noted that there were "five color phases in the group [the Skagit series] and represented the results of trial and error experimentation." He went on to explain that their "overstuffed doped bodies are their bid for individuality" and that he believed "impregnating with dope produces a fast sinking fly which I feel casts easier than flies weighted with lead or wire." He introduced his Kalamity K fly in 1949, named after the Kalama River and Mike Kennedy, "one of the first to prospect the fly fishing on that river and who unselfishly shared his best waters with me." Wahl and his wife, Jean, visited Schwab on the Klamath in September 1950 and soon thereafter began using some of his short shooting-heads.

By the early 1950s, Wahl had become one of the top fly fishermen in the Northwest. He traveled extensively, taking at least three trips to Alaska with Bradner and to the Kispiox and Babine with Bradner and George McLeod. It was in 1952 that he named one of his favorite flies Painted Lady. It evolved gradually from his Silver Rascal and Miss Wahleye (mid-1940s), and Wahl remembered that "from the start she had a way with big buck steelhead and lured many to their doom." He told Schwab that "if ever a steelhead fly possessed grace, poise and beauty, this was it." That same year, in March, Wahl took a 16-pounder from the Skagit that placed third in the *Field & Stream* contest. The following year, Wahl purchased a new German-made Exacta camera and his life as a photographer was immediately and dramatically changed. It was the first 35 mm single lens reflex camera made, and for the first time he could see the full size of what he was photographing through the lens. He also began shooting black-and-white film, developing his own photos and enlarging them in his darkroom. For Wahl, black and white was "more expressive" and could better "project my feelings." Photography was an important part of his fishing, and he took hundreds of photographs wherever he went. Wahl's 18-pound, 10-ounce Skagit steelhead placed fifth in the 1954 *Field & Stream* contest, and the following year his 16-pound, 12-ounce Kispiox steelhead, caught on his new Yum Yum pattern, placed sixth.

Between 1962 and 1965, Wahl developed a fly a year. He was striving for compactness and a quick, deep sink, so he used heavy hooks, up to 2/0, with heavy cement on the floss or tinsel, short wings, and sparse hackle. His Winter Fly came in 1962, followed by Paint Pot, Purple Charmer, and Wahlflower. Wahl and Bradner drove to Eugene in June 1965 for the inaugural national conclave of fly-fishing clubs and set up a photo display for the attendees. From this meeting the Federation of Fly Fishers (FFF) was formed, and Wahl became very active in this group. In fact, he said the fishermen he met there, particularly Lee Wulff, "changed my complete outlook on fly fishing. They were sincere and pointed me in the right direction." Specifically, Wahl was impressed with the concept of catch-and-release, and he "began turning back a lot of fish after this." He developed his Winter Fly Gold Body in 1966 and the Redwing the following year. Then, in early March 1967, at the Shangri-La pool with Les Townley, Wahl landed a 20-pound, 8-ounce buck steelhead on a size 4 Winter Fly and 10-pound leader. It surpassed Wes Drain's former state-record fly-caught steelhead by 1 ounce and brought considerable attention to Wahl, his flies, and the Skagit River.

Wahl's reputation as a photographer developed and spread significantly through the 1960s, with his black-and-white photos appearing in *Outdoor Life*, *Field & Stream*, *Life*, *Time*, *Argosy*, and *True*, among others. His photos were also used by a variety of editors to illustrate some of Roderick Haig-Brown's articles and books, and they became friends. They also shared a common friend in Tommy Brayshaw. Unknown to Haig-Brown, Wahl had a book idea in mind. He remembered reading Haig-Brown's classic book *A River Never Sleeps* and realized that "certain passages . . . seemed to describe perfectly some of my angling photographs . . . and found more than 60 of my photographs in his prose. . . . It seemed as if like minds had been similarly inspired, only the methods of expression had been different—a camera and pen." Wahl made two mock-ups of a book of his fishing photographs accompanied by excerpts from Haig-Brown's book, and he showed them to Haig-Brown in 1969. As Ann Haig-Brown watched her husband's reaction, she said to Wahl, "Look, Roddy's crying." Overjoyed, impressed, and surprised, Haig-Brown told Wahl, "We must get this published right away." Two years later, in 1971, *Come Wade the River* was published. Haig-Brown was "honored" and

RALPH WAHL WROTE THE TWO BOOKS SHOWN: *ONE MAN'S STEELHEAD SHANGRI-LA*, 1969 AND *COME WADE THE RIVER*, 1971

"proud and happy in the association," and referred to the book as "the concept and product of a single mind, one man's insight into something beautiful and deeply felt." The book meant a lot to Wahl, too, who told his friend Steve Raymond that it was "my monument."

Much recognition was bestowed upon Wahl and his many fly-fishing accomplishments during the 1970s. His photographs graced the covers of several issues of *The Flyfisher*; Trey Combs featured his photos and flies in *The Steelhead Trout* (1971) and in *Steelhead Fly Fishing and Flies* (1976); he was elected to the FFF board of directors and he became a director of the Flyfisher Foundation in Oregon; Steve Raymond wrote about him and "Mystery Lake" in *The Year of the Angler* (1973); the Museum of American Fly Fishing in Manchester, Vermont, invited him to be a trustee and hosted his photographic exhibit, "Fly Fishing the Northwest," in 1975; and, in 1977 and 1978, respectively, the Washington Fly Fishing Club honored him with their Tommy Brayshaw Award and the Letcher Lambuth Angling Craftsman Award.

In 1981, at the age of 75, Wahl began consulting his diaries and started writing about Shangri-La for *Random Casts*, the newsletter of the Fourth Corner Flyfishers in Bellingham. In all, he wrote 23 segments over five years about his once-secret spot, which had finally disappeared after years and years of flood damage. In 1987, according to Steve Raymond, publisher Frank Amato "recognized its worth as a priceless part of Northwest angling lore and expressed interest in publishing it." By the time *One Man's Steelhead Shangri-La* was published in 1989, Wahl had suffered two slight heart attacks and a stroke and was soon confined to his home in a wheelchair. Recognition and accolades continued to come Wahl's way, and his photographs were still being used to illustrate books and articles. Raymond used Wahl's photograph of the North Fork of the Stillaguamish's famous Elbow Hole for the cover of *Steelhead Country* (1991) and dedicated the book to Wahl and Bradner, his two steelhead fly-fishing mentors.

Even when Wahl was in his late 80s, he still tried to keep active in fly-fishing circles. He wrote articles for *Flyfishing* and *The Osprey*, did interviews for writers and videos, and worked with Steve Raymond to plan an exhibit for the Whatcom Museum of History and Art in Bellingham, to be called "Come Wade the River: The Nature of Northwest Fly Fishing." Wahl passed away at the age of 90, just before the exhibit opened in August 1997, but his contributions were obvious to those who attended. Tributes to Wahl appeared in several different fly-fishing publications, but none was as special as the gift of his entire personal collection of writings, photographs, movies, and tape recordings to the Center for Pacific Northwest Studies at Western Washington University in Bellingham by his sons in 2001. It will remain as a permanent remembrance of one of the Northwest's true pioneers in winter-run steelhead fly fishing and an artist who captured through his camera lens the thrill, beauty, and grandeur of being close to fish and rivers.

Selected Bibliography

"Abraham Rites Set for Today—Prominent Resident Widely-Known Sportsman." *Morning Oregonian* (September 30, 1936): 15.

Alsup, Dan. *Driftboats: A Complete Guide.* Portland, OR: Frank Amato Publications, 2000.

Amato, Frank. "The Original Inspiration Behind *Salmon Trout Steelheader.*" *Salmon Trout Steelheader* (July 1982): 7.

Arnold, Robert C. The Story Behind the Development of Today's Modern Steelhead Fly Lines." *Salmon Trout Steelheader* (October/November 1980): 22–27.

———. "Homage to Ken McLeod." *Flyfishing* 8 (January/February 1986): 42–43.

———. "Ralph Wahl's Shangri-La." *Flyfishing* 11 (November/December 1988): 6–12.

———. "Enos Bradner: Our Three Occasions." *Flyfishing* 13 (November/December 1990): 70–71, 78–80.

Auger, F. S. "General Money." *The Creel* (Official Newsletter of the Fly Fisher's Club of Oregon) 10 (December 1973): 17–19.

Barnes, Bill. "Sabalo Aqui!" *Double Haul* 8 (Fall/Winter 1976): 4–7.

Barnes, Duncan. "Ted Trueblood, 1913–1982." *Field & Stream* 87 (November 1982): 9.

Barrett, Peter. "The Real Ted Trueblood." *Field & Stream* 75 (December 1970): 42–43, 94–100.

———. "The Trout Flies of Ted Trueblood." *Field & Stream* 91 (May, 1986): 129–30, 134.

Bates, Joseph D., Jr. *Streamer Fly Fishing in Fresh and Salt Water.* New York, NY: Van Nostrand, 1950.

———. *Streamers and Bucktails: The Big-Fish Flies.* New York, NY: Alfred A. Knopf, 1979.

Baughman, Michael. *A River Seen Right: A Fly Fisherman's North Umpqua.* New York, NY: Lyons & Burford, 1995.

Beckham, Stephen D. *Land of the Umpqua: A History of Douglas County, Oregon.* Roseburg, OR: Douglas County Commissioners, 1986.

Bergman, Ray. *Trout.* New York, NY: Alfred A. Knopf, 1952.

Berryman, Jack W. "Classics of Angling Literature—Roderick L. Haig-Brown's *A River Never Sleeps* (1946)." *Salmon Trout Steelheader* 20 (June/July 1987): 44–47.

Blanton, Dan. "King Salmon: California & Oregon Style." *American Angler* (July/August 1992): 32–39, 64–66.

———. "Shooting Heads: Broadening Your Saltwater Fly Fishing Horizons." *Saltwater Fly Fishing* (April 1993): 50–55, 68–69.

———. *Fly Fishing California's Great Waters.* Portland, OR: Frank Amato Publications, 2003.

Bradner, Enos. "The Bugs of Bunyan." *Forest and Stream* 100 (July 1930): 498–99, 527-529.

———. "Steelheads from the Stilly." *Field & Stream* 48 (May 1943): 20–21, 71, 93.

———. *Northwest Angling.* Portland, OR: Binfords & Mort, 1969.

———. *Fish On!* Seattle, WA: Superior Publishing, 1971.

———. *The Inside on the Outdoor*s. Seattle, WA: Superior Publishing, 1973.

Brayshaw, Tom. "Hints on Making Wooden Fish Models." *The Creel* 5 (April 1967): 8–10.

Brooks, Joseph. *Salt Water Fly Fishing.* New York, NY: Putnam, 1950.

———. *The Complete Book of Fly Fishing.* New York, NY: Outdoor Life, 1958.

———. *Trout Fishing.* New York, NY: Outdoor Life, 1972.

Bulfinch, Kent. "Queen Bess Bucktail and Silver Demon." *Fly Tyer Magazine* 4 (February 1982): 40–41.

Carter-Hepworth, Mary, Sarah B. Davis, and Alan Virta. *The Ted Trueblood Collection at Boise State University: A Guide to the Papers of One of America's Foremost Outdoor Writers and Conservationists.* Boise, ID: Boise State University, 2000.

Cave, Robert B. *Roderick Haig-Brown: A Descriptive Bibliography.* Citrus Heights, CA: By the author, 2000.

Chatham, Russell. "Striped Bass with a Fly." *Field & Stream* 75 (April 1971): 62–63, 203-209.

———. "By the Cellblock and the Bay." *Sports Illustrated* 39 (November 12, 1973): 60–66.

———. "The World's Best." *Sports Illustrated* 41 (December 2, 1974): 91–102.

———. *The Angler's Coast.* Garden City, NY: Doubleday & Co., 1976.

———. *Silent Seasons.* New York, NY: E. P. Dutton, 1978.

———. *Dark Waters: Essays, Stories, and Articles.* Livingston, MT: Clark City Press, 1988.

———. "A Life, and a Loss: Bill Schaadt, 1922–1995," *California Fly Fisher* (March/April 1995): 20–21.

Checchio, Michael. *Being, Nothingness, and Fly Fishing.* Guilford, CT: Lyons Press, 2001.

Clement, Skip, and Andrew Derr. *Fly Fishing the Florida Keys: The Guide's Guide.* Portland, OR: Frank Amato Publications, 2005.

Combs, Trey. "Ralph Wahl, Fly Fisherman, Photographer." *Salmon Trout Steelheader* (December/January 1972): 13.

———. "Washington's Pioneering Winter Steelhead Fly Fisherman." *Salmon Trout Steelheader* (February/March 1972): 12.

———. "Brigadier General Noel Money: Canadian Angling Great of Vancouver Island, Part I." *Salmon Trout Steelheader* (April/May, 1972): 21.

———. "Brigadier General Noel Money: Canadian Angling Great of Vancouver Island, Part II." *Salmon Trout Steelheader* (June/July 1972): 21–23.

———. *Steelhead Fly Fishing and Flies*. Portland, OR: Frank Amato Publications, 1976.

———. *The Steelhead Trout: Life History, Early Angling, Contemporary Steelheading*. Portland, OR: Frank Amato Publications, 1988. (1st ed. 1971.)

———. *Steelhead Fly Fishing*. New York, NY: Lyons Press, 1991.

Conley, Clare. "Where He Longed to Be." *Outdoor Life* 170 (November 1982): 1.

Conley, Jackson R. "Introducing Ken McLeod." *Northwest Sportsman* 1 (June 1931):14.

"Dan Bailey, 1903–1982: A Last Talk." *Trout* 23 (Summer 1982): 20–22.

de Yonge, John. "Bradner Wrote Bible for Fishers." *Seattle Post-Intelligencer* (January 18, 1984): A-7.

"Enos Bradner, Outdoor Writer." *Seattle Post-Intelligencer* (January 14, 1984): B-8.

"A Farewell to Dan Bailey and Lou Bell." *Flyfisher* 15 (Summer 1982): 23.

Ferguson, Bruce, Les Johnson, and Pat Trotter. *Fly Fishing for Pacific Salmon*. Portland, OR: Frank Amato Publications, 1985.

Gadbow, Daryl. "The Trials and Tribulations of a Legendary Fly." *Missoulian* (June 7, 1990): C-1–2.

Grant, George F. "The Historic Montana Trout Fly—From Tradition to Transition." *American Fly Fisher* 1 (Spring 1974): 20–21.

———. "Franz Pott: Western Original." *American Fly Fisher* 7 (Spring 1980): 21–23.

———. *The Master Fly Weaver*. Portland, OR: Champoeg Press, 1980.

———. "Bunyan Bugs." *American Fly Fisher* 8 (Summer, 1981): 12-14.

———. *Montana Trout Flies: A Study, Discussion and Review of Most of the Popular Trout Flies*. Portland, OR: Champoeg Press, 1981.

———. "Don Martinez: Western Dry Fly Master." *American Fly Fisher* 9 (Spring 1982): 8–14.

———. "Some Fragments of Trout Fly History: Walton to Whitlock." *Fly Tyer* 5 (November 1982): 54–55.

Green, Ranny. "The State's Oldest Sportsmen's Club." *Seattle Times* (October 22, 1978): Pictorial, 11–15.

Grescee, Paul. "Crusader in Hip Boots." *International Wildlife* 7 (January/February 1977): 36–39.

Grey, Loren. *Zane Grey: A Photographic Odyssey*. Dallas, TX: Taylor Publishing, 1985.

Grey Zane. *Tales of Fishes*. New York, NY: Harper & Brothers, 1919.

———. *Tales of the Angler's Eldorado New Zealand*. New York, NY: Harper & Brothers, 1926.

———. *Zane Grey: The Man and His Work—An Autobiographical Sketch, Critical Appreciations & Bibliography*. New York, NY: Harper & Brothers, 1928.

———. *Tales of Fresh-Water Fishing*. New York, NY: Harper & Brothers, 1928.

———. *Rogue River Feud*. New York, NY: Grosset & Dunlap 1929.

Gruber, Frank. *Zane Grey: A Biography*. New York, NY: World Publishing, 1970.

Haig-Brown, Roderick L. *A River Never Sleeps*. New York, NY: W. Morrow & Co., 1946.

———. *The Western Angler: An Account of Pacific Salmon & Western Trout in British Columbia*. New York, NY: William Morrow & Co., 1947. (1st ed. 1939.)

———. *Measure of the Year*. New York, NY: Morrow, 1950.

———. *Fisherman's Spring*. Toronto: Collins, 1951.

———. *Fisherman's Summer*. Toronto: Collins, 1959.

———. *Fisherman's Fall*. Toronto: Collins, 1964.

———. "My Friend, Tom Brayshaw." *The Creel* 5 (April 1967): 6–7.

———. "Winter Steels and the Fly." *Outdoor Life* 140 (November 1967): 36–39, 93–97.

———. "Tom Brayshaw: Artist—Craftsman—Flyfisher." in Starkman, Susan B., and Stanley E. Read, comp., *The Contemplative Man's Recreation: A Bibliography of Books on Angling and Game Fish in the Library of the University of British Columbia*. Vancouver, BC: The Library of the University of British Columbia, 1970, 15–52.

———. "The Evolution of a Steelhead Fly." *Roundtable* (January/February 1976): 12–14.

———. *Bright Water, Bright Fish. An Examination of Angling in Canada*. Vancouver, BC: Douglas & McIntyre, 1980.

Haig-Brown, Valerie, ed. *From the World of Roderick Haig-Brown: The Master and His Fish*. Seattle, WA: University of Washington Press, 1981.

————. *Deep Currents: Roderick and Ann Haig-Brown.* Victoria, BC: Orca Book Publishers, 1997.

Hardin, Thomas. "Wizard of West Coast Flies." *True* (April 1952): 54–56, 65–70.

Harris, Ron. "Zane Grey Rediscovered—Part 1." *Fly Rod & Reel* 13 (January/February 1992): 54–55, 72–76.

————. "Zane Grey Rediscovered—Part 2." *Fly Rod & Reel* 14 (March 1992): 64–70.

Hedge, Marvin. *Accurate Fishing and Long Distance Fly Casting Made Easy.* Portland, OR: Privately printed, circa 1960.

Helvie, H. Kent. *Steelhead Fly Tying Guide.* Portland, OR: Frank Amato Publications, 1994.

Hidy, Pete. "The Flyfisher's West." *American Fly Fisher* 7 (Spring 1980): 2–8.

Hidy, V. S. "The Champion from Oregon." *The Creel* 3 (July 1964): 7–12.

Hogan, Dec. *Steelhead River Journal: Skagit-Sauk.* Portland, OR: Frank Amato Publishing, 1995.

Hughes, Dave. "The Importance of Polly Rosborough." *Fly Fisherman* 15 (December 1983): 42–44.

————. "Polly Rosborough, 1902–1997." *Fly Fisherman* 29 (May 1998): 32, 34.

Hunt, Richard C. "The Paradoxical Firehole." *Anglers Club Bulletin* 27 (January 1948): 32–34.

Hutchison, Bruce. *The Fraser.* Toronto: Clarke, Irwin, 1950.

Inland Empire Fly Fishing Club. *Flies of the Northwest.* Portland, OR: Frank Amato Publications, 1998.

Jennings, Adele F. "Our Trip West." *American Fly Fisher* 11 (Spring 1984): 20–21.

Jennings, Preston J. *A Book of Trout Flies; Containing a List of the Most Important American Stream Insects & Their Imitations.* New York, NY: Crown, 1935.

"The Jim Pray Steelhead Flies." *American Fly Fisher* 7 (Spring 1980): 12–13.

Johnson, Les. *Sea-Run.* Portland, OR: Frank Amato Publications, 1979.

Johnson, Walter C. "Fairy Wands and Fighting Steelhead." *Salmon Trout Steelheader* (August/September 1982): 70, 61–62.

Johnston, Greg. "Bradner Recalled as Good Fisherman, Writer." *Seattle Post-Intelligencer* (January 17, 1984): B-4.

————. " 'Father' of State Department of Game Dead at 89." *Seattle Post-Intelligencer* (October 27, 1987): D-4.

Keith, W. J. "Roderick Haig-Brown." *Canadian Literature* No. 71 (Winter 1976): 7–20.

Korich, Chris. "Profile/Jim Green." *The Creel* 3 (1980): 3–4.

Krieder, Claude M. *Steelhead.* New York, NY: G. P. Putnam's Sons, 1948.

Lambuth, Letcher. "Salt Water Fly Fishing." *American Fly Fisher* 2 (Spring 1975): 14–15.

————. *The Angler's Workshop.* Portland, OR: Champoeg Press, 1979.

————. "McKenzie River Rainbows: Oregon Trout Fishing in the 1930's." *American Fly Fisher* 7 (Spring 1980): 10–11.

Lampman, Ben Hur. "Champion Fly Caster Hails from Portland." *Oregonian* (March 22, 1936): magazine section, 1ff.

"The Late Peter Schwab on Rods, Lines, and Casting." *Fly Fisherman* 4 (December/January 1973): 18–23.

Leonard, J. Edson. *Flies; Their Origin, Natural History, Tying, Hooks, Patterns and Selections of Dry and Wet Flies, Nymphs, Streamers, Salmon Flies for Fresh and Salt Water in North America and the British Isles, Including a Dictionary of 2200 Patterns.* New York, NY: A. S. Barnes, 1950.

"Letcher Lambuth . . . Artist and Pioneer in Angling Niceties." *The Creel* 11 (December 1974): 11–12.

Lilly, Bud, and Paul Schullery. *Bud Lilly's Guide to Fly Fishing the New West.* Portland, OR: Frank Amato Publications, 2000.

Lingren, Arthur James. *Fly Patterns of Roderick Haig-Brown.* Portland, OR: Frank Amato Publications, 1993.

————. *Fly Patterns of British Columbia.* Portland, OR: Frank Amato Publications, 1996.

————. *Famous British Columbia Fly-Fishing Waters.* Portland, OR: Frank Amato Publications, 2002.

————. *Kispiox River: River Journal.* Portland, OR: Frank Amato Publications, 2004.

"The Longest Cast on Record." *Oregonian* (June 11, 1937): 8.

Love, Glen, ed. *Fishing the Northwest: An Angler's Reader.* Corvallis, OR: Oregon State University Press, 2000.

Lowenstein, Steven. *The Jews of Oregon, 1850–1950.* Portland, OR: Jewish Historical Society of Oregon, 1987.

Macdowell, Syl. *Western Trout.* New York, NY: Alfred A. Knopf, 1948.

Maclean, Norman. *A River Runs Through It and Other Stories.* Chicago, IL: University of Chicago Press, 1976.

"Major J. L. Mott Dies on the Coast." *New York Times* (June 4, 1931): 27.

Martinez, Don. "The Right Dry Fly." *Field & Stream* 58 (June 1953): 68–72.

McAllister, Tom. "Mooch." *The Creel* 9 (December 1971): 18–21.

————. "Mike Kennedy 1910–1995." *Steelhead Fly Fishing Journal* 1 (Spring 1994): 8–11.

McClane, A. J. *The American Angler.* New York, NY: Holt, 1954.

McDonald, John. "The Best Vacation Trout Fishing." *Sports Illustrated* 1 (August 16, 1954): 54–56, 102–3.

————. "Dan Bailey: 1904–1982." *Fly Rod & Reel* 4 (May/June 1982): 46–47.

McFarland, Ron, and Hugh Nichols. *American Author Series: Norman Maclean.* Lewiston, ID: Confluence Press, 1988.

McGuane, Thomas. *The Longest Silence: A Life in Fishing*. New York, NY: Alfred A. Knopf, 1999.

McLeod, Kenneth. "The End of the Rainbow." *Field & Stream* (August 1924): 34, 96.

———. "Deer Creek—Home of the Rainbow." *Outdoor Life* (March 1926): 192–94.

———. "Steelhead Fishing with a Fly." *Taft's Sportsman's Guide and Handbook*. Seattle, WA: 1928: 145–49.

———. "Fishing for Sea-Run Cutthroat." *Northwest Sportsman* 1 (June 1931): 10–11.

———. "Caught in the Act: A Steelhead Story of the Stillaguamish." *Northwest Sportsman* 1 (August 1931): 8–9.

———. "Fly Fishing for Big Trout." *Northwest Sportsman* 1 (August 1931): 10.

———. *Steelhead on a Fly?* Scientific Anglers, 1962.

———. "Game's New Deal—1933–1983." *Washington Wildlife* (Fall 1983): 12–15, 35.

McMillan, Bill. "A Book with a Yellow Cover: The Influence of the Man's Life in Mine." *Wild Steelhead & Salmon* 3 (Spring 1997): 32–34.

Menke, Frank. *The Encyclopedia of Sports*. New York, NY: A. S. Barnes, 1975.

Merritt, Jim. "Dan Bailey." *Fly Rod & Reel* 3 (November/December 1981): 30–35.

———. "Norman Needn't Have Worried: On the Set for the Filming of 'A River Runs Through It.'" *Fly Rod & Reel* 13 (January/February 1992): 56–59.

Meyer, Deke. "Roderick Haig-Brown's Favorite Steelhead and Cutthroat Flies." *Salmon Trout Steelheader* 17 (June/July 1984): 18–21.

Monroe, Bill. "Polly Rosborough: Legend of the West Passes Away." *Flyfishing* 21 (March/April 1998): 32–33.

Mort, Terry. *Zane Grey on Fishing*. New York, NY: The Lyons Press, 2003.

Mott, Major Lawrence. "Steelheads on 2 1/4 Ounces of Bamboo: The Umpqua River Steelhead Is a Tricky Savage Fighter." *Forest and Stream* 100 (January 1930): 16–17, 80.

———. "Umpqua Salmon." *Forest and Stream* 100 (April 1930): 250–51, 278–80.

———. "Umpqua Steelheads." *Forest and Stream* 100 (July 1930): 496–97, 529–31.

Nauheim, Bob. "The Kings Come to the Smith." *Outdoor Life* 146 (October 1970): 90–93, 197–98.

———. "An Angler's Christmas: Gift of the Gualala." *Outdoor Life* 146 (December 1970): 50–51, 130–32.

———. "A Season of Giants." *Outdoor Life* 150 (September 1972): 72–75, 156, 159–60.

———. "The Line on Big Fish." *Outdoor Life* 150 (October 1972): 86–89, 164.

———. "The Portable Boat Man." *Outdoor Life* 151 (January 1973): 58, 94–99.

———. "Chinook Fly-Fishing in Theory and Practice." *Fishing World* (September/October 1973): 26–27, 49–51.

———. "A Life, and a Loss: Bill Schaadt, 1922–1995." *California Fly Fisher* (March/April 1995): 20–21, 49–50, 52.

Netherton, Cliff. *History of the Sport of Casting: People, Events, Records, Tackle and Literature—Early Times*. Lakeland, FL: American Casting Education Foundation, 1981.

———. *History of the Sport of Casting—Golden Years*. Lakeland, FL: American Casting Education Foundation, 1983.

Newell, Bob. "Bunyan Bug." *Fly Tyer* 5 (August 1982): 36.

"No More Line—Maurice Abraham." *Oregon Journal* (September 30, 1936): 23.

Nordstrand, John E. "California Steelhead Fly Fishing." *Salmon Trout Steelheader* (February/March 1997): 42–43, 70–71.

———. "Spectral Steelheading on California's Eel River: The Great-Granddaddy of Them All." *Wild Steelhead & Salmon* 4 (Winter 1998): 69–77.

Patrick, Roy A. *Pacific Northwest Fly Patterns*. Seattle, WA: Patrick's Fly Shop, 1964.

Pero, Tom. "The Grand Old Man." *Trout* 23 (Summer 1982): 4.

Phillips, Roger. "Ted Trueblood: Outdoor Writer Set the Benchmark." *Idaho Statesman* (March 28, 2002).

Pochin, W. F. *Angling and Hunting in British Columbia*. Vancouver, BC: Sun Directories Ltd., 1946.

Pratt, Alan. "Steelhead Flies . . . 30 Years of Evolution." *Seattle Times* (February 24, 1974): Pictorial, 32–36.

Randolph, John. "In the Bucket: Bill Schaadt, 1924–1995." *Fly Fisherman* 26 (May 1995): 4–5.

———. *Becoming A Fly Fisher: From Brookie Days to the Tenth Level*. Guilford, CT: The Lyons Press, 2002.

Raymond, Steve. *The Year of the Angler*. New York, NY: Winchester Press, 1973.

———. "Letcher Lambuth, 1889–1974." *American Fly Fisher* 1 (Fall 1974): 22–23.

———. *Kamloops: An Angler's Study of the Kamloops Trout*. Portland, OR: Frank Amato Publications, 1980. (1st ed. 1971.)

———. "Enos Bradner, Outdoorsman, Dies: Retired Times Outdoor Editor Shared His Knowledge Generously." *Seattle Times* (January 13, 1984): F-3.

———. *The Year of the Trout*. New York, NY: Winchester Press, 1985.

———. *Backcasts: A History of the Washington Fly Fishing Club, 1939–1989*. Seattle, WA: Washington Fly Fishing Club, 1989.

———. *Steelhead Country.* New York, NY: Lyons & Burford, 1991.

———. "Rediscovering Bill Nation." *Flyfishing* (November/December 1995): 20–21.

———. *Rivers of the Heart: A Fly-Fishing Memoir.* New York, NY: Lyons Press, 1998.

———. "Ralph Wahl Remembered." *Osprey* 46 (September 2003): 8–9.

———. *Blue Upright: The Flies of a Lifetime.* Guilford, CT: The Lyons Press, 2004.

Read, Stanley E. *Tommy Brayshaw: The Ardent Angler-Artist.* Vancouver, BC: University of British Columbia Press, 1977.

Reiger, George. *Zane Grey: Outdoorsman.* Englewood Cliffs, NJ: Prentice-Hall, 1972.

———. *Profiles in Saltwater Angling: A History of the Sport—Its People and Places, Tackle and Techniques.* Engle wood Cliffs, NJ: Prentice-Hall, 1973.

———. *The Undiscovered Zane Grey Fishing Stories.* Piscataway, NJ: New Century Publishers, 1983.

Richardson, Lee. *Lee Richardson's BC: Tales of Fishing in British Columbia.* Forest Grove, OR: Champoeg Press, 1978.

Rivkin, Mike. *Big-Game Fishing Headquarters: A History of the IGFA.* Dania Beach, FL: IGFA Press, 2005.

Robbins, Jim. "Fishing: A Love Story." *USA Weekend* (October 9–11, 1992): 4–7.

Robertson, Anthony. *Above Tide: Reflections on Roderick Haig-Brown.* Madeira Park, BC: Harbour Publishing Co., 1984.

Rosborough, E. H. "Polly." *Tying and Fishing the Fuzzy Nymphs.* Manchester, VT: The Orvis Co., 1969.

———. "Rosborough on Rosborough." *Flyfishing the West* 1 (March/April 1978): 33–34.

———. *Tying and Fishing the Fuzzy Nymphs.* Harrisburg, PA: Stackpole Books, 1978.

———. *Reminiscences from 50 Years of Flyrodding.* Caldwell, ID: Caxton Printers, 1982.

———. *Marten I Have Known.* OR: n.p., circa 1983.

"The Russian River's Steelhead." *Sunset* 121 (October 1958): 40, 42.

Schneider, Norris F. *Zane Grey: The Man Whose Books Made the West Famous.* Zanesville, OH: By the author, 1967.

Schullery, Paul. *American Fly Fishing: A History.* New York, NY: Lyons Books, 1987.

———. "Western Fly Fishing: The Discovery of a Great Tradition." *American Fly Fisher* 23 (Spring 1997): 2–4.

Schwab, Peter J. "Steelheading Diary (1)." *Sports Afield* 115 (April 1946): 22–23, 78–80.

———. "Steelheading Diary (2)." *Sports Afield* 115 (May 1946): 26–27, 80–82.

———. "Bucktails for Steelheads (1)." *Sports Afield* 115 (June 1946): 20–21, 82–85.

———. "Bucktails for Steelheads (2)." *Sports Afield* 116 (July 1946): 46–47, 72–75.

Schwarzkopf, Chet. "Genius of the Fishing Flies: C. Jim Pray, Eureka Sportsman." *Humboldt Standard* (December 14, 1950): 17.

Schwiebert, Ernest. "The Orchard and the River." *Fly Fisherman* (Spring 1978): 61–73.

"Sets Fly Casting Mark—Hedge Averages 141 Feet to Break 11-Year-Old Record." *New York Times* (August 24, 1934): 20.

Sheldon, Charles H. *The Washington High Bench: A Biographical History of the State Supreme Court, 1889–1991.* Pullman, WA: Washington State University Press, 1992.

Shewey, John. *Steelhead River Journal: North Umpqua.* Portland, OR: Frank Amato Publications, 1995.

———. *Oregon Blue-Ribbon Fly Fishing Guide.* Portland, OR: Frank Amato Publications, 1998.

Sloan, Stephen, ed. *Fly Fishing Is Spoken Here.* Guilford, CT: The Lyons Press, 2003.

Smedley, Harold. *Who's Who and What's What in Fly and Bait Casting in the United States, 1864–1941.* Muskegon, MI: West Shore Publications, 1941.

Staples, Bruce. *Snake River Country Flies and Waters.* Portland, OR: Frank Amato Publications, 1991.

———. *Trout Country Flies from Greater Yellowstone Area Masters.* Portland, OR: Frank Amato Publications, 2002.

Stewart, Dick, and Farrow Allen. *Flies for Steelhead.* Intervale, NH: Northland Press, 1992.

Sturgis, William B. *Fly-Tying.* New York, NY: Charles Scribner's Sons, 1940.

"Supreme Court Judge Olson Dies of Stroke." *Seattle Times* (January 16, 1955).

Swanson, Ronald S. "Fish Models, Plaques, and Effigies." *American Fly Fisher* 18 (Summer 1992): 7–13.

Swisher, Larry. "Ted Trueblood: Dean of Outdoor Writers Dies at 69." *Idaho Statesman* (September 14, 1982): A-1, A-8.

Tapply, William G. "A Horrible Looking Grub." *Fly Tyer* 6 (Spring 2000): 42–43, 65–66.

Tax, Jeremiah. "Lucky Readers Get a Second Crack at a Classic About Early Montana." *Sports Illustrated* 59 (October 17, 1983): 17.

Taylor, C. W., Jr. *Eminent Judges and Lawyers of the Northwest, 1843–1955.* Palo Alto, CA: By the author, 1954.

Trotter, Pat. "Matching the Pacific Northwest Hatch—Letcher Lambuth: The Pacific Northwest's Answer to Jennings, Flick and Marinaro." *Salmon Trout Steelheader* 8 (June/July 1975): 22–27.

———. "Evolution of the Steelhead Fly." *Flyfishing the West* (July/August 1978): 60–70.

———. "Deschutes Salmonfly Hatch." *Salmon Trout Steelheader* 12 (June/July 1979): 41–43, 50.

———. "Winter Flies—Winter Water." *Salmon Trout Steelheader* (December/January 1979): 45–49.

———. "Knowing Your Bugs with 'Western Hatches.'" *Salmon Trout Steelheader* 15 (April/May 1982): 40–41.

———. "Woolly Worms and Woolly Buggers." *Salmon Trout Steelheader* 19 (November 1985): 40–42.

———. "The Lord Iris Steelhead Fly." *Salmon Trout Steelheader* 21 (December/January 1988): 94, 85-87.

———. "Bucktails for Salmon in the Salt." *Salmon Trout Steelheader* 22 (August/September 1988): 59–61, 71.

———. "Hen Hackle: Other Thoughts for Next Season's Dry Flies." *Salmon Trout Steelheader* 24 (December/January 1991): 54–56.

"Trueblood Named Conservationist of the Year." *Field & Stream* 79 (June 1974): 110.

Trueblood, Ted. *The Angler's Handbook*. New York, NY: Thomas Crowell, 1949.

———. *Fishing Handbook*. Greenwich, CT: Fawcett, 1951.

———. *How to Catch More Fish*. Greenwich, CT: Fawcett, 1955.

———. "Heads for Shooting." *Field & Stream* 62 (March 1958), 16–17.

———. "Fly Lines Made Easy." *Field & Stream* 66 (May 1961): 26, 108–9, 157–59.

———. "Flies for Sophisticated Trout." *Field & Steam* 68 May 1963): 24–28.

———. "The Most Delightful Fishing." *Field & Stream* 68 (August 1963): 14–15, 105–6.

———. "Steelhead Fly Fishing." *Field & Stream* 68 (October 1963): 16, 20, 22, 88–89.

———. "The Low-Down Fly Line." *Field & Stream* 69 (May 1964): 24, 28, 30, 115–16.

———. "An Eclipse, and Other Strange Things." *Field & Stream* 84 (June 1979): 10, 26–27.

———. "The Rewards of Experimenting." *Field & Stream* 84 (July 1979): 8–10.

Van Fleet, Clark C. *Steelhead to a Fly*. Boston, MA: Little, Brown, 1954.

Wahl, Ralph. "Winter Steelheads on Flies." *Field & Stream* 47 (February 1943): 34–36, 51–52.

———. "Camera on the Kispiox—Fisherman's Scrapbook." *Seattle Times* (December 18, 1955): Pictorial, 12–14.

———. "The Judge and I." *The Creel* 2 (December 1962): 22–28.

———. *Come Wade the River: The Photography of Ralph Wahl with Excerpts from "A River Never Sleeps" by Roderick Haig-Brown*. Seattle, WA: Superior Publishing, 1971.

———. *One Man's Steelhead Shangri-La*. Portland, OR: Frank Amato Publications, 1989.

———. "Journey to Harrison Lake." *Flyfishing* (April 1992): 68–72.

———. "Ralph Wahl on the Skagit." *Osprey* 46 (September 2003): 17.

Waller, Pat and Gary. "Peter J. Schwab Fly Tyer, Fly Designer, and Fly Rod Designer." *Fishing Collectibles* 7 (Spring 1996): 13–17.

Waterman, Charles F. "Streamers & Near-Streamers." *Fishing World* 26 (November/December 1979): 2–5.

———. *A History of Angling*. Tulsa, OK: Winchester Press, 1981.

———. "Dan." *Fly Fisherman* 14 (December 1982): 40.

———. *Mist on the River: Remembrances of Dan Bailey*. Livingston, MT: Yellowstone Press, 1986.

Wendelburg, Tom. "The Flies That Won The West." *Fly Fisherman* 7 (Spring 1976): 62–66.

Whitehouse, Francis C. *Sport Fishing in Canada*. Vancouver, BC: By the author, 1945.

———. *Sport Fishes of Western Canada, and Some Others*. Toronto, ON: McClelland & Stewart, 1946.

Williams Arthur Bryan. *Rod and Reel in British Columbia*. Vancouver, BC: Progress Publishing Co., 1919.

———. *Game Trails in British Columbia: Big Game and Other Sport in the Wilds of British Columbia*. New York, NY: Scribner's, 1926.

———. *Fish & Game in British Columbia*. Vancouver, BC: Sun Directories, Ltd., 1935.

Wood, A. H. E. *Greased Line Fishing for Salmon*. Portland, OR: Frank Amato Publications, 1982.

Wiltshire, Bob. "IFFC Features Peter Schwab Display." *Flyfisher* 31 (Summer 1998): 24–25.

Wulff, Lee. "Dan Bailey & the Great Depression." *Fly Rod & Reel* 8 (May/June 1986): 64–63.

Wurdemann, Col. Harry Vanderbilt. "Fly Fishing for Pacific Salmon." *Northwest Sportsman* 1 (July 1932): 10.

Zern, Ed. *Zane Grey's Adventures in Fishing*. New York, NY: Harper & Brothers, 1952.

———. "Is There Really a Ted Trueblood?" *Field & Stream* 67 (October 1962): 144.

———. "Trueblood Is Thicker Than Butter." *Field & Stream* 84 (May 1979): 200, 130.

Index

Page numbers with *f* indicate
    photographs.

Abraham, Madge, 111–113, 114, 115
Abraham, Maurice "Mooch," 110–115,
    136
Air Cel lines, 181
Alevin (Brayshaw's), 23
Allcock Limerick hooks, 43
Allen, Zeke, 119, 120
Amato, Frank, 33–34, 192
Anderson, Ben, 55
Anderson, N. H., 156
Andrus, Cecil, 77, 79
Arnold, Robert, 141, 175, 183
Asam, Fred, 120
Ash River, 14–17
AT Specials (Pott's), 86
Auger, Fred, 13, 14, 18
awards/honors: British Columbia
    legends, 11, 14, 27, 35;
    Idaho's Trueblood, 78–79;
    Montana's Bailey, 107;
    Oregon legends, 114,
    120, 122*f,* 133, 146, 148;
    Washington legends, 158, 163,
    167, 183

Backus, William F., 112, 113, 135
Bacon, Sanford, ix, 164
Badger series (Pott's), 86, 87
Bailey, Dan, 84, 100–107
Bailey, Helen, 102, 107
Bailey, John, 107
Bailey Muddler, 103
Bair, Fred, 49, 53
Bair's series (Pray's), 49
bamboo rods, 90, 153–154
Bardon, Claude, 129
Barker, Thomas, 96
Barrett, Peter, 77
Bates, Joseph D., Jr., 40, 53
Baughman, Michael, 122
Bayley Pool, Smith River, 66
Beaty, Wilbur "Bill," 84
Bellamy, George, 42, 44
Bellamy fly (Schwab's), 44
"belly reel," 38, 42
Belmont Creek, 92*f*
Benn, John, 56
Bergman, Ray, 40, 96, 97–98, 122
Berisa, John, 48
Betten, H. L., 56
Bi-Fly (Bailey's), 103
Big Grey Stone Fly (Means'), 89

Big Hole River, 86, 92
Birch's Favorite (Martinez's), 97
Bi-Visible flies (Bailey's), 102
Black, Orange, and Jungle Cock
    (Money's), 17
Black, Tippet, and Yellow (Money's),
    17
Black Ant (Means'), 89
Black Creeper (Grant's), 84
Black Demon (Pray's), 48
Black Drake Nymph (Rosborough's),
    144, 145
Blackfoot River, 92–93
Black Jack (Pott's), 86, 87
Black Optic (Pray's), 46, 50, 64
Black Wulff (Bailey's), 102
Blanton, Dan, 68
Block, William C., 112, 114, 138
Blond Goofus Bug (Bailey's), 104
Bobbie Dunn (Schwab's), 43, 44, 45
Boehme, Jack, 83–84
Boise River, 73
Boldt, George, 182
Boss fly (King's), 64
Bradley M. (Martinez's), 97
Bradner, Enos "Brad": biography,
    160–167; and British
    Columbia legends, v, 33; and
    Montana's Means, 89–90; and
    Washington legends, 33*f,* 174,
    180, 183, 186, 190–191
Brass Hat (Schwab's), 44, 45
Brat series (Bradner's), 160, 161–162
Brayshaw, Tommy, v, 20–27, 30, 158, 186
Brenan, Dan, 42
British Columbia legends, 5–35
Brooks, Joe, 67, 104, 105
Brown Caddis (Means'), 89
Brown Nymph (Schaadt's), 65
BT Specials (Pott's), 86
"bucket," casting, 178
Bucktail, McLeod's, 181
Bucktail Camp, 164, 165, 166–167
Buddy Mite (Pott's), 85, 87
Bulkley River, 174
Bumble Bee (Means'), 89
Bunyan Bugs (Means'), 84, 88–93
Burnham, Fred, 48, 49, 129, 131

Cable Hole, Smith River, 66
Cains River Steelhead Streamer
    (Pray's), 48
Calhoun, Mr., 130*f*
California legends, 37–69
Camp, Ray, 101

Campbell River: Brayshaw's fishing/ flies, 21, 22; Grey's fishing, 127; Haig-Brown's fishing/flies, 28, 30, 33; Money's fishing, 14
Camp Water, North Umpqua River, 120, 122, 132
Candlefish, Lambuth's, 152, 156
Carlon, Dick, 112
Carlson, W. E., 112
Carmichael, Bob, 99
Carson, Sumner, 56
Carter fly (Pray's), 47, 49–50
Carter-Hepworth, Mary, 79
carvings, Brayshaw's, 22, 24, 26
cast-and-strip technique, 59
casting skills/techniques: Abraham's, 114; competitions, 64, 113, 114, 135, 136–141; Hedge's, 134–141; Hornbrook's, 59; McLeod's, 178, 179; Schaadt's, 67, 69; Trueblood's teaching, 76
catch-and-release advocacy, 98, 114, 120, 141, 191
Cedar Borer (Haig-Brown's), 30
Chambers Creek, 2
Chatham, Russell, 59, 66, 67–68, 69
Chatt, George C., 136
Checchio, Michael, 122
Chetco River, 66
Chocolate Dun (Martinez's), 97
Church, Frank, 77, 79
Clackamas River, 2
Clearwater River, 76, 78
Cliff Specials (Pott's), 86
Cligan Bass Bugs (Martinez's), 98
Cock Robin Optic (Pray's), 51
Coho series (Haig-Brown's), 28, 30, 35
Combs, Trey (writing on legends): British Columbia's, 13, 17, 19; California's, 40, 56, 65, 68; Oregon's, 115, 122, 141; Washington's, 175, 180, 192
Comet (King's), 64
competitions: casting, 113, 114, 135, 136–141; McLeod's fishing/ flies, 177, 181–182; Olson's flies/fishing, 170, 171, 172–174; Pray's flies, 48, 50, 57, 59; Schaadt's fishing, 65; Wahl's fishing/flies, 53, 186, 187, 190
Connett, Eugene V., 155, 157, 158
conservation work: Abraham's, 113–114; Bailey's, 105, 107; Bradner's, 162, 163–164, 180; Grey's, 131, 132; Haig-Brown's, 32, 34; Lambuth's, 157; Martinez's, 98; McLeod's, 179–180, 181, 182–183; Rosborough's, 145–146; Trueblood's, 73, 77–79
contests. See competitions
Conway Special, 161

Copper Colonel (Rosborough's), 145
Copper Colonel (Schwab's), 44
Coquihalla River, 23–24, 26
Coquihalla series (Brayshaw's), 20, 24, 25–26
Cowlizt River, 181
creels, Lambuth's, 154, 155
Creeper series (Bailey's), 103
Cummings pattern, 186
Curtis, Alan, 64

dam opposition, 73, 107, 181
Dandy Green Nymph (Bradner's), 164
Dari's Hopper (Bailey's), 103
Dark Caddis (Haig-Brown's), 30
Davis, Sarah, 79
Dedini, Art, 55
Deer Creek: Bradner's fishing/ conservation efforts, 161, 163–164; Grey's fishing, 127; Haig-Brown's fishing, 29; McLeod's fishing/conservation efforts, 176–178, 179, 181
Devine Rod Company, 153–154
Dick's Fly (Money's), 17, 18
Dina Mite (Pott's), 85, 87
Donaldson, Lauren, 164
Donkey Hole, Gualala River, 64
double-haul technique, 76, 114, 137, 140–141
Dower, Walter, 74
Drain, Wes, 173, 187, 191
drawings/paintings, Brayshaw's, 21, 24, 25f, 26, 27, 159f
Drury, Esmond, 17
Duncan's, Russian River, 65
Dungan's Pool, Eel River, 59
Dunham (Martinez's), 98
Dunn, Bobbie, 42, 44

Early Hole, Smith River, 66
Eel River: competitions generally, 174, 190; Hornbrook's fishing/flies, 54–55, 56–60; Pray's fishing/ flies, 47, 48, 49–51, 57, 59; watershed description, 55–56
Egan, Van Gorman, 33
Elbow Hole, Stillaguamish River, 167, 192
Elevation Pool, Umpqua River, 60
Elmore, Ann (later Haig-Brown), 30, 34–35
Emidas (Martinez's), 98
Esopus River, 101
Evans, John, 79
Ewell, John, 119
Explorer (King's), 66

Fall Favorite Optic (Silvius'), 64, 65
Fan Wing flies (Bailey's), 102

Farrington, S. Kip, Jr., 74
Federation of Fly Fishers: and British
     Columbia's Brayshaw, 26–27;
     and Idaho's Trueblood, 77;
     and Oregon legends, 141,
     145–146; photograph, v; and
     Washington legends, 165,
     190–191
Feeler Flies (Schaadt's), 65
Ferenz, John, 64
Ferguson, Bruce, 156
Fibber flies (Pott's), 86, 87
Finline Tackle Company, 87
Fizzle flies (Pott's), 86, 87
flies: Abraham's, 112–113, 114; Bailey's,
     100, 102–105; Bradner's,
     160, 161–162, 163, 164–165;
     Brayshaw's, v, 20, 22–23, 24,
     25–26, 27; Grey's favorites,
     129, 130, 132; Haig-Brown's,
     28, 30, 32; Lambuth's, 152,
     155–157; Martinez's, 94–99;
     McLeod's, 176, 180, 181–182;
     Means', 88–93; Money's, 16,
     17–18; Mott's favorites, 120;
     Nation's, 6, 8–9, 11; Olson's,
     168, 171–173, 175; Pott's,
     83–87; Pray's, 47–53, 57, 59,
     60, 64; Rosborough's, 142–149;
     Schaadt's, 62, 65, 66; Schwab's,
     38, 39, 43, 44–45, 53; Silvius',
     40, 64, 65; Trueblood's, 72, 73,
     75–76; Wahl's, 53, 170, 184,
     185, 190–191; Wulff's, 101, 102
Fly Fisher's Club, 26, 141
fly fishing, historical overview, 1–2
Freezeout, Russian River, 65
Fulmore Pool, Eel River, 59
Fuzzy Bear Yellow and Brown
     (Bailey's), 103
Fuzzy Nymphs (Rosborough's), 147

gamebooks, Money's, 13
Gammarus (Haig-Brown's), 30
Gapen, Dan, 103
Garcia River, Pray's flies, 50
General Fry (Haig-Brown's), 32
General Money series (Money's), 16,
     17–18
General Practitioner (Drury), 17
General's Pool, Stamp River, 15
Gingrich, Arnold, 1–2
Glorius Run, Umpqua River, 116
Godart, Albert, 138
Godfrey Special, 112
Golden Demon (New Zealand's), 17,
     48, 124, 130
Golden Gate Angling and Casting
     Club, 64, 76, 138
Golden Girl (Haig-Brown's), 32
Golden Goose (Schaadt's), 62, 66

Golden Quail (Martinez's), 98
Golden Red (Money's), 16, 17
Gold Nymph (Schaadt's), 65
Gordon, Clarence, 120
Grande Ronde River, 76, 188–189
Grandy Pool, Skagit River, 170, 186
Grant, George (flies of), 84
Grant, George (writing on): Bailey,
     105; Martinez, 96, 97, 99;
     Means', 90, 92, 93; Pott, 85–87
Gray, Howard, ix, 164
Gray, Romer Carl "Reddy," 125, 127,
     129, 130
Grayback (Bailey's), 103
Gray Nymph (Schaadt's), 65
"greased line technique," 19
Great Pool, Stamp River, 15
Green, Milton James "Jimmy," 64, 139, 140
Green Drake (Bailey's), 104
Greenhill, H.M., 29
Green River, 181
Gregory, Myron, 64
Grey, Lina Elise Roth, 125–126
Grey, Loren, 127, 132
Grey, Romer, 132
Grey, Zane, 40, 48, 118, 122, 124–133
Grey Fly (Money's), 17
Grizzley Wulff (Bailey's), 102
Gualala River, 64, 65

Haig-Brown, Alan, 34
Haig-Brown, Ann, 30, 34–35, 191
Haig-Brown, Roderick: biography,
     28–35; on British Columbia
     legends, 7–8, 17–19, 22–23,
     26, 27; and Washington
     legends, 157–158, 191–192
Haig-Brown, Valerie, 34, 35
Hairwing Variant (Martinez's), 97
Hamilton Bar, Skagit River, 186
Hamley, Frederick G., 175
Hardin, Thomas (Ted Trueblood), 53,
     60
Harkley & Haywood (store), 17
Harrison Lake, 169, 170
Headrick, Frank, 164
Hedge, Marvin K., 114, 115, 134–141
Herman, Jack, 113
Herring, Lambuth's, 156
Herters hooks, Means' bugs, 91
historical overview, fly fishing, 1–2
Hjortsberg, William, 105
Holden, George P., 153
Honeyman, Walter (and store), 112,
     113, 114, 136
hooks: Bradner's, 162; Martinez's, 97;
     Means', 91, 93; Money's, 17;
     Pott's, 86, 87; Pray's, 48, 49, 51,
     52; Rosborough's influence, 146;
     Schaadt's, 65; Schwab's, 43, 45;
     Trueblood's, 75; Wahl's, 190

Hornbrook, Dave, 58, 59
Hornbrook, Harry, 54–60, 174
Horner, Jack, 145
Hosfield, David "Skip," 27
House Pool, Stamp River, 15
Hughes, Dave, 146, 148
Humpback Fry (Haig-Brown's), 32
Hunt, Lynn, 74
Hutchens, Jim, 56

Idaho legend, 71–79
Improved Governor Bucktail (Pray's), 50
Integration (Trueblood's), 76
International Fly Fishing Center, 45, 99
Irresistables (Martinez's), 98
Izaak Walton League, 39

Jackman Creek, 186
Jennings, Preston: and Montana
        legends, 96, 98, 102, 105;
        and Pray's flies, 50; and
        Washington legends, 154–155,
        157, 158
Johnson, Les, 156, 187
Johnson, Walt, 141
Johnston, Greg, 167
Jollymore, Bill, 11
Jones Line Company, 139
Junction Pool, Stamp River, 15

Kalama Special (Abraham's), 113, 114
Kalamity K (Wahl's), 190
Kamloops region, 6–11, 22
Kaufmann, Randall, 149
Kennedy, Jay Winfield "Mike," 114,
        115, 190
King, Grant, 64
Kingfisher Creek, 30
Kinzer, William L., Jr., 113
Kispiox River, 162f, 174, 181, 184f, 190
Kitchen Pool, North Umpqua River,
        120, 122
Klamath Country Flycasters, 145
Klamath River: Grey's fishing, 128f,
        129; Pray's flies, 47, 48, 49–50;
        Schwab's fishing, x, 40–41,
        42, 44
Knudson, Al, ix, 173, 174, 187
Krieder, Claude, 45, 64, 122

Lady Godiva (Olson's), 168, 170,
        171–173, 175
Lady Hamilton (Wahl's), 53, 170, 190
Lady Mite (Pott's), 85, 87
Lake Ballinger, 180–181
Lambuth, Benjamin Letcher, 24, 33,
        152–159, 180, 186

Langlie, Arthur, 173
lead-core lines, 64, 65, 66–67
Ledge Pool, Grande Ronde River,
        188–189
"Leetle Feller" series, 41
Leisenring, James E., 149
Light Caddis (Rosborough's), 144
Lilly, Bud, 84, 91–92, 95–96, 99, 105
Limerick hooks, 43
line designs: Hedge's, 136–137,
        139–141; McLeod's, 181;
        Schaadt's, 66–67; Schwab's,
        41–42; Trueblood's, 76
Lingren, Arthur (writing on): Brayshaw,
        22, 25–26, 27; Haig-Brown,
        30; McLeod, 181; Money, 13,
        17, 19; Nation, 8
Little Qualicum River, 14
Little River series (Brayshaw's), 22–23
London, Jack, 118
Lord Hamilton (Wahl's), 53, 170, 184,
        190
Lord Iris (Jennings'), 157
Lord Jim pattern (Trueblood's), 73
Lower Park, Smith River, 66

Macdowell, Syl, 87
Mack, J. G., 111–112
Mack, Mollie, 111, 112
Mackie, Austin, 21–22
Mackie, Hugh, 21–22
Maclean, Norman, 92–93
Maclean, Paul, 92–93
Madison River, 92, 98
Mad River, 50
Maggot (Brayshaw's), 23
Maggot (Pott's), 87
Mansfield, Walter, 136
Marabou Muddler (Bailey's), 100, 103, 104
Marbury, Mary Orvis, 47
Martinez, Donald S., 94–99
Martuch, Leon, 181
Martuch, Leon P., 76
Mausser, Ken, 181–182
McAllister, Tom, 115
McCarthy, Call, 39
McClane, A. J., 60, 65, 140–141, 173,
        174
McCloud River, 2
McDonald, John, 101, 104–105
McEwan, Alex, 29
McGuane, Tom, 67
McLeod, George, 179, 180, 181, 183
McLeod, Ken, ix, 162, 170, 176–183, 183
McLeod's Bucktail, 181
McLeod's Ugly, 181–182
McMillan, Bill, 33, 34
Means, Norman, Jr., 92–93
Means, Norman Edward Lee, 84, 88–93
Meier & Frank Dept. Store, 112, 145
Meloche, Gilbert, 102

Meloche (Bailey's), 102
Merritt, Jim, 107
Miller Pool, Eel River, 58
Missoulian Spook (Bailey's), 105
Miss Wahleye (Wahl's), 190
Mite series (Pott's), 85–86, 87
Money, Noel, 12–19, 30
Monical, Louise, 104
Monical, Red, 102, 104, 107
Montana legends, 81–107
Morrill, Jack, 11
Morris, James C., 112
Mossback series (Bailey's), 84, 102
Mossy Creeper (Bailey's), 103
Mott, Jordan Lawrence, III, 116–122, 131
Mottley, Charles, 7–8
Mr. Mite (Pott's), 85, 87
Muddler series (Bailey's), 103, 104
Multi-colored Variant (Martinez's), 97
Multnomah Anglers' and Hunters'
        Club, 112, 113, 114, 135
museum displays: British Columbia
        legends, 11, 27; California's
        Schwab, 45; Montana's
        Martinez, 99; Washington
        legends, 158, 159, 192
Museum of American Fly Fishing, 158,
        159, 192
Museum of Modern Fly Fishing, 99
Mustad hooks, 49, 52, 75, 86
Mystery Lake, 171, 186

Nasty Nymph (Schaadt's), 65
Nation, Arthur William "Bill," 6–11, 30
Nauheim, Bob, 65–67, 68, 69
Nimpkish River, 29, 30
Nite Owl pattern (Silvius'), 40
Nooksack River, 181
North Forks. See Stillaguamish River;
        Umpqua River
Norwich Line Company, 139
Nylon Nymph (McLeod's), 181
Nymph flies (Schaadt's), 65

Ober, Harold, 30
Olive Badger (Pott's), 86, 87
Olive Creeper (Bailey's), 103
Olive Drake (Means'), 89
Olive Sedge (Brayshaw's), 22
Olson, Charles, 173
Olson, Dan, 173
Olson, Ralph O., 168–175, 186, 187
Optic series (Pray's), 40, 50–52, 58, 59,
        60, 64
Orange Badger (Pott's), 86, 87
Orange Caterpillar (Haig-Brown's), 30
Orange Creeper (Bailey's), 103
Orange Optic (Pray's), 51
Orange Steelheader (Schwab's), 44
Orange Stone Fly (Means'), 89

Orange Wing (Olson's), 172, 175
Oregon legends, 109–149
Orleans Barber (Pray's), 47–48
Oso Pool, Stillaguamish River, 182f
Otter Shrimp (Trueblood's), 72, 75
Owl-Eyed Optic series (Pray's), 50–51

Paint Brush Bucktail (Schwab's), 38,
        39, 43, 44
Painted Lady (Wahl's), 53, 190
Paint Pot (Wahl's), 190
Palmer fly, 96
Pass Lake, 157, 162, 180
Patrick, Roy, v
Paul, Joe, 64
Paul Lake, 7–8, 10–11
Peet, Fred, 39
Perla (Haig-Brown's), 32
photography, Wahl's, 185, 188–189,
        190, 191–192
Picket Pin (Boehme's), 84
Pictorial mayfly series (Martinez's), 97
Pine Squirrel (Trueblood's), 76
"pin vise," 94, 96
Polly's Pride (Rosborough's), 145
Pope, Decimus, 29
Pop-Eye Sawtooth Orange (Bailey's),
        103
Portland Casting Club, 114, 138
Pott, Franz B. "Frank," 82–87
Powell, Edwin C., 136
Pratt, Alan, 163, 165
Prawn Fly (Money's), 17, 18
Pray, C. James "Jim," 40, 46–53, 57, 58,
        59, 60, 63; biography, 46–53;
        and Schwab, x
Prill, Ray, 87
Princess (Schwab's), 44
Puget Bug (Bradner's), 165
Purple Charmer (Wahl's), 190
Purple Peril (McLeod's), 180

Qualicum Beach, 15–19
Queen Bess (Schwab's), 43, 44, 45, 49
Queen Mary (Brayshaw's), 23
Quill Adams, 97
Quinsam Hackle (Haig-Brown's), 32

Rainbow (Money's), 17
Randolph, John, 69
Raymond, Steve (writing on): British
        Columbia legends, 8–9, 11,
        27; foreword by, xi–xiii;
        Washington legends, 157, 158,
        159, 165–166, 180, 192
Read, Stanley, 27
Red and Yellow Optic (Pray's), 51
Redden, John, 165
Red Fly (Van Luven's), 39

Red Optic (Pray's), 50, 59, 60, 64
Red Phantom Streamer (Rosborough's), 142, 145
Red Variant (Bailey's), 103
Redwing (Wahl's), 191
reels, Schwab's, 38, 42
Reiger, George, 133
Reversed Caddis (Martinez's), 97
Rice, Ed, 67
River of No Return Wilderness Council, 77
A River Runs Through It (Maclean), 92–93
Rock Creek, 91–92
Rock Worm (Pott's), 86, 87
rods: Brayshaw's, 22, 24, 27; Brenan-built, 42; and casting contests, 136, 137; Grey's, 129, 132; Lambuth's, 153–154, 158, 159; Means', 90; Trueblood's, 76; Wilson's, 136, 137; Winston-built, 41
Rogue River: Grey's fishing/writing, 127, 129–130, 135; Hedges' writings, 135–136; Mott's fishing, 118; Pray's fishing/flies, 47, 49–50
Rosborough, E. H. "Polly," v, 67, 68, 142–149
Rosborough, Goldie, 143–144
Rose, Daniel, 93
Rose, Richard, 93
Rosenberg, Stephen, 58, 59, 60
Roth, Lina Elise (later Grey), 125–126
Rough Water series (Martinez's), 98
Royal BC Museum, 27
Russian River, 64–66, 69

salmonfly pattern (Means'), 88, 90, 91–92, 93
Salmon River, 76, 77
Samish River, 185
Sandy Mite (Pott's), 85, 86, 87
San Francisco Bay, 66
Sapp, Gene, 48, 57
Satre, John, 87
Sax & Fryer's store, 84–85
Schaadt, William E. "Bill," 62–69, 174
Schmidt, Stanwood, 53
Schullery, Paul, 56, 83–84, 92, 99, 156
Schwab, Peter J.: biography, 38–45; and California's Pray, x, 49, 51, 53; and Oregon's Rosborough, 145; and Washington legends, 173, 190
Schwiebert, Ernest, 149
Schwinden, Ted, 107
Scientific Anglers, 76, 146, 181, 182
Seattle Casting Club, 179
Servatius, Rae, 95
Shad Roe (Schaadt's), 65

Shangri-La pool, Skagit River, 185, 186, 191, 192
Sheldon, Charles H., 175
Shewey, John, 122
Shoff, Clarence, 132
shooting-heads, 64, 67, 76, 181
Silver Demon (Pray's), 48, 49
Silver Garland Marabou Streamer (Rosborough's), 144
Silver Rascal (Wahl's), 190
Silvius, Lloyd, 40, 56, 64
Singley Pool, Eel River, 59, 60
Sink-Tip lines, 76
Skagit River: McLeod's conservation efforts, 181; Olson's fishing/flies, 169–171, 172–173, 174; Wahl's fishing/flies, 53, 185–186, 187*f*, 190, 191
Skykomish River, 179
Skykomish Sunrise (McLeod's), 176, 181–182
Smedley, Harold, 17
Smith River, 50, 62, 65, 66, 67
Snag Hole, Gualala River, 64
Snag Pool, Eel River, 59
Somass River, 14
Special (Geib's), 66
Spiders (Bailey's), 102
Sprague River, 143
Sproat hooks, 43
Sproat River, 14
Spruce Fly (Godfrey's), 112
Spuddler pattern (Bailey's), 105
Squalicum Creek, 185
Stamp River, 14–17, 174*f*
stamps, commemorative, 27, 35
Staples, Bruce, 107
Starkman, Susan, 27
Steamboat Creek, 119, 120
Steelhead Bee (Haig-Brown's), 32, 35
Steelhead Trout Club, 162, 178, 180, 183
Stickleback (Haig-Brown's), 32
Stillaguamish River: Bradner's fishing/flies, 161, 164, 167; conservation efforts, 157, 162, 180; McLeod's fishing, 182*f*; Wahl's photography, 192
Stimson, Harold, 153–154
Stoner, Lew, 40, 41, 44, 49, 136
Sturgis, William Bayard, 50
Sullivan, Virgil, 64
Swan, James, 2
Synder, Gene, 87

Takahashi, George, 129
Tarantino, Jon, 64, 67
Teeny, Jim, 67
Telephone Wire Fly (Hornbrook's), 58
Teton Special (Martinez's), 97
Thompson River, 24, 26
Thoresen, Walter J., 48, 56, 57

Thor fly (Pray's), 48–49, 57
tippet colors, 76
Tommy Award, 27, 192
Tongue River, 2
Townley, Les, 185, 191
Trotter, Pat, 156, 158, 159, 175
Trout Unlimited, 79, 105, 107
Trude, A. S., 2
Trueblood, Cecil Whitaker "Ted," 49,
    53, 60, 72–79, 105, 145
Trueblood, Jack, 79
Trueblood Fledermaus, 76

Ugly, McLeod's, 181–182
Umpqua River: Grey's fishing/writing,
    122, 131–132; Hornbrook's
    fishing, 60; magazine articles,
    40; Mott's fishing/writing, 116,
    119–121

Van Fleet, Clark, 45, 56, 59–60, 122, 158
Van Luven, Harry, 39
Van Luven (Schwab's), 44
Van Zandt, Josh, 56
Variant flies (Bailey's), 102
Virta, Alan, 79
vises, 43, 94, 96, 143

Wahl, Ralph: biography, ix, 184–192;
    and British Columbia legends,
    24, 33; and California legends,
    44–45, 53; and Washington's
    Olson, 169–171, 173–174, 175
Wahlflower (Wahl's), 190
Wahl's Cutthroat, 185
Waller, Gary, 45
Waller, Pat, 45
"wall fish" tradition, 101, 102, 103, 104,
    105, 107
Washington Fly Fishing Club: Bradner's
    activity, 162–163; Brayshaw's
    association, 26, 27; Lambuth's
    work, 156–157, 158, 159;
    McLeod's work, 180, 183;
    membership photograph, ix;
    and Oregon's Rosborough,
    148; Wahl's work, 186, 192
Washington legends, 151–192
Waterman, Charles, 102, 107, 136
Watson's Log, Russian River, 65
Wendelburg, Tom, 105
Weston, J. J., 23
Wet Cel lines, 181
Wethern, Bob, 26, 141, 158, 163
Wet Tip lines, 146
Wharton, Joe, 129, 132
Whatcom Creek, 185
Whatcom Museum of History and Art,
    11, 192

Whitcraft variant (Martinez's), 97
Whitehouse, Francis C., 23
White Moth (Means'), 89
White Muddler (Bailey's), 105
Wiborn, J. Auburn, 127
Wickwire, Bob, 67
Wilkerson, Mike, 87
Willapa Bay, 2
Williams, A. Bryan, 23
Williams, R., 93
Williamson River, 143, 144, 145f, 149
Willmarth Company, 144
Wilson, John, 135, 136, 137
Winch, Frank, 118–119
Winkle Bar, Rogue River, 130
Winston Rod Company, 40, 41, 136
Winter Fly series (Wahl's), 190, 191
Winther, Robert, 136
Wintring, J. W. (Ted Trueblood), 73
Wood Pussy Bucktail (Schwab's), 39,
    44
Woodruff Pool, Smith River, 66
Woolly Worm (Martinez's), 94, 96–99
Worden Company, 42
Wright, Dwain, 87
Wright & McGill, 146
writings (of legends): Bradner's, 89–90,
    163, 164–165, 167; Grey's,
    122, 125–133; Haig-Brown's,
    7, 22–23, 29–34, 191–192;
    Hedge's, 141; Lambuth's,
    157, 158–159; Martinez's, 95,
    98, 99; McLeod's, 177–179,
    182, 183; Money's, 13; Mott's,
    117–119; Rosborough's, 144,
    145–146; Schwab's, 39, 40–42,
    44, 53; Trueblood's, 53,
    73–75, 105; Wahl's, 170–171,
    175, 186, 192
Wulff, Lee, 76–77, 92, 101, 102, 107, 191

Yellow Creeper (Bailey's), 103
Yellow Jacket (Means'), 89
Yellow Stone Fly (Means"), 93
Yellow-Stone Nymph (Bailey's), 104
Yellowstone River, 84–85, 86, 92, 105, 107
Yolk Sac (Brayshaw's), 23
Yum Yum pattern (Wahl's), 190

Zahner, Donald, 40
Zern, Ed, 76–77, 133